DATE LOANED

THE TUSCAN REPUBLICS

DANTE ALIGHIERI, FROM THE FRESCO BY GIOTTO, FLORENCE.
(After a Photograph by Brogi.)

THE STORY OF THE NATIONS

THE
TUSCAN REPUBLICS

(FLORENCE, SIENA, PISA, AND LUCCA)

WITH

GENOA

BY

BELLA DUFFY

NEW YORK
G. P. PUTNAM'S SONS
LONDON: T. FISHER UNWIN
1898

COPYRIGHT, 1893
BY G. P. PUTNAM'S SONS
Entered at Stationers' Hall, London
BY T. FISHER UNWIN

PREFACE.

No history of the Italian communes could be considered in any sense complete which disregarded the recent researches of German historians into the origin of these little Republics. The reader will find the views of Hegel, Pawinski, and Ficker embodied with as much succinctness as possible in the introductory chapter of this work; and should he desire to penetrate further on his own account into the subject, he would derive much assistance from the four valuable volumes of original documents with copious annotations, published by Ficker.

As regards Florence alone, and from one point of view, Florence must always be the most interesting of the Italian Republics, articles of extreme interest on the beginnings of the commune have been contributed to the "Nuova Antologia," by Professor Pasquale Villari, and form, it may be hoped, the prelude to a larger work.

As an example of sudden spontaneous growth, yielding original and splendid social results, the Italian Republics are unique in history. Politically speaking, other countries offer a spectacle of more epic grandeur. The legendary personage, great king, or great warrior, and statesmen is absent from the annals of the towns which strove so passionately to preserve their independence against Pope and Emperor, and against each other; but, on the other hand, the commune itself becomes an unit of fascinating individuality and force.

Genoa has been included in these pages partly because of the close rivalry in which it stood to Pisa in the most brilliant period of both republics; and in a lesser degree because of the contrast afforded by its dreary annals to the distinction in Art and Literature of the Tuscan towns. Taken altogether there are no more instructive examples of self-help and self-destruction, of rapid rise and complete extinction, than are offered by the Commonwealths which for five hundred years controlled the destinies of Tuscany and Liguria.

BELLA DUFFY.

CONTENTS.

I.

                                                        PAGE

INTRODUCTORY 1–10

Small beginnings—Imperial Concessions—Commencement of the Trade Guilds—Rival Rulers.

II.

THE UPRISE OF PISA AND GENOA . . . 11–21

Activity of Pisa—Beginning of Faction—Expeditions to the Holy Land—Splendour of Pisa—Rivalry of Genoa.

III.

LUCCA AND PISA 22–27

The rise of Lucca—Attack of Pisa on the Balearic Isles—Florentine chivalry.

IV.

GENOA 28–32

Consuls of the Commune—Feudatories of Genoa.

V.

HOW THE COMMUNES GREW 33–42

Destruction of Amalfi—Character of the Communes—Genoa proceeds against the Moors—First appearance of Barbarossa.

VI.

THE ORIGIN OF FLORENCE 43–56

Obscurity of its early years—Religious Feuds—Spontaneous growth of the Commune—Its Democratic basis—Early struggles between classes—Guilds and Towers.

VII.

THE TUSCAN COMMUNES AND GENOA IN THE TIME OF BARBAROSSA 57–62

Their self-seeking Policy—A brief Peace.

VIII.

THE EXPANSION OF FLORENCE . . . 63–69

Discontent among the Barons—Pretensions of the Podestàs—The Pope and the Republics.

IX.

FLORENCE IN THE THIRTEENTH CENTURY . . 70–85

Real nature of the Podestàs—Factions in Siena—Buondelmonti and Amidei—Frederick II.—Fighting Companies—War with Siena—Battle of Mont' Aperti—Disastrous consequences.

X.

FLORENCE IN THE THIRTEENTH CENTURY (continued) 86–105

Farinata's Protest—Ghibelline Cruelties—Battle of Benevento—Alarm of the Ghibellines—Institution of the Twelve—The Guelph Party formed—General Discord—Confusion of Parties—Practical Ideals—Constant change of Office-holders.

XI.

GENOA, PISA, AND LUCCA DURING THE THIRTEENTH CENTURY 106–120

Prosperity of Lucca—External power of Genoa—Struggles with Frederick II.—A Captain of the People—Battle of Meloria—Ghibellinism at Arezzo—Battle of Campaldino.

XII.

FLORENCE IN THE FOURTEENTH CENTURY AFTER GIANO DELLA BELLA'S REIGN OF TERROR 121–140

The Ordinances of Justice—True Guelphs and Ghibellines at an end—Giano's Unpopularity—Popular Outbreak—Blacks and Whites—Intervention of the Pope—Feuds among Kinsfolk—Florence half destroyed by Fire—Death of Corso Donati.

XIII.

EVENTS IN LUCCA AND PISA. FLORENCE IN THE FOURTEENTH CENTURY (*continued*) . . 141–149

War with Castruccio—Battle of Altopascia—Sack of Pistoja—Prohibitions laid upon Officials.

XIV.

GENERAL EVENTS 150–161

General Depression—The Duke of Athens summoned—Made Lord of Florence—Fall of the Duke—The Bardi attacked.

XV.

FLORENCE IN THE FOURTEENTH CENTURY (*continued*); **AND AFFAIRS IN LUCCA, PISA, AND SIENA** 162–181

Further Humiliation of the Grandi—Rise of the Visconti—Revolution in Siena—A faithless Emperor—The " Admonitions"—The Eight of War—Events in Bologna—A Religious Revival—Unpopularity of the Eight.

XVI.

FLORENCE IN THE FOURTEENTH CENTURY (*continued*). THE CIOMPI RIOTS 182–197

A Popular Revolt—Conspiracy of the Ciompi—Demands of the Insurgents—The Revolutionary Eight—Defeat of the Ciompi—Palace of the Podestà attacked—Purchase of Arezzo.

XVII.

FLORENCE IN THE FOURTEENTH CENTURY (*continued*). THE STRUGGLE WITH GIOVAN GALEAZZO VISCONTI 198–222

Charles of Durazzo threatens Florence—The Intrigues of Visconti—Hawkwood and Jacopo del Verme—Pisa at Visconti's mercy—Persecution of the Alberti—Visconti's triumphs—Gian Galeazzo dies—The indispensable Condottieri—Pisa sold to Florence—Pisa starved into surrender—War with Ladislaus—Events in Bologna.

XVIII.

GENOA FROM 1288 TO 1410 223–235

Simone Boccanera—War with Venice—Adorno and Montaldo—Advent of Boucicault—He establishes Peace—His Fall.

XIX.

COMMERCE, MANUFACTURES, AND FINANCE . 236–252

Rise of the Cloth Trade—Foundation of the Guild of Wool—Florentine Banking—Loan to English Kings—The First Galleys—Charitable Institutions—Fairy Tales of Commerce—Bank of St. George.

XX.

INTELLECTUAL AND ARTISTIC DEVELOPMENT UNTIL THE CLOSE OF THE FIFTEENTH CENTURY   253–278

Rise of Poetry—Early Tuscan Singers—Folgore da San Gemignano—The "Divina Commedia"—Its Subject—"The Decamerone"—Architecture and Sculpture—A Group of Great Names—Masterpieces and Renaissance—Tuscan Painting—Luca Signorelli.

XXI.

FLORENCE AND GENOA IN THE FIFTEENTH CENTURY   279–292

Government by Tyrants—The Genoese defeat Alfonso—Cosimo de' Medici—Cosimo's noblest Victim—Death of Cosimo.

XXII.

FLORENCE UNDER THE MEDICI (*continued*)   .   293–314

Useless Struggles—Lorenzo and Giuliano—Strange Contrasts—Last Liberties suppressed—The Pazzi embittered—Conspire against the Medici—The Hour of Mass chosen—Failure of the Plot—Jacopo de' Pazzi's death—Lorenzo's position.

XXIII.

GENOA FROM 1435 TO 1488   315–323

The Genoese expel the French—Genoa loses Caffa—Genoa's long disease—And discord.

XXIV.

FLORENCE UNDER LORENZO DEI MEDICI (*continued*)   324–333

Murder of Girolamo Riario—Lorenzo's Financial difficulties—Savonarola—Summoned to Lorenzo's deathbed—Lorenzo dies unshriven.

XXV.

THE HUMANISTS IN FLORENCE, AND THE POETS AND HISTORIANS WHO GATHERED ROUND THE MEDICI 334–340

Poggio Bracciolini—Pico dello Mirandola—The Morgante Maggiore.

XXVI.

FLORENCE UNDER THE INFLUENCE OF SAVONAROLA 341–362

Charles VIII. of France—Enters Pisa as a Deliverer—The Medici fly—Charles in Florence—Piero Capponi—Proposed Grand Council—Supported by Savonarola—Parliaments of the People abolished—Savonarolo's Visions—Superstitions of the Renaissance.

XXVII.

FLORENCE UNDER THE INFLUENCE OF SAVONAROLA (*continued*) 363–380

Charles abandons Pisa—But Pisa still resists—Conspiracy to restore Piero—Savonarola excommunicated—Ordeal of Fire suggested—The Day for it fixed—Siege of St. Mark's Convent—Death of Savonarola.

XXVIII.

GENERAL EVENTS FROM 1498 TO 1512 . . 381–393

Cæsar Borgia's Plan—Destroyed by Death of Pope—Entry of Louis XII. into Genoa—Pisa surrenders to Florence—Restoration of the Medici—Entry of Giuliano into Florence.

XXIX.

THE SIEGE OF FLORENCE. DECADENCE AND END OF THE REPUBLICS 394–436

Pope Leo's cruelty—Advance of the Constable of Bourbon—The Medici again expelled—Andrea Doria—The Plague in

Florence — A vain Religious Revival — Kingly bad faith— The Emperor crowned in Bologna—Francesco Ferruccio— Baglione's Treachery—Final Return of the Medici—Assassination of Alessandro—Decay of the Republics—Dying Struggles—Siege of Siena—Genoa incorporated with Sardinia—Concluding Events in Florence.

CHRONOLOGICAL TABLE OF EVENTS . . 437-446

INDEX 447

LIST OF ILLUSTRATIONS.

	PAGE
DANTE ALIGHIERI, FROM THE FRESCO BY GIOTTI, FLORENCE. (AFTER A PHOTOGRAPH BY BROGI) .	*Frontispiece*
CHURCH OF ST. LORENZO, GENOA. (AFTER A PHOTOGRAPH BY BROGI)	29
INTERIOR OF SAN MINIATO, FLORENCE. (FROM A PHOTOGRAPH BY BROGI)	66
COMMUNAL PALACE AT SIENA. (FROM A PHOTOGRAPH BY BROGI)	72
VIEW OF FLORENCE. (FROM A PHOTOGRAPH BY BROGI)	79
BASILICA OF ST. FREDIANO, LUCCA. (AFTER A PHOTOGRAPH BY BROGI)	102
MAP OF FLORENCE	122
STREET IN OLD MARKET, FLORENCE, NOW DESTROYED	128
COURT OF BARGELLO, FLORENCE	154
PALACE OF THE PODESTÀ OR BARGELLO, FLORENCE	157
VIEW OF SIENA	171
GATE OF ST. GEORGE, FLORENCE, IN THE OLTRARNO QUARTER. CONSTRUCTED IN 1324. (AFTER A PHOTOGRAPH BY BROGI)	184
OLD MARKET PLACE, FLORENCE	189
MAP OF LIGURIA	220
DUCAL PALACE, GENOA. (FROM A PHOTOGRAPH BY BROGI)	232

LIST OF ILLUSTRATIONS.

	PAGE
MEDAL SHOWING DANTE. (FROM DIE ITALIENISCHEN SCHAUMÜNZEN DES FÜNFZEHNTEN JAHRHUNDERTS. (1430–1530.) VON JULIUS FRIEDLAENDER. BERLIN. 1882)	254
VIEW OF THE PIAZZA DEL DUOMO, AT PISA. (FROM A PHOTOGRAPH BY BROGI)	266
WEST GALLERY IN THE CAMPOSANTO AT PISA. (AFTER A PHOTOGRAPH BY PISANO)	268
CHURCH OF SANTA CROCE. MONUMENT TO CARLO MARSUPPINI	270
CHAPEL OF THE MADONNA DELLA SPINA, PISA	272
STUDY BY BENOZZO GOZZOLI, IN THE UFFIZI GALLERY, FLORENCE	274
STUDY FROM THE LIFE, BY LIONARDO DA VINCI, IN THE UFFIZI GALLERY. (AFTER A PHOTOTYPE BY ALINARI)	276
LIONARDO DA VINCI, IN HIS MAJESTY'S COLLECTION	277
MEDAL OF COSIMO DE' MEDICI. (FROM DIE ITALIENISCHEN SCHAUMÜNZEN DES FÜNFZEHNTEN JAHRHUNDERTS. (1430–1530.) VON JULIUS FRIEDLAENDER. BERLIN, 1882)	283
PITTI PALACE, FLORENCE. (AFTER A PHOTOGRAPH BY BROGI)	290
MEDAL OF SIXTUS IV. (FROM DIE ITALIENISCHEN SCHAUMÜNZEN DES FÜNFZEHNTEN JAHRHUNDERTS. (1430–1530.) VON JULIUS FRIEDLAENDER. BERLIN, 1882)	300
MEDAL OF PIUS II. (FROM DIE ITALIENISCHEN SCHAUMÜNZEN DES FÜNFZEHNTEN JAHRHUNDERTS. (1430–1530.) VON JULIUS FRIEDLAENDER. BERLIN, 1882)	339
MEDAL SHOWING ST. PETER'S	392
MICHAELANGELO	404
DAWN. (FROM THE MONUMENT TO LORENZO DE' MEDICI, BY MICHAELANGELO, AT FLORENCE)	406

LIST OF ILLUSTRATIONS.

	PAGE
EVENING. (FROM THE MONUMENT TO LORENZO DE' MEDICI, BY MICHAELANGELO, AT FLORENCE)	408
NIGHT. (FROM THE MONUMENT TO LORENZO DE' MEDICI, BY MICHAELANGELO, AT FLORENCE)	411
SALTCELLAR, BY BENVENUTO CELLINI, IN THE UFFIZI GALLERY, FLORENCE. (AFTER A PHOTOTYPE BY ALINARI)	422
JUDITH, BY BOTTICELLI IN THE UFFIZI GALLERY, FLORENCE. (AFTER A PHOTOGRAPH BY ALINARI)	424
SWOON OF ST. CATHERINE, CHURCH OF ST. CATHERINE, SIENA	427
ARCHITECTURAL DETAILS, BY BALDASSARRE PERUZZI, IN THE UFFIZI GALLERY. (AFTER A PHOTOTYPE ALINARI)	429
ALFONSO D'ESTE. (FROM DIE ITALIENSCHEN SCHAU-MÜNZEN DES FÜNFZEHNTEN JAHRHUNDERTS. (1430–1530.) VON JULIUS FRIEDLAENDER. BERLIN, 1882)	430
FRANCIS SFORZA. (FROM DIE ITALIENISCHEN SCHAU-MÜNZEN DES FÜNFZEHNTEN JAHRHUNDERTS. (1430–1530.) VON JULIUS FRIEDLAENDER. BERLIN, 1882)	431
CASA GUIDI. (THE HOUSE ELIZABETH BARRETT BROWNING OCCUPIED IN FLORENCE)	434
MEDAL OF LEO X. (FROM DIE ITALIENISCHEN SCHAU-MÜNZEN DES FÜNFZEHNTEN JAHRHUNDERTS. (1430–1530.) VON JULIUS FRIEDLAENDER. BERLIN, 1882)	435

THE TUSCAN REPUBLICS.

I.

INTRODUCTORY.

AMONG historians of the Italian Republics the origin of the communes has been a much disputed point. From Sigonius to Sismondi, from Sismondi to Savigny, from Savigny to various living writers, Italian and German, the question has been argued, and although much still remains doubtful at least it now seems generally agreed that the communes were not, as at one time believed, the lineal descendants of the Roman Municipalities.

Roman institutions in Lombardy, Liguria, and Tuscany were either swept away by the Langobards, or disrupted by successive tides of invasion, which receded only to reveal all the ruin they had worked, and caused the panic-stricken inhabitants of the devastated lands to build themselves new, walled towns, and form isolated associations for defence. The Langobard kings and their powerful vassals were forced by the difficulties of their own position to leave maritime towns like Genoa and Pisa to defend themselves against the Saracen invaders, who continually ravaged the coasts; and the hardy race of seamen whom these necessities developed, soon began to navigate on their own account, and laid the foundations of Italian trade. The towns along the seaboard were thus the first to rise into importance, but so gradual was their evolution that the date of their constitution as communes remains unknown. And the same may be said of the inland towns, where struggles of another sort, that is, against other aggressors, resulted in a similar independence.

In some towns like Pisa and Lucca, the origin of the commune was aristocratic, being the work of nobles who aspired to free themselves from the interference of the Marquis. In other places, notable in Lombardy, the German emperors, finding an obstacle to their own designs in the power of the Marquises, were glad to seek a makeweight in the authority of the bishops, and encouraged the popular revolts of which these ecclesiastics were the leaders. Geographical position, richness or poverty of soil were minor factors, which yet had their importance. Genoa, for instance, with the arid territory surrounding it offered slight temptation to Teutonic settlers, and consequently suffered comparatively little from foreign occupation; while, on the other hand, its command of the seaboard made it useful to such non-maritime folks as the Langobards, who in return for services rendered might remit a portion of their usual exactions. Florence again, although for reasons to be explained it developed more tardily than its neighbours, owed its final great prosperity to its position midway between the Mediterranean coast and Rome, which caused an ever-growing stream of traffic, and established commercial relations so wide-reaching that the Florentine merchants ended by obtaining a monopoly of the banking business of the Holy See. Finally, when Hildebrand, Matilda, and Henry the Fourth filled the scene, the necessity laid upon each commune of choosing between pope or emperor had an incalculable influence upon the destinies of the towns, by forcing them to play parts, out of all proportion to their size, upon the troubled scene of European politics. These separate impulses, once given, lasted all through the Middle Ages and until the accession of Charles V., and, while preventing the consolidation of Italy into a kingdom, exposed it to the misery of constant invasion, but encouraged that growth of individuality among the communes to which the world owes such marvellous results.

For the rest the commune seems to have been everywhere an unnoticed growth from small beginnings. First, we have the Marquis, or his representative the viscount, of Teutonic origin, presiding in the courts, surrounded by his *Scabini*, or judges, who, although in one sense imperial officers, seem nevertheless to have been chosen usually from among the inhabitants of each town and territory, and not to have travelled about in the suite of the overlord. They were doubtless originally the descendants of the ancient freemen, whom Charlemagne had done his best to protect against the tyranny of his own lieutenants, and who in Tuscany, where, with two exceptions, the power of the bishops remained insignificant, probably only attained to some relative well-being at last by union with the trading classes, as soon as these became rich. Be this as it may, we must accept the relative independence of the Scabini as forming the starting-point of the future commune. For as time elapsed, the Marquis frequently absented himself from the deliberations of the courts, and delegated his functions more and more apparently to the Scabini, who would naturally come by degrees to regard themselves as constituting a kind of local self-government.

And the absence of the overlord had another result, that, namely, of affording to a group of ambitious nobles the opportunity of interposing themselves between the feudal governor and the Scabini, and when necessary seeking a justification of their action in an appeal to a general assembly of the people. When things had reached this point, and the Marquis came to look again into the affairs of the town, he found that they had passed virtually out of his control, and as he usually had ambitions of his own to further being enveloped by the complicated machinery of European politics, he consented to confirm by statutes the liberties which had sprung up without his ken. This was the case in Genoa as far back as 958, when Berengarius and Adalbert, joint "kings" of Italy, conferred upon the town sole possession to the property to which it then laid claim, and guaranteed it from all interference on the part of Crown functionaries. If this does not prove that there was as yet any regular form of communal administration in Genoa it shows at last that the town had customs which its superiors found it advantageous to respect.

Much more significant are three documents relating to Savona, and dated respectively A.D. 1059, 1061, and 1062, wherein it is expressly stated that the citadel shall be held by the *Majores*, or prominent citizens, with prohibition to the Marquis and his officers from entering it. A yet earlier document ensures safety of person and property to the people of Savona, and engages in the name of the Marquis that no fortified place shall be erected by him upon their territory, providing at the same time that all disputes concerning property shall be decided, not as heretofore, by single combat, but by an appeal to the courts and the testimony of sworn witnesses.

From these beginnings, which seem to have been much the same everywhere the commune rapidly developed. In the strife between Gregory VII., his ally the Countess Matilda, and the Emperor Henry IV., Pisa and Lucca, mindful of the long oppression they had endured under Matilda's father, Duke Boniface, espoused the imperial cause and were rewarded by a formal recognition of their rights and customs on the part of Henry. In a diploma dated from Rome, June 23, 1081, he expressly assured to Lucca, for instance, absolute security within the double circle of her walls, allowed her to prohibit the building of castles or fortified places inside the city or for six miles round, and released her from the obligation to erect an imperial palace. He furthermore promised that no imperial officer (*missus*) should be sent to pronounce sentences in Lucca, unless the Emperor himself, the Emperor's son, or the Chancellor of the Empire were present within the town. In the same year, by another diploma, he guaranteed the exercise of her ancient practices (*consuetudines*) to Pisa; undertook that no foreign (*i.e.*, non-Pisan) count should be empowered to pronounce sentences within the city or its territory; and agreed to appoint no Marquis whose nomination had not been ratified by twelve citizens or *Buoni uomini*, elected in a full parliament of the Pisan people. Here, then, we have the form of government existing in the earliest Italian communes, namely, a popular assembly and an elective body constituted by twelve principal citizens, who are variously distinguished as *Buoni uomini, Sapientes*, or *Majores*.

Thirty years or so later, these Buoni uomini are fewer in number, and have received the title of Consuls; the communes are already conscious of their youthful strength, and their history as independent entities has begun. The smaller republics are as full of narrow and intense civic patriotism as the larger ones, but almost in their hour of birth Genoa, Pisa, Lucca, Florence felt the impulse of expansion which led them gradually to conquer and absorb their neighbours. Individualism and self-assertion are the keynotes of Italian mediæval history, and struggle between commune and commune, class and class, family and family, long-continued, ever-renascent struggle was the breath of the people's being. Starting all equal in the race, or if unequal, favoured by advantages not immediately apparent, some communes distanced the others through the remote consequences of this unceasing competition, supported as it was by a liberty of individual action far superior in developing power to the most wisely organized machinery of administration.

To the towns where the bishops, strong in their immunities, had re-established some kind of order, and where the Roman *Scholæ* had reappeared in the looser form of trade guilds under powerful patrons, the conquerors of Italy fled for refuge whenever a fresh tide of invasion swept over the land. Thither came the Langobards when vanquished by the Franks, who in their turn sought safety there, from the Avar hordes. In the schools, the cloisters, and workshops of these towns, a new life had already begun, which was independent of the feuds of rulers or the dreams of invaders. And it is not too much to say that even in the tenth century the backbone of these young societies was trade. Langobards and Franks, aristocratically devoted to warfare and the chase, had naturally left the supply of their material wants to the bondsmen and the half-free, with whom, in course of time, there associated themselves such freemen as did not despise the comparatively honourable callings of goldsmiths and armourers. Humbly and unobserved fisherfolk, weavers, and carriers built up the wealth of the towns, and the calling of a merchant soon became of such importance as to receive formal recognition even by Langobardic legislators.

A great impulse to trade was originally given by the Arab settlers along the southern coasts of the Mediterranean, whose demands for arms, slaves, building materials, clothing, wood, hemp, &c., soon raised Amalfi to importance. Such an example was not likely to be wasted on a keen-witted people, and the unceasing stream of strangers who on various errands, political, religious, and commercial, passed through the peninsula, soon freshened an enterprising spirit which had perhaps never been wholly dormant. The slave trade for a while supplied what was wanting in manufactures, the captives, mostly Germans, whom the perpetual fighting among the Teutonic nations had exposed to the fortune of war, being transferred to the Levant through the offices of Jewish middlemen. Of agricultural produce Italy was the great centre, and as far back as 629 Lombard merchants carried their wares to Paris there to exchange them with the supplies brought to the same mart by Anglo-Saxon, Provençal, and Spanish traders. These causes, all working imperceptibly throughout centuries of external strife, contributed to the gradual evolution of the communes which, with the germ of their future greatness already lying within them, presented themselves as facts to be dealt with to Otho the Great upon his descent into Italy. Long anarchy had preceded this event, and no profounder intellectual gloom ever wrapped Italy than during the tenth century.

Louis II., grandson of Charlemagne, died in 875 without heirs, and immediately two rival monarchs found supporters, Pope John VIII. attaching himself to the party of Charles the Bald, King of the West Franks, while another faction upheld the German Ludwig in his pretensions. Charles being eventually successful, the Pope crowned him Emperor, and assisted him, with further help from the Archbishop of Milan and the Langobard party there, in overcoming Ludwig's successor, Karlmann. Shortly afterwards the whole Frankish kingdom was united by simple inheritance under Charles the Fat, but his incapacity bred fresh discord. In Italy the Marquis Berengarius of Friuli and Duke Guido of Spoleto both claimed kingly authority, and Guido eventually obtained it. He and his son Lambert were successively crowned, but recognized the German Arnulf as overlord. The latter twice invaded Italy, and reduced opposition by cruelty. The opportunity of Berengarius came when Guido and Lambert died, and under his rule the unhappy land might have enjoyed some peace had it not been for the terrible invasion of the Hungarians. The Italians were thoroughly beaten in the open field, and almost simultaneously found themselves confronted by the Saracens, who effected settlements in Northern and Southern Italy. Berengarius called upon Louis of Provence and Rudolph of Upper Burgundy for help, but had no sooner obtained it than he allied himself with the Hungarians against these princes. This perfidy availed him nothing in the end, as he finally lost all of his kingdom but Verona; Rudolph establishing himself in Lombardy and becoming utterly enslaved by Hermengard, widow of the Markgrave Adelbert of Ivrea. A party hostile to Rudolph and to the woman who governed him then called in Count Hugo of Provence, who eventually exchanged that possession with Rudolph for Lombardy. When Rudolph died Hugo married Hermengard, and gave her daughter Adelheid to his son and successor Lothar.

He ruled with great energy, and was especially a redoubtable foe of the Saracens.

But Berengarius of Ivrea plotted with the bishops of Lombardy against Hugo, and, on the death of the latter, as of Lothar, he had himself proclaimed king, and endeavoured to marry Adelheid to his son Adalbert. On her refusal she was imprisoned, but escaped, and appealed to Otho of Germany, known as the Great. He invaded Italy; was acknowledged as king at Pavia, and crowned in Rome A.D. 962.

He was a great prince; but the nascent Communes were already too strong for him. He recognized their existence, and was the first of the German sovereigns to purchase their allegiance by timely concessions. They started then each on a separate life, and the key to their peculiar history lies in the fact that they never once entertained the idea of any federation or recognized the possibility of uniting for any length of time in a common effort or against a common foe. Had the communes ever desired federation, or had the Visconti or any other prince succeeded in establishing a kingship, the Italian towns must have been lacking in the strenuous individuality to which even the smaller among them owed an early and splendid civilization.

II.

THE UPRISE OF PISA AND GENOA.

IT is difficult in the beginning to dissociate the history of Genoa and Pisa, the permanent rivalry between the two republics being in fact attributable to the identity of their aims and aspirations.

Both emerged fairly from obscurity during the period of the Saracen raids upon the coast, and after the permission, constantly refused by the Langobards, had been finally obtained to build walls and fortifications, which gave to each of the isolated towns a special and separate activity, the necessity of scouring the Mediterranean in pursuit of the alternately victorious and vanquished Pagans, accustomed the Genoese and Pisans equally to adventurous enterprises, and suggested the commercial expansion which, beginning with Sardinia and Corsica—the first wrested by Pisa, and the second conquered for a time by Genoa, from the Moors—eventually extended itself, as we shall learn, by sea and land to the very heart of Asia. Both republics sent armaments of their own to the crusades, and each, like Venice, only in a more disinterested spirit, acted as carriers of foreign troops to the Holy Land. Both had to contend against great disadvantages, Genoa in an unfertile soil, and Pisa in a geographical position which prevented expansion inland, and to both, therefore, the only future lay towards the sea, with its hazards, its possibilities, and its fascination.

Even socially, and so to speak, psychologically, there was a resemblance between the two towns. They shared alike in traditions, vague, yet imposing, like all traditions, which reached them in faint echoes from Roman days, and gave a kind of solemnity to the narrow patriotism resulting from the action of the Langobards who, not amalgamating with the Italians as the Goths had done, but dwelling as a conquering race in the midst of the conquered, had accustomed the inhabitants of each province or district to cling together, Romans with Romans, Ligurians with Ligurians, Etrurians with Etrurians. The crusades also had their share of influence in increasing the impoverishment of the nobles which began during the anarchy following on the death of Charles the Fat. During that long chaos all the great fiefs had changed hands or been broken up: the resources of the devastated land remained to a great degree undeveloped, and unfed by territorial wealth, feudalism, always an exotic in Central Italy, languished. The nobles from their mountain fastnesses began to turn their eyes towards the towns; but the towns were already self-conscious and strong, and would not admit the nobles unconditionally. The terms offered and accepted constituted a new basis; the nobles became carriers, merchants, administrators; but mindful of their origin, and accustomed to command, they endeavoured to turn each commune into an oligarchy almost in the hour of its birth.

Pisa seems to have been the first of the two republics to rise to real importance, for it was to her that Otho II., when proceeding against Magna Græcia in 980, applied for vessels to carry his troops. The Pisan port was at that time well adapted for the light ships of the period, and the town had already a record for seafaring enterprise extending over some centuries. Pisan merchants had established counting-houses as far south as Calabria, and Pisan galleys were formidable in the eyes of Moorish invaders. Pope John XVIII., beset by Saracens who had appeared in the Tiber, appealed for help to Pisa, which had already inflicted a great defeat on the enemy at Civita Vecchia in 1003, and followed it up by another beating at Reggio in 1006. This last expedition was undertaken to punish the Moslem for a descent upon the town of Pisa in the previous year. The descent was a surprise, and might have been successful but for the energy, as old chronicles relate, of a woman, Chinzica Sismondi, who perceived the enemy's sail in the distance, and roused her apathetic fellow-townsmen: a service, in grateful memory of which the quarter of the town in which she dwelt was called Chinzica after her. The Sismondi, Gualandi Lanfranchi, Godimari, Orlandi, Verchionesi, seem at this time to have been the leading citizens of Pisa, and haughtily claimed a German origin, which meant really that they had aristocratic tendencies, and were destined eventually to be known as Ghibellines. But internecine struggles were for the present only germinating in Pisa. The external activity of the town was entirely directed to keeping off the Saracens ; or in attacking them in their strongholds of Sardinia and Corsica. These expeditions were usually undertaken at the request of the Pope, and sometimes in conjunction with Genoa. About 1021 the forces of the allied towns put the Moorish leader Musetto for the twentieth time to flight, and it was then, according the Pisan annalists, that Sardinia was divided into four parts, under four rulers, sometimes called judges, and sometimes kings, the districts thus created being respectively Cagliari, Gallura, Arborea, or Turrita. Muratori, who is always inclined to be sceptical where Pisan exploits are concerned, maintains that this division was of earlier date, and had taken place quite independently of Pisa. It is certain that the so-called "kings" were not at all submissive subjects, and in fact there always seems to have been a party of native nobles in Sardinia who approved of the Pisans or Genoese just as little as they did of the Moors—perhaps even less so—and who made the island anything but an easy possession to govern. For a century, in fact, Pisa's rule over the islanders was merely nominal, for as soon almost as the galleys were out of sight, the Moors re-appeared and established themselves in their former quarters. And there is not any sign that the Sardinians ever complained of this, the expeditions of Genoa and Pisa being always undertaken out of sheer intolerance of the Infidel as a neighbour.

As the Pisans increased in strength they tried to root out the poisonous growth of Moslemism in what might be called its own soil, and they are reported to have descended in force upon the coast of Barbary and captured the King of Carthage, whom they caused to be forcibly baptized by the Pope previously to reinstating him in his kingdom. A more authentic story describes them as proceeding against Bona, the ancient Hippo of St. Augustine, and at any rate it seems pretty clear that Pisan enterprise did at this time carry the war-galleys of the nascent commune as far as the African coast.

Whatever may be the amount of legend which found its way into the early chronicles of the Republics, there is no doubt about the main fact: namely, that during a hundred years or so both Genoa and Pisa had to struggle for dear life against the Infidels, and owed their development in great part to these combats. But such a struggle could not take place without evoking the spirit of internecine rivalry, whose birth indeed was contemporaneous with the uprise of the commune itself. For combined efforts against a common foe were not possible without obedience to leaders who on the narrow stage of city politics speedily became predominant, and then began the famous street fights of Italy which deluged Pisa and other towns with blood. The nobles, the Buoni uomini, in a word the leaders under whose command the Saracen had been conquered in Sardinia, in Africa, in Sicily, threatened one another from their sky-kissing towers, and filled the narrow ways of the town with the sound of war-cries and the clash of arms. The mere fact that they dwelt in fortified places, and had built themselves such lofty towers as symbols of strength and pride, proves that for a long time before we see them fighting these nobles must have been armed against each other. But a foreign foe had kept them busy, and it was when external danger for a moment ceased to threaten them that they turned upon each other. At last Daibert, Bishop of Pisa, and soon to be Patriarch of Jerusalem, interposed. The Church spoke with an authoritative voice in those days, and all Italian mediæval history demonstrates how profound was the influence exercised on the town by their bishops. Daibert succeeded in formulating conditions of peace to which the citizens of Pisa subscribed ; reconciliation took place between the contending factions, and Daibert established a government which the people swore to maintain.

The nobles even agreed that with two exceptions (that of Viscount Hugo and Albizi's sons) all towers should be of equal height, and that no houses should be demolished, in the way of reprisals, without the permission of the *Commune Colloquium Civitatis* in other words, the parliament of the people. Here then we have the city appearing as a collective entity endowed with public functions and exercising its authority to hinder acts of individual vengeance. The rule of the Marquis or Count was virtually a thing of the past. The nobles who, in some places, as the bishops in others, had formed a sort of provisional government found themselves confronted with the necessity of establishing a stable one ; and while it seems pretty clear that in Pisa, at any rate, the aristocratic element prevailed, still the determination to humble the pride of the few by reducing all towers to the same height, and the necessity of obtaining the consent of the majority before any houses could be demolished prove that among the nobles themselves the instinct of self-preservation had developed a tendency towards democracy.

In 1087 Pisa, now at peace internally, Genoa, Rome, and Amalfi descended as allies on the African coast in an expedition against the Saracen king. Viscount Hugo—Matilda's delegate—led the Pisan army, and, if an old rhyme is to be believed, with him were four consuls. This is the first occasion on which such a word appears in any annals of the town, and consuls are not again mentioned until 1094. By this time they are fairly on the scene, and about the same date similar officers under an identical denomination figure in the chronicles of Genoa. The towns now began to call themselves communes, the word being suggested probably by the *Commune Colloquium* or parliament, and springing naturally out of the idea of common efforts made for the common weal.

Shortly after the promulgation of his celebrated *Concordia* (or peace) Daibert profited by the happier condition of Pisa to lead the citizens to the Holy Land, and from thence he wrote an urgent letter to the Genoese, imploring them to cease their quarrels and join the army of the Cross. For Genoa seems to have gone, only a very few years later, through exactly the same crisis as Pisa, being torn by internecine feuds which, when allayed, resulted in a government by consuls. The feuds were between nobles, and the new administration when formed was evidently in the hands of a few conspicuous families whose names recurred again and again throughout a long subsequent period. But the first trustworthy annals of Genoa begin with the year 1100, and consequently the commune, as a German historian has remarked, suddenly springs from obscurity, armed and powerful like a new Minerva.

Some trace of a previous government under the Bishop may be found in certain privileges, such as that of holding the episcopal stirrup on public occasions, which were claimed by particular families, and were symbolical of a dependence that could not have been simply moral. The consuls of Genoa, also, on taking office swore to respect the *honorem*, of the Archbishop, and this of itself implied the possession by the prelate in question of material authority, *honor*, in mediæval days, signifying sometimes fief or posession, and sometimes district or territory. Moreover, for a time the treaties made by Genoa are in the joint name of Archbishop and consuls, and any feudal lord, any inhabitant of the city or the *contado* who was admitted to a *campagna*, swore fealty first to the Archbishop and then to the Consuls. The campagna was a curious institution in Genoa, being the union of a certain number of persons who joined together for purposes of mutual protection for a definite period of three or at most four years. When a campagna lapsed it could be, and generally was, renewed, and as long as it lasted it was presided over by the consuls whose term of office expired with the campagna. The members of these unions belonged to the most conspicuous families, and any person of less importance whom they admitted to their number had to be qualified for election by some special utility, aptitude, or power. The poorer citizens (*minores*) and priests were *ipso facto* excluded as associates from the campagna, which nevertheless undertook to protect them : whereas even this protection was denied to strangers and to certain people who, owing to their feudal or family relations, the commune regarded as its enemies. The individuals thus banned were not infrequently of great social power and formed a class apart, which was only not as important as the campagna because numerically weaker.

In Genoa, then, as in Pisa the bias of the commune was aristocratic and the chief difference, so far as it is faintly discernible between the two, is that Genoa appears to have developed rather more spontaneously. By the beginning of the twelfth century in the last-named city the authority of Marquis and Bishop had become a memory, while in Pisa as long as the great Matilda lived the viscounts whom she appointed, and who frequently presided over courts of justice in her name, constituted a visible reminder of sovereignty. As we have seen Viscount Hugo was allowed to keep a tower of greater height than that of his neighbours, and when the Pisan army marched out to war he led it in virtue of his office.

But though the shadow of feudal rule projected itself for a longer time over Pisa than over Genoa, it in no way dimmed the splendour of the former. Pisa was rich, powerful, and luxurious almost from the moment that her achievements pass from the dim twilight of the earlier annals into the broad light of history. A modern historian says in reference to her : " Merely from these conquests "—that is, Sardinia,

Corsica, and the Balearic Isles—" one can perceive that the Pisans from the beginning of the twelfth century were in possession of the whole trade of the western coast of the Mediterranean. One usually fails to realize how magnificent was the life of Pisa at this period. The fortified houses, the numerous retainers, the ever-extending warehouses, the wealth and independence of these princely Pisans were not of a nature to incline them towards the humbler habits of a middle class."

When Beatrice, the mother of Matilda, died, and was buried at Pisa in April, 1076, Donizone a monk of Canossa broke out into bitter invective against this place of sepulture, so wrongly chosen, as he conceived, in preference to his own pure and pious Canossa: and the principal reason of his wrath seemed to be that Pisa, the famous emporium and free port, was defiled by the presence of Infidel traders from the East and from Africa. This curious explosion of religious intolerance on the part of a monk affords a fugitive glimpse into the many-coloured life of Pisa, as well as into the complex spirit of the Middle Ages in Italy, with all its strange contrasts of luxury and superstition, besides being interesting as showing how far the town had developed through its commerce even as far back as days when the name of the great Countess was still a power in the land.

Genoa had the same aspirations as her neighbour, but constantly found that neighbour in the way. The overweening might of Pisa on the sea finally compelled the Genoese to their attacks upon her; nor were these as unsuccessful as might have been expected. The very extent of Pisa's wealth and outlaying interests made her vulnerable to the onslaught of an energetic foe whose force though smaller could be more easily concentrated, and the Genoese were also indirectly assisted by the ever-watchful jealousy against Pisa of Lucca.

III.

LUCCA AND PISA.

THE early history of Lucca differs from that of Pisa and Genoa, and yet the stages of its evolution were much the same as those of the sea republics. The tyranny of Boniface predisposed it against the rule of the Duke, and it took sides against Matilda in her struggle with Henry IV. After her death a series of Dukes were appointed to Lucca, but none enjoyed real authority. Finally, in 1160, Guelph VI. of Este, the uncle of Barbarossa, sold his rights over the town of Lucca and its territory (*contado*) in consideration of 1000 soldi to be paid yearly for ninety years by the consuls to the Duke and his successors. Two years later Barbarossa conferred a diploma of freedom on the commune, in return for an oath of fealty, sworn to by the five consuls and confirmed by a Parliament of the people, as well as an engagement to supply twenty knights for the campaign against the Pope and to pay a due share of tribute towards the expenses of the Imperial court and army. The consuls who were elected yearly had to repeat this oath on taking office, and received their investiture from the Emperor, he having come into possession of all the titles in Italy of Duke Guelph, who had renewed on a larger scale the bargain already struck with Lucca, and parted with all his honours for a consideration.

Lucca, consequently, like Genoa and Pisa, had now consuls, a Senate composed of the consul's advisers, and a Parliament of the people, the " people," however, being in all cases not the "plebs," but a majority of the rich and powerful citizens.

The commerce of Lucca must already have had a certain importance, for Henry IV. had conferred on the town the privilege of trading freely throughout his dominions, and this fact explains the passionate jealousy of Pisa, which, desirous of expanding inland, found an insurmountable obstacle to this aspiration of its neighbour ; while Lucca, in its turn, could not but look with an envious eye on a rival whose name was already famous in the marts of the East. The result was an ever-recurrent war between the two republics.

About 1112, the Pope turned his attention to Majorca and Minorca, where the presence of the Saracens vexed his soul, and he addressed an urgent appeal to the Pisans to dislodge them. The Archbishop of Pisa, Daibert's successor, preached the crusade, and on Easter Day himself assumed the cross and gave it to the crowd of devotees whom his preaching had inspired. The Pisans then elected twelve consuls for the preparation and conduct of the war. An embassy, headed by the Archbishop, was sent to Rome, there to receive the crucifix and a benediction from the pontiff, who empowered the Archbishop, on his return home, to remit the sins of the whole army. Thus purified and full of holy enthusiasm the crusaders set out—alone, say the Pisan chronicles; accompanied by a Genoese force, say the Genoese historians. Lucca had also been invited to take part in the expedition, and joined it at first, but soon, being discouraged, returned home. The enterprise, indeed, proved more difficult than had been anticipated by the Pisans, who found themselves forced to winter at Barcelona; and even when the operations against Nazaredech, King of Majorca, at last commenced, they hung fire until the arrival of the reinforcements, which had been ordered to supply the place of some Pisan galleys destroyed by being dragged ashore in stress of weather.

The first attack was made on Iviza, which was vigorously defended by Abulmanzar, second in command to the king. Stones, javelins, and poisoned arrows were launched against the undaunted Pisans, but a breach was at last made in the outer circle of the walls. Through this entered first two noble Pisans, Hugo Visconti and Duodo Duodi, followed by a soldier belonging to the small force brought by the Count of Barcelona, who had joined in the expedition. The Saracens took refuge behind a very narrow passage, which admitted only one man at a time, and at the entrance of this a valorous Moor, scimitar in hand, confronted a crowd of Pisans. A blow from the sword of Ildebrando Eufrasico cut the Moor in half, and the Pisans entering massacred all the Saracens.

The assault of the second circle followed, each consul heading his company and urging on the soldiers. On both sides the voices of the combatants reached the stars. Finally for that day the Pisans had to desist and remained within the first circle. They buried their own dead with all due honours, and piously burnt the bodies of the Infidel. Seven days the siege of the second circle lasted. On the eighth day the well-nigh exhausted Pisans mounted the walls at dawn, and at sight of them the Moors fled within the fortress. The Pisans descended and put the women and children, who alone were left, to the sword. At last, on the 10th of August, the day of St. Laurence Martyr, the city capitulated, and as soon after as possible the victors marched to Cabrera, whence they could see the walls of Majorca.

Then the Archbishop Pietro, stretching out his hand, thus addressed the soldiers:—

"Behold, O valorous warriors, that city which has the aspect of hell. It is the goal you have longed to reach, and where our Lord languishes in miserable servitude. To release him from his bondage who would not willingly fight?"

The legate Buorzo, with tears in his eyes, made another speech in a similar strain, and the Pisans were raised by these exhortations to a pitch of passionate heroism. The people of Majorca, says the chronicler, were stupified at the sight of the enemy's great fleet, and the king, the demon ruler of the Paynim, looked forth with lowering brows. Terror invaded his soul, but he concealed this feeling and summoned his people to arms. To the Christian Pisans fear was unknown, and a falling star, which seemed to typify the impending ruin of Majorca, inspired them with even more than their natural courage. Nevertheless, the final triumph did not come until the spring, when, one day, seven Pisans scaled the walls and planted there the banner of their town. The defence was fierce, individual Pisans fighting single-handed against innumerable Moors, but the assailants at last reached the foot of the fortress, where they found Ugo Visconti standing in a lake of Saracen blood, all shed by him alone. The victors were in the highest spirits. A Moor put his head through a hole in the wall, and, dragged forth immediately amid general jubilation, was gaily beheaded. All is related with youthful enthusiasm. The taking of the Majorca is an epic; the Pisans are like heroes of Illium. For them the God of the Christians fights, while on the side of the Infidels are arrayed the powers of hell. A romantic enthusiasm was the keynote of the sentiments animating these republics in their first young strength. The Pisans, when departing for this expedition, begged the Florentines to defend their town, which they feared might be attacked by Lucca. The Florentines complying, encamped two miles outside Pisa, and published an order that not one soldier should penetrate within the walls, on pain of instant death; the object of the prohibition being to protect the honour of the Pisan women. One man alone dared to violate the command, and he was condemned to die. The Pisans interceded for him, but the Florentine leaders were inexorable, and when the Pisans as a last resort refused to allow a capital punishment on their soil, the Florentines bought a piece of territory, and caused the unhappy offender to be executed there. The Pisan army, on its return, as a mark of gratitude for such stern chivalry offered the loyal allies their choice between two bronze doors from the Balearic Isles and two porphyry columns. The Florentines chose the columns, which still stand in the square of San Giovanni.

This story, although probably apocryphal, is repeated by nearly all historians, and is valuable, if for nothing else, at least for local colour.

IV.

GENOA.

IN 1222, the preponderance of a few families was already felt as an evil in Genoa, and an effort was made to redress matters by limiting the consulate to one year. It was hoped by this means also to check the farming out of the public revenues by the consuls for the whole of their term of office, which practice tended ever more towards the concentration of wealth in a few hands. Perhaps it was this growing corruption which led, in 1130, to the appointment of consuls of justice, who, with a few exceptions, decided civil suits, while the consuls of the republic reserved to themselves the right of deciding finally in all criminal and some civil matters. They could revoke their own decisions, but nobody else had the right to appeal against them. Both the consuls of the commune and the consuls of justice received a fixed annual stipend, which was paid to them out of the proceeds of taxes on provisions, on the public weights and measures, and out of harbour dues. On special occasions extraordinary sums were allotted to them, but they and their wives were rigorously forbidden to accept presents for any object connected with their official capacity.

The number of consuls of the commune varied at different periods, but was eventually fixed at four; one, that is, for each quarter of the city. The consuls of justice were seven or eight, corresponding

CHURCH OF ST. LORENZO, GENOA.
(*After a photograph by Brogi.*)

to the number of *campagne* into which the citizens were divided.

All questions brought before the consuls of the commune were decided by vote. If the votes were equal on both sides, then a stranger (of whose opinion the consuls were ignorant) was called in, and having had the point with which he was previously unacquainted explained to him, he gave the casting vote.

On assuming office the consuls of the commune swore in the presence of their predecessors to respect the rights of the Church and the town. Originally they were chosen by the campagne or by the Parliament, which appointed electors for the purpose, but after a time they designated their own successors. Their jurisdiction extended not only over the town of Genoa and its neighbourhood, but included the coast from Porto Venere to Monaco.

The power of the consuls in Genoa, however, as in Pisa and in Pistoja, was held in check by the Council of Conciliators, to which, in some Italian towns, the title of "Credenza" (signifying confidence or secrecy) was later given, and which was composed of men wise and experienced in public matters, and technically learned in the law. It constituted then a kind of senate (such being, in fact, the name given to it by the Pisans in the twelfth century), and controlled the action of the consuls in all questions of peace and war, or where a subsidy was to be demanded, or a public prohibition to be pronounced.

The Parliament of the people in Genoa presumably consisted at first only in the members of the campagne, or efficient members of the state. It was called together by the consuls on certain fixed occasions, or when affairs of great moment were to be discussed. On surrendering office, for instance, the consuls had to appear before the Parliament at the Town Palace, there to give an account of their public acts and expenditure. That sometimes the Parliament formed a popular tribunal whose decisions were final, may be inferred from an appeal for the restoration of certain church property made to the assembly by the Bishop of Pisa in 1112; and if this may not seem to have much to do with the history of Genoa, it must be remembered that the materials for an historical reconstruction of the Italian communes are scanty, and that much reasoning in the matter must proceed by analogy.

The power of Genoa gradually increased through absorption of the surrounding feudal nobles and their lands, as in the case, for instance, of the Lords of Vizzano, who sold Porto Venere to the republic for one hundred lire, and bound themselves to military service within a limited district. Every feudatory desiring to trade under Genoese protection was allowed to invest a certain sum in the maritime enterprises of the commune, on condition of first swearing fealty and binding himself to military service. In this way one turbulent neighbour after another was won over, and if his acquisition was sometimes a doubtful blessing he did not, at least, show himself a more unruly subject of the republic than many a native born son.

In 1119 a war broke out between Genoa and Pisa concerning Corsica, which both claimed to have conquered from the Moors. But as the latter generally reoccupied the islands as soon as the victorous galleys had disappeared, these conquests did not amount to much. And as both Corsica and Sardinia formed part of the pretended donations of Constantine, the popes were perpetually interfering in their affairs. As regards Corsica, Pisa was on the whole most favoured by the Holy See, and the irritation of Genoa rose to fever heat when Pope Gelasius II. made the bishops of the island suffragans of the Archbishop of Pisa. The two communes flew to arms; but Calixtus II. on his accession sought to re-establish peace by summoning a Lateran Council, whither went Caffaro, Genoa's earliest annalist, as one of the delegates from his native commune. He describes the negotiations, the efforts made by the Pope to satisfy both parties, and how his final decision in favour of Genoa so enraged the Archbishop of Pisa, that he threw his cap and ring at the feet of the Pontiff, exclaiming, "No longer will I be Archbishop or Bishop of thine," then rushed out followed by all the Pisans.

After this, naturally, the war continued until put an end to by the Pope Innocent II., who was in difficulties and wanted assistance from both the sea communes.

V.

HOW THE COMMUNES GREW.

THE complexity of Italian history at this period, the confused strife of ambitions, the views of popes and antipopes, of emperors and Normans, all had their share in the growth of the communes which again interacted upon each other, so that any help given to wandering emperor or fugitive pontiff by Genoa and Pisa had consequences if not immediate, at least eventual, for Lucca and Florence.

In February, 1130, died Pope Honorius II., when a portion of the cardinals, supported by the powerful Frangipani, chose as his successor Gregory Papareschi, a native Roman.

But this did not suit the majority of the electors, or of the party whom they represented, and their choice fell upon Peter Leone, who in spite of his Jewish origin possessed enormous influence in Rome, and he was raised to the papal chair by his adherents under the name of Anaclet II. He held the Castle of Sant' Angelo, the Vatican and Trastevere generally; while his rival, now designated as Innocent II., dwelt in the Lateran in such partial security as the armed retainers of the Frangipani and their friends could afford him. Out of Rome his party was strong, being composed of Ravenna, Parma, Pavia, and the towns allied to these—also of the King of France, and eventually of Lothair of Germany, while Anaclet had chiefly to attach himself to the Normans in Sicily. This country had been conquered by Roger Guiscard, whose brother Robert possessed himself of Puglia and Calabria. William, Duke of Puglia, a grandson of Robert, died without children, and then Roger II., of Sicily, conceived the design, eventually successful, of uniting the dominions of his kinsmen to his own. Campania had been settled by the Greeks, and the towns founded by them developed communal institutions even earlier than Genoa and Pisa, being assisted in their development by precisely the same cause, namely, the unceasing incursions of the Saracen. Amalfi especially had a brilliant history and had early roused the jealousy, and brought on herself the attacks of Pisa, who saw in the southern republic a rival of her own commercial wealth and splendour.

Anaclet had established a friendly understanding with Roger II., whose usurpation of Puglia and Calabria displeased Innocent II. as it had done his predecessor, for the reason that the popes claimed dominion over the south, and by supporting the Barons who had revolted against Roger, delayed the fruition of the latter's plans.

This was the state of affairs in the autumn of 1132, when Lothair, who wished to be crowned emperor in Rome, came from Germany as far as Roncaglia to have an interview with Innocent II.

The Pope was fully alive to the necessity of procuring allies in Italy against Anaclet and Roger, and consequently turned his attention to the two sea communes whose fleets could best serve his purpose.

The first thing was to make peace between them, and this he succeeded at last in doing by coming to Pisa and winning the rulers there to his views. He divided Corsica between the two republics, and decreed that the Bishop of Genoa, who up to this time had been a suffragan of the Archbishop of Milan, should receive the high rank and be given the diocese of Corsica, while the diocese of Sardinia fell to the share of the Archbishop of Pisa.

At the end of the following March Lothair entered Rome, but could only get himself crowned in the Church of the Lateran instead of at St. Peter's, from whence there was no evicting Anaclet. The Pisan and Genoese ships indeed conquered the Roman seacoast for Innocent, but that was not much help to him, and when Lothair some months later was driven by heat out of Rome, the Pope felt his own position there to be insecure and returned once again to Pisa.

In 1135 the Barons of Sicily were anew in revolt against Roger, and found allies in Sergius, the military governor of Naples, in Rainulf of Alifa and Robert of Capua.

The chief event in this third war between the insurgents and Roger is the destruction of Amalfi by the Pisans. The brilliant and cultured town was taken and sacked by its ruthless rivals, and as owing to altered circumstances the commercial supremacy of Amalfi had already begun to wane, the blow struck by the Pisans was to all intents and purposes a fatal one.

As far as Innocent II. was concerned, the help lent him by Genoa and Pisa was of no particular use. After the death of Anaclet Innocent bought off all his other opponents and, being then generally recognized as Pope, felt himself strong enough to proceed in person to Benevento for the purpose of entering into negotiations with Roger. But the negotiations fell through : both parties took the field, and Innocent soon found himself a prisoner. From this undignified position he was released on condition that he should recognize Roger as King of the Two Sicilies— and after doing this he returned to Rome, and his allies were again able to attend to their own affairs. Perpetual fighting against each other, varied by foreign enterprises was now the order of the day among the communes : it may be said indeed that strife internal and external was a condition of their existence. Nothing short of the intense individualism thus developed would have enabled them within such narrow limits, on such restricted strips of territory, to have played the lofty part they did and which was soon to fill the courts of Europe with their ambassadors and the marts of the known world with their traders.

They were governed instinctively in all their actions by the state necessity of protecting their freedom against superior aggression and against each other ; they obeyed a spontaneous economical instinct in the successful effort to supply by commerce the wealth which there was no homogeneous territorial aristocracy to create for them; and they had inherited from the Dark Ages, when men's souls had so long been oppressed by the terror of coming doom, a robust belief in the supernatural, in the nearness of God and the punishment of the damned. Enterprises against the Infidel constituted their ideal, the poetry, the glory of their lives; and they undertook these crusades with a joyful fervour that was very different from the savage exultation with which the Pisans attacked the Lucchese and the Genoese fell foul of the Pisans. One hardly understands these youthful communes until one has reflected on these contrasts in their character; how ardent they were yet how practical; how hard-headed, yet how valiant; how personal in their patriotism; how unselfish in their enthusiasm. Pisa could not but regard with jealousy every fresh acquisition made by Lucca whose vicinity condemned her to the sole outlook towards the sea, and all through the first half of the twelfth century Lucca was perpetually gaining ground by the conquest of surrounding castles, or the voluntary cession to the commune of territory by feudal nobles, like the two Viscounts of Versilia, Uguccione, and Walter, who were wise in their generation, and made a merit of necessity.

The shadowy Marquises or Margraves, Conrad, Rempret, Engelbert, Henry of Bavaria, Welf, who succeeded one another in rapid succession, served no purpose apparently but that of demonstrating with what impunity their feudatories might be dispossessed; and Florence, like Lucca, was quick to profit by the opportunity. In 1129 the Florentines took possession of the castle of Vignale in Val d'Elsa ; in 1135 they destroyed that of Monteboni, the cradle of the Buondelmonti who were forced to submit to the commune, to bind themselves to defend it in time of war, and to inhabit the city during some months of every year.

In 1144 Florence had attacked Siena, and the Lucchese, going to help the latter, were fallen upon by the Pisans at the instigation of the Florentines. On this occasion the Pisans were victorious ; a few months later, at Vorno, it was the Lucchese. In vain Pope Eugenius III. sent the celebrated Peter, abbot of Clugny, into Tuscany, with the object of reconciling the contending parties. Pisa and Lucca at any rate would not listen to him, and in 1148 war was raging again between them with such fierceness that not even in Holy Week would they lay down their arms.

The next struggle of the Lucchese was against Count Guido Guerra, one of the most powerful of the independent nobles of Tuscany, whom they vanquished to their no small satisfaction, and the great chagrin of the Pisans. But Lucca was by this time really strong, having an army of five hundred cavalry and twenty thousand foot, besides five thousand auxiliary cavalry, furnished doubtless by the once menacing neighbours whom she had gradually reduced to her rule.

During a portion of this period Genoa had been busy with an expedition against the Moors in Almeria. This had long been a great stronghold of the Infidel, renowned for its silk manufactures, and for general wealth and splendour. The Visigoth king of Spain wrote to Pope Eugenius III., urging him to initiate a crusade against the town, and he addressed a letter on the subject to the Genoese impressing on them the importance of the enterprise, in which they were to have the co-operation of the kings of Castille and Navarre, as well as of Raymond Berengarius, Count of Barcelona. The last named, however, did not intend to embark on the undertaking without a previous bargain, and it was agreed between him and the consuls of Genoa that he should keep two-thirds, and the republic one-third, of the territory to be annexed in Tortosa and the Balearic Isles, the consuls stipulating nevertheless for a Genoese commercial settlement with exemption from dues and taxes in the future dominions of the Count. These preliminaries settled, a Parliament was summoned in Genoa, and the project laid before it. The prospect of such a holy enterprise mixed with material advantages excited the liveliest enthusiasm. At the suggestion of the consuls peace was made between all enemies, and sworn to before the altars of the city amid tears and embraces. It was decreed that any person refusing to join in the crusade should be branded with infamy—himself and his children—that no campagna should count him among its members, and no taxes be remitted to him. In other words, he was to be deprived of Genoese citizenship, and treated as a foreigner. Women brought their jewels as a contribution toward the expenses of the armament. Among the male population young and old sought to join; all volunteered to assist in the preparation of the ships; and so great were the efforts made that in five months sixty-three galleys, one hundred and sixty-three smaller sail, and thirty thousand troops were equipped. By the end of August, 1147, the Genoese arrived at Capo de' Gatta, but formed no allies. Alfonso, king of Castille and Leon, had gone home again owing to want of means, and Don Garcia of Navarre would not fight without him. After a time Count Raymond appeared, and success having attended the first unassisted efforts of the Genoese, the allies presently returned, but were so nearly bought off by the Moors, that the consuls, who suspected their baseness, hurried on the assault. On the 26th of October, at dawn, the city was stormed with brilliant results, the Genoese taking, it was said, ten thousand prisoners and an enormous booty. The commune assigned Almeria for thirty years as a fief to Ottone Buonvillano, who undertook to hold the fortress with a garrison of three hundred men. A further force of one thousand was left to him, and the Genoese fleet sailed for Barcelona and there wintered. The enthusiastic Parliament at home, as soon as the news of these events reached it, clamoured for the despatch of further reinforcements, and with the help of these, the Genoese, a few Pisans and the Counts of Barcelona and Montpelliers, took the town of Tortosa in the following year. The fortress capitulated only a year and more later, and the credit of this strenuous victory was chiefly due to the Genoese, as Raymond's soldiers, not having been paid, deserted. Tortosa, like Almeria, was formed into a fief and given, on the usual conditions, to a group of Genoese citizens.

The triumphant armament then returned home, but the glory it had achieved was momentarily obscured by the anxiety now possessing all men's minds at the approach of the redoubtable Barbarossa.

With the instinct of liberty and self-aggrandizement which at present never deserted them, Genoa and the Tuscan communes immediately felt the importance of the struggle then beginning between the emperor and the free towns of Lombardy. Frederick's design was a great one, in as much as he desired to recover, and to endow with fresh vitality those imperial prerogatives in Italy which his careless or feeble predecessors, from the time of Henry V., had allowed to pass out of their possession. His claims were not more unreasonable than most pretensions of the sort, and by the decision of the jurists of Bologna they were soon to receive the stamp of legality. His pretexts, in short, were plausible, and half a century earlier, if advanced by as great a man as he, they might have prevented the communes from developing, and would have made the world poorer by the loss of all that Milan and Venice and Florence were to teach it. But the time for that was happily now over : the communes were self-conscious and strong in a knowledge of their own aims ; their wealth made them important, the moral power of conviction made them invincible, and from the date which we have now reached until three hundred years later their history, through all its superficial contradictions and changes, even through what sometimes looks like treachery and baseness, is a narrative of intelligent self-preservation and valiant self-defence.

But before proceeding to describe the attitude of the republics towards Barbarossa, we must return to an earlier period, and relate the origin and development of Florence, latest-born but most glorious of all the great Tuscan towns.

VI.

THE ORIGIN OF FLORENCE.

THE documents for reconstructing the origin of Florence are very scarce, and it is only in the twelfth century that some annals began to be written, and even these only recorded some of the more important events, with dates and names of places and people. To about the same period belong lists of the consuls, who were duly followed later by the Podestà. We know, therefore, that Florence had a consular government like Genoa and Pisa, but we are in ignorance of the stages of development which led to this result. In Florence, as soon as any consuls are heard of, it seems that they were changed every year, and this fact alone proves a certain maturity in the form of government. For the first tendency of men is certainly to appoint a permanent leader; the distrust which suggests frequent change is a sentiment born of experience.

Legends clustered thick round the origin of Florence, which was supposed to have been founded by Julius Cæsar. Catiline, after his conspiracy, fled to Fiesole, and was pursued by a Roman force under Metellus and Fiorinus who were routed, the last named being killed. Julius Cæsar besieged Fiesole, razed it to the ground, and built a new city on the spot where Fiorinus had fallen. Catiline was overtaken in the mountains near Pistoja, and defeated in a battle so bloody that a plague followed on the mortality whence the name of Pistoja from *pestis*. It may be remarked in passing that a legendary derivation was found for the names of all the principal Tuscan cities; Pisa being suggested by *pesare* because the Romans received their tribute there; Lucca, by *lucere*, because it was the first town to receive the light of Christianity; Siena, by *Senæ-Senarum*, because the Franks, when marching against the Langobards, had there deposited all their old people.

Fiorinus, Fluentia (a reference to the flowing Arno) and Flowers (of which the soil bore abundance) were all offered as explanations of the name of Florence.

That city was built, still according to the legend, like Rome with a Capitol, a Forum, a theatre, and baths. It flourished for five hundred years till destroyed by Totila who rebuilt Fiesole. At the end of another five hundred years Florence, having apparently risen again and preserving a long memory for old injuries, assaulted and destroyed Fiesole. In all this the one grain of truth seems to be that Florence really owed its origin to the Etruscan town of Fiesole which, from a very early time, founded an emporium for its traders at the junction of the Mugnone and the Arno. The huts then built eventually became a town, being perhaps favoured in its development by the Romans when they began to make roads in the valley of the Arno as a protection against the invading Ligurians. Strabo, who alludes to Pisa as one of the bravest of Etruscan towns, makes no mention of Florence, but Tacitus and Pliny speak of it, and recent excavations in bringing Roman remains to light prove that in the time of Sylla the town really merited its appellation of *Municipium splendidissimum.* Its first circle of walls probably dates from the time of Augustus, who restored the town. Oltr' Arno was the portion of the city beyond the Old Bridge, and although originally only a suburb, became eventually included in the second circle of the walls. These, according to the historian Villani, were built in 1078, and as he himself was present during the construction of the third and last circle (now in their turn almost entirely destroyed) which were begun in 1299, it may be concluded that he was correct in his assertion.

After the brilliant Roman dawn a period of complete obscurity envelopes the history of Florence. Flashes here and there reveal an invasion by the Goths under Radagaisus in 405, and a victory over them carried off by Stilicho; further, frightful cruelties committed in 545 by Totila who, however, contrary to the legend, did not destroy Florence; then the occupation in 570 by the Langobards during the period of whose reign the darkness becomes greater than ever. The commerce of Florence was completely ruined, and so many families migrated to Fiesole that in the middle of the eight century that town had again risen to superior importance, and Florence seems to have been included in it as a sort of suburb. From this degradation it was rescued gradually during the rule of the Franks, when, security returning, the descendants of the former emigrants returned from the hills to the valley, and over Florence a Count was set whose jurisdiction extended almost as far as Prato, and was limited by the various districts of Lucca, Volterra, and Fiesole.

The territory thus attached to Florence was called its *contado*. Charlemagne really came to Florence at Christmas 786, where his visit formed the foundation of the legend that he had built Florence up again after its pretended destruction by Totila some two hundred and forty years previously.

From the time of the Frankish rule, Florence prospered, thanks for one thing to a geographical position which connected her with Rome, and was very favourable to commerce. Several churches had already been built within the walls and outside them by the end of the tenth century—one among these being the lovely San Miniato: and, as Professor Villari observes, Florence speedily became one of the chief centres for the reform of the cloisters, a movement which beginning at Cluny spread to other countries, and in Italy bore later a complex growth in the strange mysticism of Joachim and the tender teachings of St. Francis.

When to material advantages such as Florence already possessed in its renascent and increasing commerce, a spirit of moral enthusiasm is joined, the keen vitality of a people, thus roused to struggle in different departments, proves itself independent of any form of government; and the feudal husk still enclosing Florence was powerless to hamper its development. Old rights seemed chiefly to have served as confirmation after the fact, and it is curious to observe that the first internecine war in Florence was of religious and not of political origin. San Giovanni Gualberto, founder of the reformed Benedictine Order of the Monks of Vallombrosa, preached in the streets of the town against the Bishop of Florence, Pietro da Pavia, who he affirmed had obtained his high position through a large sum of money paid into the imperial and margravian coffers. These charges roused the monks and the people to frenzy against the bishop, who with an armed force besieged the convent of San Salvi, wrecked the altars, and killed several of the brothers. Five years the struggle lasted, and St. Peter Damian, sent by Pope Alexander II. to try and restore peace in a letter addressed to the citizens of Florence, "beloved in Christ," positively asserted that nearly a thousand people had preferred to die without the sacraments of the Church rather than receive them from the hands of the priests ordained by the simoniacal bishop. His attempts at pacification were fruitless; the monks who at his instance had gone to Rome to submit their complaint to a council, only appeared before the latter to declare that they desired the question of the bishop's guilt or innocence to be decided by a judgment of God; or, in other words, a trial by fire. The Pope and council highly disapproved of this suggestion, and ordered the turbulent monks to retire to their convents. San Giovanni Gualberto, consternated at the storm he himself had raised, would fain have induced them to obey the command, but the monks were unruly, and the people of Florence no sooner heard of the proposed ordeal than they passionately clamoured for it.

The champion selected was a monk named Peter, formerly a herdsman at Vallombrosa. His impatience to enter the flames was overpowering; and not even the threats of the bishop, who, strong in the support of Duke Godfrey and Beatrice, ordered that all rebellious priests and laymen should be bound with cords and dragged before the ruler of the town, availed to quench the religious fervour of the champion or the frantic eagerness of the populace. The trial by fire finally took place at the Badia of S. Salvi at Settimo, five miles from Florence, on the 13th of February, 1068. An enormous crowd of men, women and children gathered there, having filled the way for miles around with the sounds of prayers and hymns as they advanced. This preparation was favourable to the production of a miracle, and it is not surprising to learn that Peter was seen to issue unharmed from the flames. The news flew to Rome; the Pope necessarily submitted to such testimony and the vanquished bishop had to retire to a convent. The poor monk was made a cardinal and bishop of Albano, and adored after his death as a saint under the name of Peter Igneus.

Religious zeal, commercial interests centred in Rome, and the neighbourhood of numerous feudal nobles whose raids imperilled the lives and goods of their traders—all tended to make Florence Guelph. These nobles were of Germanic descent, while the population of Florence was largely of the artizan class, Roman in origin and tradition.

The feudal barons were secure in their castles, and had nothing to gain by descending to inhabit the town where wealth was only beginning, and which, having no fleets, offered no advantages for foreign enterprise, or opportunities for spoil. The Donati, the Caponsacchi, the Uberti, the Lamberti and others who sat in Matilda's tribunals and later composed the consulate, were neither counts, marquises, nor dukes, like the Counts Cadolingi, Guidi, Alberti who inhabited the contado, some of whom were descendants of the Cattani Lombardi (Lombard captains) whose origin was distinctly Teutonic. The leading Florentine citizens were not real nobles, but conspicuous persons (grandi) of superior wealth, but addicted, at the time we are considering, to no trade:—a fact proved by their belonging to the cavalry which did not include artizans. Later the grandi engaged extensively in commerce, and were heads of the Major Guilds, as soon as these became definitely organized. Their opportunity was made by the slackness of margravian rule, which produced in Florence the same results as in Pisa, Genoa, and Lucca, the city when left to its own devices spontaneously organizing itself into associations, and forming a local government to which the later institution of the consuls only set an official seal. Out of these associations the commune built itself, unobserved, by a slow process of absorption and aggregation; but there remained outside it some unassimilated groups who constituted its first difficulties and dangers. At Pisa, for instance, where the commune was of aristocratic origin, the artizan class or members of the Arti Minori remained so long an unabsorbed element, that as late as 1226, they were ordered to submit their statutes for correction to the magistrates of the commune, and deprived of the right of naming their own consuls or rectors.

In Florence the process was different, in so far as the government there was of popular origin. It owed little to the feudal ruler, and less to the feudal nobility, but everything to its own commerce and industry; and how the impulse to this commerce might be given by the old Roman *Scholæ* it is easy to understand.

As Hegel says, there can be no doubt that among the populations which had originally flourished under Roman rule a tradition of the *Scholæ* would remain. Their essential character of course vanished at the same time as the State with which they were bound up, but what probably survived were associations for self-defence, under an influential patron for whom the members of the society were bound to work. Certain rules and regulations connected with trade are more likely to have continued unchanged through several centuries, than to have been subjected in the Dark Ages to a process of reconstruction. The very word, Arte, by which the guilds were distinguished is found in its Latin form in a letter addressed by Gregory the Great to the soapboilers of Naples, in which *Ars* is used in the identical sense as *Schola* the word more generally employed in Rome, Ravenna, and other towns of the same region. Now Florence, as we have learnt, had enjoyed a period of prosperity under the Romans, and as soon as the dark veil which enveloped her history during the centuries of barbarian rule is lifted, we find her already engaged in a commerce of sufficient importance to make her traders a desirable prey for the feudal lords. The Langobards and Franks were certainly not commercial in their aptitudes and must have depended in great measure for their wants upon the working population of the town. In Florence, this population, untrammelled by feudal interference, and unseduced by the possibilities of foreign enterprise, offered to Genoa and Pisa, became from the first an important class; and if the period of incubation of this, the greatest of Tuscan communes was longer than that of its neighbours, the reason was that in its multiplying workshops and growing streets it slowly educated the future rulers who in other towns were imported from the mountain eeries of Langobardic barons and Frankish knights.

But the sources of Florentine commerce were in flocks and land, the possessors of which, forming a comparatively leisured class, were naturally the first to emerge into visible importance, and to be intrusted by Matilda with conspicuous posts. These grandi, for the moment identical in their interests with the people, were later to form associations of their own, known as the companies of the Towers. But their energies were at present altogether employed in making war upon their dangerous neighbours, the inhabitants of the castles. Already in 1107 they assailed the Monte Orlando near Lastra a Signa, a possession of the formidable Cadolingi. The same year, assisted by Matilda, they destroyed the castle of Prato which belongs to Counts Alberti, and three years later in the Val di Pesa a fresh victory was obtained over the Cadolingi, who ruled over a territory extending from Pistoja almost to Lucca on one side, and from the lower valley of the Arno almost to Florence on the other. Between 1113 and 1119 attacks were made, with final success, upon Monte Cascioli yet another stronghold of the same family, and by these successive victories the Florentines had opened a way for their trade by Signa, by Prato, and by Val d'Elsa.

After the death of Matilda in 1115 circumstances caused the grandi to be recognized as consuls of the now regularly constituted commune.

Matilda, as is known, had left her vast possessions to the Church. In reality she was only entitled thus to bequeath her allodial lands the remainder being imperial fiefs. But as it was not always easy to distinguish between the two sorts, and the popes were naturally anxious to get as much as they could, a fresh source of contention was added to the constant quarrels between the Empire and the Church.

" Henry IV. immediately despatched a representative into Tuscany, who under the title of *Marchio*, *Judex*, or *Praeses*, was to govern the Marquisate in his name." " Nobody," says Professor Villari, " could legally dispute his right to do this : but the opposition of the Pope, the attitude of the towns which now considered themselves independent and the universal confusion rendered the Marquis's authority illusory. The imperial representatives had no choice but to put themselves at the head of the feudal nobility of the contado and unite it into a Germanic party hostile to the cities. In the documents of the period the members of this party are continually described as *Teutonici.*"

By throwing herself in this juncture on the side of the Pope, and thus becoming the declared opponent of the empire and the feudal lords, Florence practically proclaimed her independence. The grandi, having the same interests with the working classes, identified themselves with these; became their leaders, their consuls in fact if not yet in name. Thus was the consular commune born, or, rather, thus did it recognize itself on reaching manhood; for born, in reality, it had already been for some time, only so quietly and unconsciously that nobody had marked its origin or, until now, its growth. The first direct consequence of this self-recognition was that the rulers were chosen out of a larger number of families. As long as Matilda had chosen the officers to whom the government of the town was entrusted, the Uberti and a few others who formed their clan, their kinsmen, and their connections had been selected, to the exclusion of the mass of the citizens. Now more people were admitted to a share in the administration: the offices were of shorter duration, and out of those selected to govern each family had its turn. But those who had formerly been privileged—the Uberti and others of the same tendencies and influence—were necessarily discontented with this state of things, and there are indications in Villani of burnings and of tumults such as later, when the era of faction fights had fairly begun, so often desolated the streets of Florence.

In 1125 the Florentines marched out against Fiesole, took and destroyed it. The immediate cause of the war was the spoiling by the inhabitants of Fiesole of a Florentine merchant who was passing through their town with his wares; but, if we are to trust Villani, the old hatred between the two cities had of late been greatly increased by the fact that Fiesole formed a refuge for robber nobles, descendants of Langobardic captains, who were at the head of bands of highwaymen and malefactors and thus rendered the district near Florence insecure for traders. For the rest, by their victory the Florentines overthrew more than their enemies: since of course every successful enterprise of the commune strengthened the tenure of its newly-acquired independence.

By the year 1138 the consuls of Florence are mentioned in documents: for some time after this they were nominated only for brief periods such as a month or two months, and their number corresponded to the divisions of the town, there being usually two consuls for each Sestiere, consequently twelve in all. When they came to be appointed for a year, the election took place always in January.

Two out of the twelve (or whatever might be the number, for this was not invariable) were elected by turns to preside over the others, and they were called *Consules priores*.

By about the middle of the century the Guilds or Arti, as we shall henceforth call them, were already constituted, and so were the Associations of the Towers. The Arti were composed of merchants and artizans, while to the Towers belonged the grandi. The component members of such association lived in adjoining houses, above which rose the tower of defence that all possessed in common, and to the expenses of which all contributed. Every association was ruled by two or three rectors to whom sometimes the appellation of consuls was given, and who settled disputes and chose their own successors. These rectors and those enrolled with them were at present the class out of which exclusively the rulers of the city itself were chosen. This did not prevent their being also in some instances consuls of the Guilds and, indeed, many grandi became merchants. The Societies of both sorts were democratic in their nature, were formed, apparently, for mutual self-defence and possessed not a trace of feudalism. The party which, like the Uberti and others, might have introduced a feudal constitution were for the present almost totally excluded from power.

The Guilds were already so thoroughly organized that, as Villani relates, the work of building the church of San Giovanni in 1150 was entrusted to the Guild of the Wool Merchants (Arte di Calimala), who had risen, through their wealth and the extension of their commerce, to such importance that, in a treaty of alliance concluded in 1184 between Florence and Lucca, it was expressly stated that any alteration of the articles might be made either by the Florentine consuls, or by twenty-five councillors among whom the rectors of the wool merchants were to be included.

We have consequently got to represent Florence to ourselves as now governed in effect by associations and guilds who, for all matters connected with war or finance or justice, were represented by annual consuls : these being assisted, as in Pisa and Genoa, by a Senate or Council of Good Men (who in Florence numbered a hundred), and having the right, as elsewhere, to summon on great occasions a Parliament of the people.

From this government were at present excluded the working classes and lower orders or plebs as well as the inhabitants of the contado. Professor Villari seems to think that the Parliament was theoretically composed, even from the beginning, of the entire city population, but points out that as it often met in a small piazza or even in a church, only a limited number of persons can really have taken part in it. It must be remarked that the council was not distinctively a legislative assembly, nor were the consuls solely the executive. They judged and governed, and sometimes even promulgated laws without reference to the council, which, on its side, often dispensed with the ceremony of discussing the laws submitted to it for approval. The Parliament in general gave its sanction without any clear comprehension of the question it had been summoned to consider ; and government generally was of a free and elastic description, such as suited voluntary combinations of men who administered the affairs of their town in much the same resolute and ready spirit as they did the business of their warehouses, their shops, and their towers.

VII.

THE TUSCAN COMMUNES AND GENOA IN THE TIME OF BARBAROSSA.

IN 1162-3 Frederick Barbarossa, perceiving the authority of his uncle Guelph or Welf to be illusory, despatched the Archbishop Reinhold, of Cologne, to Tuscany, with orders to restore the imperial supremacy upon a new basis. Barbarossa's object, as is well known, was to recover the Regalia and other privileges which his predecessors, in their struggles with the Church or their acquiescence in the *status quo*, had either been deprived of or had allowed to lapse. How these views involved Frederick in a cruel war upon the Lombard towns, and led eventually to the establishment of German Podestàs as his representatives, are facts which belong to the commonplaces of history.

Frederick saw that the feudal rule was a thing of the past, and sought by fresh means to re-establish the authority which he conceived himself, in his imperial capacity, to possess. He partially succeeded, only eventually to fail, and his concessions to Genoa and the Tuscan towns were in reality a recognition of their power and a confession of his own weakness.

In the meanwhile Reinhold filled the principal castles round Florence with German counts or Podestàs and German garrisons: building new castles where none previously existed or where the old ones had been demolished, and choosing San Miniato—called since then San Miniato al Tedesco—as the centre of his foreign government. When Reinhold went, he was succeeded by Christian, Archbishop of Mayence, and the same policy continued. Everywhere we find the German Podestàs, but nowhere less than in Florence do we find that they hindered the development of the communes in Central Italy. In the contado, indeed, the presence of these imperial officers with their garrisons created a Teutonic party among the feudal castellans, between whom and the consuls of the towns there were unceasing disputes.

Even the communes, which like Pisa and Lucca declared for the Empire, had no notion of parting with their liberty to Frederick; so that in reality there were three factions: the party of the Empire, the party of Barbarossa, and the party of the people, which, as far as supporting the Church against the Emperor went, meant also the party of the Church.

Frederick confirmed both Pisa and Lucca in their independence, and promised them security in their conquests. Genoa had early taken alarm at the presence in Italy of Barbarossa, and when he demanded the usual regalia, began hastily to arm. Men, women, children, helped in the fortifications, which were made so impregnable that Frederick renounced all idea of a struggle. He allowed the Genoese to keep their consular government, and waived his claims to their possessions even those which had been imperial fiefs, only exacting in return that the republic should take the oath of fealty and pay twelve hundred silver marks. After the siege and destruction of Milan a fresh treaty established that in return for investiture with the whole Riviera from Monaco to Porto Venere (with reserve only of the jurisdiction of the Marquis of Montferrat, the Counts of Lavagna, and a few other feudal lords), Genoa would furnish the Emperor with a fleet for the conquest of Sicily, Puglia, and Calabria, &c. But it must be clearly understood that what lay at the bottom of all treaties between the communes and German sovereigns was simply the determination of the former to preserve their independence and their commerce, not only against a foreign foe, but also against each other. No sentimental attachment to a cause influenced these republicans at any time, and Genoa was quite as willing to sell the Emperor, if necessary, at any moment, as Florence was to desert its allegiance to the Church. Genoa was at this period, as always, desolated by faction fights, but her spirit was stubborn, and in spite of all difficulties she made an energetic stand against the Pisans in Sardinia, and succeeded in occupying one half of the island. The Pisans retaliating laid Arborea waste: then both combatants appealed to Frederick, who accepted thirteen thousand lire from Pisa as a retainer, but finding the Genoese too difficult to deal with, abstained from any decision, and by keeping both rivals in suspense induced them to lend him equal help in his expedition against Rome; for the Eternal City was again divided between two

Popes, Alexander III. and Pope Paschal III., the former opposing the Emperor and the latter supporting him.

In the summer of 1167, Frederick marched upon Rome and took the Leonine city. Paschal made a solemn entry, and on the 1st of August crowned Frederick and his wife. Alexander was practically a prisoner in the neighbourhood of the Colosseum, and the Roman people swore fealty to Kaiser and Antipope. Barbarossa's triumph seemed complete, and it was just in this hour of success that what looked like a judgment of God overtook the ruthless Hohenstaufen, for Roman fever suddenly laid his army low. In the morning the Germans were alive, says an historian; in the evening they were dead. The Emperor, leaving a garrison to protect Paschal, quitted the fatal city as quickly as possible and went to Lucca, losing, it is said, yet another two thousand men by the way. This disaster gave fresh courage to the Lombard communes, and in the spring of 1168, the League was so fully formed that Frederick, to escape with his life, had to flee in disguise across the Alps with only five companions. He carried with him a conviction of the strength of the allied republics, and remained some years in Germany while preparing a force powerful enough, as he hoped, to crush the combination.

His departure was the signal for the central republics to turn against each other, Lucca drawing Genoa into an alliance against Pisa which was beset by sea and land. Versilia and Garfagnana overrun by contending troops were the scenes of many battles, in which one castle after another fell to triumphant Lucca, who either destroyed or gave them to the flames. On the water Pisa had better luck, taking Motrone to the chagrin of Genoa, and Viareggio to the dismay of the Lucchese.

The latter then induced Siena, Pistoja, and Count Guido to enter into a league against the common foe; on which the Florentines required little persuasion to conclude an alliance for forty years with the Pisans, who not only gave them an opportunity to wage war against Count Guido, but accorded various commercial advantages precious to an inland State like Florence. Archbishop Christian, who had been left in Tuscany as Imperial Vicar, at last interposed to conclude peace, but as Pisa refused to give up the prisoners she had taken unless indemnified, the first negotiations fell through and the stubborn commune was excommunicated. Christian renewed his efforts a little later, and in a Parliament held at Pisa on the 1st of June, 1173, he formulated terms which were solemnly agreed to by all the contending parties.

This happy state of things lasted for two months, when it was put an end to by an unexpected action of Christian himself. He invited the consuls of Pisa and Florence to appear before him at San Genesio on the 4th of August, and on their obeying he had them seized and thrown into prison. The much-disputed reason of this move appears to have been a secret treaty concluded by Pisa and Florence with some malcontent refugees from San Miniato al Tedesco, who in the palace of the Bishop of Florence swore to hand over their castle to the two allied towns, if these could succeed in driving out the German garrison. Christian, on discovering these facts, thought himself entitled to consider that neither Florence nor Pisa desired peace, and he gave effect to this conviction by imprisoning their consuls. A Florentine force, already assembled at Castel Fiorentino, was strengthened by two hundred and twenty-five knights sent by the Pisans, from Pontedera, under the leadership of two consuls. Christian advanced on his side with Count Guido and the Lucchese; but the latter had soon to desert him and return to their own territory which was being laid waste by the Pisans : in spite of his dwindled numbers, however, the Archbishop would not retreat, and in the battle which followed he was beaten. The subsequent course of the war, if it continued at all, is unknown, but the following year when Frederick was again at Pavia, he summoned Pisan, Lucchese, and Genoese ambassadors to his court, and ordered them to conclude a peace in which the principal conditions subscribed to were that Genoa should have half of Sardinia, that the Lucchese should dismantle Viareggio, and that the Pisans should abstain in future from the practice they seemed to have adopted of coining money with the valuable stamp of Lucca.

On May 29, 1176, Barbarossa sustained at Legnano a crushing defeat from the armies of the Lombard League, and from that moment the danger with which his designs had threatened the communes of Tuscany was over.

VIII.

THE EXPANSION OF FLORENCE.

THE expansion of Florence, like that of all the communes, was achieved by a constant annexation of castles and a corresponding increase of territory. Sometimes these castles belonged to nobles, sometimes to rival towns. In 1170, the Florentines carried off a victory with all its contingent advantages over the inhabitants of Arezzo, who were friends of Count Guido; and some years later they had a successful struggle with Siena for the possession of Asciano, a fortified place in the neighbourhood of Arezzo, of which the inhabitants had submitted partly to the Florentines and partly to the Sienese. The latter wished to annex the whole, but sustained a disastrous defeat in which the Florentines took a thousand prisoners. Long negotiations followed, but in the end the Florentines were recognized as sole masters of all the contado around Florence and Fiesole, and were assigned a portion of the Sienese possessions in Poggibonsi, the people of Siena promising at the same time to aid the Florentines in all their wars except such as were waged against the Emperor or his delegates (*missi*).

These various triumphs were not regarded with

identical feelings by all classes inside the walls of Florence. Every fresh acquisition of territory meant an increase of immigrant nobles, who not being admitted at once to all the rights of citizenship could take no share in the government, and consequently attached themselves to the excluded nobles, the clan, that is, of the Uberti and their relatives or dependents, and to other malcontents. After a time these immigrant nobles became citizens in the proper sense of the word, but as they remained hostile to the predominant party of the Grandi they formed a powerful opposition, which by infusing fresh spirit into the malcontents brought about one of the earliest civil wars in Florence.

These faction fights have often been made a subject of reproach to the Italian communes as though accidental and avoidable. But when one considers that the government had originated in, and reposed on, the popular will, it is obvious that faction was a condition of the communes' being, and had its favourable side in the strenuous individuality that for three hundred years survived foreign and domestic disaster. From 1177 to 1179, therefore, Florence burnt and sacked, " shone o'er with civil swords," the chief citizens and their followers of all classes waging war against the consuls, lords and leaders of the communes, and the whole city being divided into clans which fought one against the other from their towers. "Warfare became so habitual," says Villani, " that one day the citizens fought and the next they ate and drank together boasting mutually of their deeds of prowess."

Exhaustion produced peace at last, but the Uberti had gained a fresh accession of strength, and were able to introduce a more aristocratic element into the government of the town. The commune was still too vigorous to be weakened by these divisions, and as soon as peace reigned within the walls, the old enterprises in the surrounding country recommenced. About 1183, the Florentines allied themselves with Lucca against Pistoja, and presently achieved a great triumph in reducing to submission the haughty Alberti, who had to swear obedience to the commune, to promise an annual tribute of a taper and a pound of pure silver to the Church of St. John the Baptist, and to demolish various castles in the Elsa and Arno Valleys. The head of the family also undertook that his sons should reside in Florence for two months during wartime and for one month during peace. After such successes it is not to be wondered at if the commune began to be detested as well as feared by the still unsubdued nobles, and when Frederick returned he was assailed with complaints from the chieftains who gathered round him at San Miniato.

The same lamentations were poured into his ears about Lucca, and the chroniclers go so far as to relate that he deprived all the towns except Pisa and as some say Pistoja, not only of the territory they had recently conquered, but of all comprised in their own contado, leaving them not a rood outside their walls. Of late years, however, the truth of this has been repeatedly called in question, nor indeed on the face of it does it seem very probable. With the power which Lucca and Florence had then attained to, they

INTERIOR OF SAN MINIATO, FLORENCE.
(From a Photograph by Brogi.)

would certainly not have submitted tamely to a measure of the sort; and there is no trace in any extant document of the order having being given, far less of an attempt to carry it out. But, on the other hand, there exist diplomas in 1184, by Henry VI., King of the Romans, Frederick's son, in which in return for tribute he accorded jurisdiction to the Florentines over their town and a limited portion of contado three miles in one direction, one in another, and ten in the remainder. Similar " privileges " were at the same time and in the same form given to Lucca, to Siena, and to Perugia, restrictions being expressly imposed in favour of the nobles and garrisons, over whom, even in the territories named, the towns were to enjoy no power. The fact that Henry should thus have " restored " jurisdiction to the communes has seemed to some writers a proof that Frederick had deprived them of it, while others with more plausibility argue that Henry's diplomas simply had reference to the state of things created by the office of the Podestàs.

These functionaries appointed by Frederick had never succeeded in establishing any authority in the towns, and only an imperfect amount in the contado, where between them and the consuls who governed the cities disputes had been of frequent occurrence. For the Podestàs conceived that their jurisdiction over the contado should extend to the towns, while the consuls were of opinion that the government of the city should include the government of the city's outlying territory. As long as Frederick remained in Tuscany he presumably gave an immense impulse to the authority of the Podestàs, who perhaps then did really make their power felt up to the walls of the towns. But as soon as the Emperor went the consuls probably recovered all that they had lost, and Henry VI., when confronted with this state of things, sought by his diplomas to give a legal sanction to encroachments on imperial rights which he was powerless to prevent. And it is also most likely that for strong towns like Lucca and Florence even these diplomas were a dead letter, and the hardy communes continued to take just as much as they could, without reference to king or kaiser, to Podestà or Pope. In 1190, Barbarossa was drowned in Syria, and his son Henry VI. (called Henry V. as Emperor) created his brother Philip Duke of Tuscany.

But when, seven years later, Henry died, and Philip returned in haste to Germany, where his election was contested, the influence of the Empire in Tuscany rapidly lost ground, while the popes sought to establish some authority by waiving their illusory claims as Matilda's heirs and seeking the friendship of the communes. Florence initiated a league against the Empire which the Pope joined, and into which the Counts Alberti and Guidi, Lucca, Siena, the Bishop of Volterra (as representing his town), Pistoja, and Poggibonsi successively entered, Pisa alone remaining steadily imperial.

The allies bound themselves to recognize nobody as emperor, king, prince, duke, or marquis, without the express order of the Church, which, on its side, was entitled to call upon the league for help if attacked, or for the recovery of any territory not possessed by the allied communes themselves.

None of the towns were to make war or peace with emperor, king, or duke without the consent of the others, and all could constrain by force of arms reluctant cities, countships, bishoprics, and villages to join the league when requested.

This alliance served several purposes. By a special clause which provided that castles and small places should only enter the union as dependents of the towns to which they "legitimately" belonged, it took advantage of the weakness of these, now that the Emperor was gone, to force them into submission; it defined and consolidated a distinctly Guelph party; and it identified the interests of the Church with those of the free communes in general, without admitting, on the part of the Pope, any prescriptive rights over the league beyond such as the members allowed him.

Of course it was free to an ambitious and clever Pontiff, like Innocent III., to interpret the conditions accepted by the Church in a sense inordinately favourable to his own aggrandisement; but as a point of fact the communes were already quite able to take care of themselves, and such submission as they made now and in the future to the Church was a mere question of policy founded on self-interest.

IX.

FLORENCE IN THE THIRTEENTH CENTURY.

WITH the year 1200 a change came over the government of the Tuscan Republics and Genoa, where, in the course of a few years, we find that to consuls had succeeded a Podestà. In Genoa, as in Lucca, the change was accompanied by bloodshed; but in Florence it appears to have come about gradually, the Podestà first appearing in 1193, in the person of a certain Gherardo Caponsacchi, who belonged to a consular family. A year or two later the consuls reappear, and for a time the two offices either alternated or co-existed, the consuls sometimes figuring as the councillors of the Podestà, and sometimes acting with all their old authority and alone.

In 1200 the Podestà is no longer a Florentine, but a foreigner (*i.e.*, a native of some town not included in Florence or its contado), and by 1207 he alone is at the head of the government. The consuls have disappeared, or rather have been merged in a new council, which in its turn brought about a change in the old council or senate, this being henceforward known as the Consiglio Maggiore (Larger Council).

It must not be imagined that the Podestàs, though

they bore the same title as the imperial officers originally appointed by Frederick, in any way represented the power, now practically defunct in Italy, of the Emperor.

They were appointed by the communes themselves, just as the consuls had been, but in spite of this they were the outcome of a change which had crept over the spirit and constitution of parties in the republics. They were, in one sense, a creation of the Ghibellines or aristocrats as distinguished from the Guelphs or democrats. When Florence admitted the feudal nobles within her walls and to a share in her government, accepting also their help in her wars upon the various castles which still remained unsubdued, it was inevitable that the power, hitherto supreme, of the grandi should be weakened.

The institution of the Podestà was aimed against them. They, on their side, naturally resisted the growing power of the Ghibelline faction, and thus began the frequent changes of government throughout which Florence obeyed an unerring instinct of independence and self-aggrandizement. But a state of things which could not wither the vital forces of a commune so happily situated as to expand continually in enterprise and wealth, necessarily arrested the development of another deprived of the same advantages. And there is no doubt that the spirit of faction, which only rendered the institutions of Florence elastic, did seriously affect the prosperity of towns like Pistoja and Siena. The independence which they pursued was a will-o'-the-wisp and prevented the development of a Tuscan State that might

COMMUNAL PALACE AT SIENA.
(From a Photograph by Brogi.)

naturally have made Florence its head. Siena was torn by three factions, known respectively as the Ordine dei Nove, the Ordine dei Dodici, and the Ordine dei Riformatori. The last named was the largest, comprising some old families and all the lowest class or *popolo minuto* as it was commonly designated in all the Tuscan towns. The prevailing spirit in Siena was intensely democratic, so that any noble admitted to the government had to call himself *popolano* (commoner). In Siena, as in Florence, there was a class of grandi, there called Maggiori, comprising, however, only five principal families with a vast number of retainers or hangers-on. These five families were the Piccolomini, Tolomei, Malavolti, Salimbeni, and Saraceni, and they enjoyed the privilege that two members of their respective houses could be in the government at the same time, while for all other families the number was limited to one.

In 1186 the Sienese obtained from the Emperor the right to coin their own money and execute their own justice. Their form of government was at this time consular, and remained so until the general institution of the Podestà, the consuls being invested by the Imperial Vicar or the Emperor himself (for which latter purpose they had to go to Germany), and paying as representatives of the communes a yearly tribute of seventy silver marks weighed in the imperial treasury. Left to its own devices, Siena would certainly have been as sturdily Guelph as Florence, and for precisely the same reason, namely, that its interests lay that way.

The Sienese merchants were the first Tuscan

bankers of the Holy See, and this was an advantage of which Florence very early determined to deprive them. Rome, owing to its relations with the Christian world, received more money than any other city of the Middle Ages, and was too rich a prey not to be coveted by a people like the Florentines, who felt within themselves the stirrings of an unusual commercial aptitude. Arezzo, Volterra, and Siena, by standing in the way of these designs were regarded less as enemies than as obstacles, and all, but especially the last named, soon felt the weight of the Florentine arm. Constant wrangles over the possession of border castles or fortified places occurred between the two communes; and the Florentines forced Montepulciano, a large district on the Sienese territory, to take the oath of obedience and promise an annual tribute. Not content with this they also constrained it to enter into an alliance offensive and defensive against Siena. The matter was referred to the League, but the Florentines, having got all they wanted out of that, had already quitted it; and very soon the association fell to pieces, every power belonging to it being now more or less an open enemy of the triumphant commune which, secure in its strength, and full of vitality, pursued a policy as imperturbable as it was astute. So poor Siena eventually went to war and got the worst of it, being forced to cede the castle of Tornano and all its rights in Montepulciano and Poggibonsi.

About 1215 Florence was distracted by the famous quarrel between the Buondelmonti and the Amidei clans. Young Buondelmonte dei Buondelmonti jilted a lady of the Amidei family for the sake of a beautiful maiden of the house of Donati. On this the kinsmen of the derelict betrothed resolved to kill him, and on Easter morning the conspirators assembled at the dwelling of the Amidei in the neighbourhood of Santo Stefano to carry out their purpose. Buondelmonte, splendidly dressed in white, and mounted on a white palfrey, approached from the other side of the Arno ; and on reaching the statue of Mars at the end of the old bridge he was dragged to the ground by three of his foes, and then despatched by Oderigo Fifanti, who cut his veins.

On this Florence flew to arms, the Guelphs taking the side of the Buondelmonti, and the Ghibellines of the Uberti (who were allied to the Amidei). This, at least, is what Villani says, but it is evident that the Buondelmonti murder was only a dramatic incident in a series of feuds of which the cause lay deeper than in private quarrels.

The city, meanwhile, prospered in spite of all ; and its commerce must already have increased immensely ; for we find that in 1214 the Marquis of Este had mortgaged all his allodial lands to Florentine money-lenders. How the wealth of the town was partly created by the wool trade will be related further on. Meanwhile a few words may be devoted to the gradual change which the expansion of Florence and of the other republics worked in the conditions of the small agricultural proprietors who, more than the Ghibelline nobles, were the unobserved and unpitied victims sacrificed by the communes to their greatness.

Florence and the other large towns not only adopted a Podestà for themselves, but placed an officer of the sort over all the small places which they annexed. The inhabitants of these townlets were chiefly rural proprietors; descendants, probably, of Teutonic freemen. In Florence they had been doubtless the ancestors of the grandi, but in the small communes their destiny formed a dreary contrast to the growing power of the Guelph leaders. The Podestà tyrannized over them unbearably, until he drove them to sell their tiny freeholds either to himself or his dependents, who then proceeded to speculate in the land thus acquired, and instead of selling it again or allowing it to be held as of old on conditions of service, let it to tenant-farmers (perhaps the former proprietors) out of whom they squeezed as much rent in kind as it was possible by any means to extort. The richer inhabitants of the same places, finding all things changed around them, and scenting gain and excitement in the growing towns, migrated there, after either selling their lands, or letting them on the same terms and in the same ruthless spirit as the Podestà. They became in short, in many instances, absentee landlords, while the places which they had deserted were inhabited after a while by only two classes—lords and louts; probably the future leaders and future rank and file of the mercenary troops which under the brilliant Baglioni, Malatesta, Sforza, and others, were in another century or so to overrun Italy.

In 1248, Frederick, Prince of Antioch, the natural son of the Emperor Frederick II., entered Florence with a company of knights in order to assist the Ghibellines there in their machinations against the Guelphs.

Frederick II., grandson of Frederick I., while constantly professing his devotion to the Church and occasionally proving it when this suited his purpose, intended nevertheless to acquire all the power he could in the Two Sicilies (which had come to him by inheritance from his mother Constance), and had no intention of abandoning any rights there to please the Pope who, as usual, claimed jurisdiction over the whole of South Italy. The Emperor was his whole life at war with successive pontiffs, and by his far-reaching dreams of ambition and his aim of establishing a great monarchy, he revived the hopes of the imperial party in Italy and deepened the division between Ghibelline and Guelph.

The object of these two parties was identical. Neither wanted Papal rule nor Imperial rule, but both wished to be predominant in the communes, and even expected, by the help of pope or emperor, to be sole gainer in the end of all the advantages reaped by the republics in the achievement of their independence.

Hence the appearance of the Prince of Antioch in Florence, and an immediate uprise of the Ghibellines.

They joined the German soldiers and fought the Guelphs from barricade to barricade until they had won every street. The Guelphs had finally to depart on February 2, 1249, but before going, they carried to his grave Rustico Marignolli, who had fallen in battle. An armed procession, fierce yet wailing, bore the body to San Lorenzo and there buried it beneath a stone which is still to be seen.

While the vanquished party retired to Montevarchi

and Capraja or to the castles and villas of their friends, the victors and the German soldiers celebrated their triumph by pulling down thirty-six houses and towers of the Guelphs, among others the lofty and famous tower of the Tosinghi adorned with marble columns. But the predominance of the Ghibellines did not last long, the people of Florence soon rising against the oppression of the Uberti and their clan. The men who by a natural process of readjustment formed the new group of potential rulers met on October 20, 1250, in the Church of San Firenze, but fearing the violence of the Uberti, who lived all congregated together in the neighbourhood, they removed later in the day to Santa Croce.

Thence, gaining courage, they marched in military array to San Lorenzo, and there elected thirty leaders, annulled a portion of the functions of the Podestà, and appointed as guardian of the new government a captain of the people, Messer Uberto da Lucca, with whom were to be associated twelve elders (two for each division of the town) as councillors for him and advisers of the people.

The captain was to be a foreigner; but the elders were to be Florentines. Among them was a shoemaker—a rich shoemaker presumably, for they called him a grande.

The fighting population was divided into twenty companies, each with a standard of its own, and the force thus created was intended, under the leadership of the captain, to defend the liberties of the people within the town. Outside Florence the army was still to be commanded by the Podestà. The captain's standard showed a red cross on a white field : to this day the ensign of the town of Florence. The nobles and the powerful burghers (*popolani*) formed a separate force—that of the knights. Each sesto or division of the town had a separate ensign for its

VIEW OF FLORENCE.
(*From a Photograph by Brogi*)

troop of cavalry, and these banners with many others were given solemnly by the Podestà on every Whitsunday.

The contado was also divided into companies under respective standards, and when called into the town fell naturally into line with the city bands.

All these changes were intended to check the power of the Ghibellines, who soon came to be so hated by the majority of the Florentines that a common banner even was felt as an intolerable evil, and the Guelph party adopted a red lily on a white field leaving the white lily on a red field (the old arms of the commune) to the opposite faction.

1254 was called the Year of Victory, because during its course Florence carried on triumphant wars against Pistoja, Siena, Volterra, and Pisa, ostensibly because of their imperialism, but really for the sake of material advantages, and to defeat the ends of Ghibelline malcontents who had gathered within their walls. Pisa was forced to open its territory and port for the free passage of Florentine wares; to adopt Florentine weights and measures; to accept a Podestà of Florentine origin for three years; and to promise not to receive any Ghibelline exiles.

These were hard terms wrung from weakness, but the imperialist party in Italy had received a severe blow on the death of Frederick in 1251, and did not begin to recover from it until Manfred occupied the throne of the Two Sicilies.

Among the many difficulties which beset this prince was the strong Guelph spirit of Florence, against which as well as against Lucca he encouraged Pisa to make war. Florence remaining victorious, the Uberti, whose hopes had thus received a check, conspired secretly with other Ghibellines for the overthrow of the government, but the plot oozed out, and the people rising thronged to the houses of the Ghibelline chiefs, killed Schiattuzzo degli Uberti, and dragged Uberto Caimi and Mangia degli Infangati to prison, where their confession of guilt did not avail to save their heads. The remainder of the Uberti with many Ghibelline families, the Fifanti, the Lamberti, the Scolari, the Amidei, and others, besides many plebeian adherents fled to Siena, while their homes and towers in Florence were razed to the ground. Even the Abbot of Vallombrosa, because he was suspected of Ghibellinism, was first tortured and then beheaded: a deed which brought excommunication upon the Florentines. The latter then turned to avenge themselves upon Siena which, by harbouring the Ghibelline refugees, had broken an agreement previously made with Florence. First, as a matter of form, Siena was haughtily requested to eject the fugitives, and when this was refused the war immediately commenced.

In the month of May, 1260, the Florentine force marched out, taking with it the famous Carroccio, or war-car, without which the republic never undertook any great battle.

The Carroccio was painted red and surmounted by two masts on which fluttered the red and white standard of the commune. It was dragged by two powerful oxen covered with cloth of the same colour as the car. These oxen were especially reserved for this office, and were kept in a stable of the Pinti Hospital, under charge of a guardian who was free of the commune. When war broke out, the counts and nobles of the contado and the knights of the town assembled to drag the car from the Church of San Giovanni to the New Market, where it was placed on a particular round stone and handed over to the charge of the people. It was led to the battlefield by the best, the strongest, and bravest of the citizens who surrounded it on foot; and as long as the fight raged the soldiers pressed thickly round this sacred ark of their liberties, the sign and symbol of all they held most dear.

For a month after the war was declared and until the march forth began, a bell, called the Martinella, placed under the gateway of Santa Maria near the New Market, rang incessantly; and when at last the army moved out, the bell was placed on the Carroccio inside a wooden tower and guided the troops by its sound. So with Carroccio and Martinella, and secure of coming victory, the Florentines marched in May against Siena, took some castles by the way, reached their destination, and encamped at Santa Petronella, where on a little hill they built a tower for their bell. In the first encounter the Florentines were successful, and the miserable reinforcement of a hundred German knights sent by Manfred lost the standard of their king, which, after being first dragged in the dust, was despatched to Florence. The Ghibelline exiles and the Sienese then borrowed twenty thousand golden florins from the Salimbeni, great bankers of Siena, and sent a fresh embassy to Manfred detailing their defeat and the dishonour done to his banner. These representations joined to the money proved successful, and presently eight hundred knights arrived to inspire the Sienese with fresh energy. They sought the help also of the Pisans and every other Ghibelline town or noble in Tuscany and soon got together a considerable army.

The Florentines on their side sought help from the Guelphs of Lucca, Bologna, Pistoja, Volterra, and other places, and sent for reinforcements to Florence which was depleted of all its fighting population. The Ghibellines were forced to accompany the army, as it was not thought safe to leave them unwatched by the Guelphs in the town. The Florentine forces marched past Siena, and encamped five miles from the city near the river Arbia, where they were joined by some Perugians and Orvietans who brought the numbers of the army up to about three thousand horsemen and several thousand foot. The night before the battle Siena solemnly dedicated itself to the Virgin as sole and everlasting patroness. The citizens crowded to the churches, where they prayed, and wept, and made peace each one with his enemy. About one on September 4, 1260, the Sienese forces and their allies set out to meet the foe, the German knights at the head under the leadership of a Count Giordano, while the remainder were commanded by the great Ghibelline Farinata degli Uberti. The Florentines were assembled at a place called Mont' Aperti, having, it is said, been induced to take up that position by false representations elaborately made to them by the Ghibellines who, instigated by Farinata, had sent two pretended secret ambassadors, Franciscan monks, to Florence to inform the government that Sienese malcontents intended to surrender the town for the purpose of shaking off the dominion of Provenzano Salvani.

The Florentines had thus been beguiled into placing themselves unfavourably, and when they saw the Sienese army streaming down the hillsides towards them and suddenly realized that they had been deceived, they lost courage, and made but a feeble defence to the first onslaught of the German knights.

The next thing to happen was that the Ghibellines from Florence quitted the ranks of their fellow-townsmen and went over to the enemy. German swords meanwhile frayed a passage through the Guelph troops, who were further discomfited by having the burning September sun in their eyes. The ensign of the knights was carried by Jacopo de' Pazzi, a valorous soldier, but he was suddenly attacked from behind by Bocca degli Abati, a Ghibelline traitor who was in his troop, and who, riding against Jacopo, took him by surprise and cut off his hand so that the ensign fell to the ground. On this the knights broke and fled; but the foot-soldiers made a better stand and gathered stubbornly round the Carroccio. This was guarded by old Giovanni Tornaquinci, a veteran of many fights and head of the Guelphs in the sesto of San Pancrazio. Beside him were his son and three kinsmen, who, with the old man, made a long and passionate resistance only to fall one after the other upon the heap of the slain. The sun went down while the battle still raged; and the darkness brought an end at last to a fight of seven hours. Two thousand five hundred Florentines were killed and one thousand five hundred taken prisoners, all belonging to the best and bravest families. The Carroccio, the Martinella, and innumerable arms fell to the possession of the victors. The Lucchese also suffered severely. The defeat was a judgment of God, avers Villani, provoked among other iniquities by the murder of the Abbot of Vallombrosa, but it was also an immense disaster in the sense that it brought about the ruin of the old governing party in Florence which for ten years had been so great and so victorious.

X.

FLORENCE IN THE THIRTEENTH CENTURY
(continued).

INFINITE was the grief in Florence when the first miserable fugitives brought the tidings of the great defeat through which the Arbia ran red with blood. The wailing of women and old men went up to heaven, for there was hardly a family but counted some dead. One thousand two hundred and sixty Guelphs rather than face the vengeance of the returning Ghibellines voluntarily expatriated themselves. Mourning, they turned their backs on Florence, going first to Lucca, but afterwards dispersing all over Italy where they stirred up enemies to the Ghibellines on all occasions. Villani gives an imposing list of names among these exiles, Bardi, Rossi, Mozzi, Gherardini, Pulci, Buondelmonti, Tornaquinci, Tosinghi, &c., and from among the great burghers (*popolani*) departed the Canigiani, Machiavelli, Rinucci, Soderini, and many others who had been admitted to power in the State.

The Ghibellines elected as Podestà of Florence Count Guido Novello of Poppi in the Casentino Valley—a personage destined to be famous in many battlefields for always running away. He made the citizens swear fealty to Manfred and destroyed five castles in the territory of Florence at the request of the Sienese. As Podestà he could bring no force nor any kinsmen into the town he was appointed to govern, consequently he provided for his personal safety as well as he could by opening out the street, still known as Via Ghibellina, from end to end so as to be able either to summon his liege-men or make his own escape if things ceased to be comfortable.

Count Giordano in command of the German troops remained as Vicar-general of King Manfred. All the property of the Guelphs went to the commune, and many of their houses were razed to the ground. Florence was in the power of the foreigner.

The Pisans, the people of Siena and Arezzo, and the heads of the Ghibelline party in Tuscany, the Counts Alberti, Guidi, Santa Fiore, the Ubaldini, and others met in a general parliament at Empoli for the purpose of dividing among themselves the expenses of the great victory, and it was on this occasion that the celebrated proposal to pull down the walls of Florence and reduce it to the condition of an open town was made and would have been carried unanimously but for the protest of Farinata degli Uberti. He declared that alone, if needs were, and sword in hand he would defend the town while there was breath in his body; and he was about to quit the assembly when Count Giordano interposed and suggested other and less atrocious means of reducing the people of Florence to submission.

Count Giordano being recalled to Sicily by Manfred, handed over his functions to Count Guido Novello, who, setting out on the campaign throughout Tuscany, occupied several castles in the Lucchese territory, but had to abandon the siege of Fucecchio after thirty days' assault, the place being vigorously defended by the flower of the Guelphs. The latter were not idle in their exile: they sent ambassadors to Conradin's mother with the vain request that they might have care of the boy until Manfred could be driven from the throne he had occupied, and they made one or two attempts to re-enter Florence by armed force, but only succeeded in bringing down upon themselves and their allies, the Lucchese, the army of Count Novello who inflicted a defeat upon them. It was in this fight that Farinata made his last apparition. The chroniclers relate that after the battle he was riding away from the field with a prisoner Cece dei Buondelmonti behind him, when the latter was brutally set upon by Piero, nicknamed the Ass, Farinata's own brother, and killed by the blow of an axe on the head. After this, history is silent concerning the noble Ghibelline who lives, however, for all time in the fiery tomb where Dante placed him, and whence he looked forth undaunted even by the terrors of hell. The self-seeking spirit of the Italian communes was well demonstrated by a secret treaty now concluded between the Lucchese and the Ghibelline chiefs. Many castles belonging to Lucca had fallen with their garrisons into the hands of Count Novello, to whom the treacherous town now proposed that these should be restored in return for a wholesale eviction from Lucca of all the Guelph exiles. The negotiations were conducted with secrecy and success, and all at once the unhappy Guelphs were ordered on pain of death to quit their refuge within three days. No prayers availed to obtain the smallest delay; already the German troops were advancing, and old and young, delicate women and children were driven forth to face all the hardships of a perilous journey through the passes of the Apennines to Modena, whence they eventually proceeded as well as they could to Bologna. A portion of the exiles went to France and, it is asserted by some, there established banking. What is quite certain is that they enriched themselves by commerce in foreign countries, and returned to Florence—such as did return,—more valuable members of the commonwealth than they had left it. Others going from Modena to Reggio and fighting all the time for the adherents of their party, collected much honour and more booty, and eventually under Forese degli Adimari formed a force of four hundred troopers— one of the earliest of the wandering armed bands with which Italy was destined to be inundated. All Tuscany had now returned into the power of the Ghibellines, but how superficial are the roots struck by faction was soon proved when the elevation in quick succession of two French Cardinals, Urban IV. and Clement IV., to the Papal throne, and the policy which they pursued brought Charles of Anjou as a pretender to the throne of the Two Sicilies across the Alps.

Every Guelph rallied to his standard, and an echo

of their sense of coming triumph is found in the words of Villani describing how the judgments of God, tardy but inexorable, was shortly to overtake the great sinner Manfred in the midst of his worldly and epicurean life ; and he goes on to relate how at Benevento, just before the battle, the king, surveying the forces of the French, asked who were the well-equipped cavalry composing the fourth division, and on hearing they were the Guelphs whom he had helped to drive from Florence and Tuscany, he exclaimed, mournfully, "Where are the Ghibellines whom I have so well served?" They were not present; and there was supposed to be treachery in his own ranks. He fell valiantly fighting amid the rout of his whole army, and for three days his body could not be found. At last it was recognized by one of his own soldiers there where the battle had been fiercest. The ruffian placed it across an ass and went on his way calling out, "Who buys Manfred?"

"Then one of Charles' knights struck the body with his stick and brought it before the French monarch who, calling all the barons, prisoners in his camp, asked them one by one if this were the corpse of their king. All timidly said it was ; only Count Giordano at the sight covered his face with his hands weeping and crying out, 'Oh! my master, what is this?' whereon the French nobles greatly commended him. And some of them begging Charles to give him (Manfred) honourable burial, the king replied, 'I would do it willingly, were he not excommunicated ;' but because he was excommunicated, Charles would not have him borne to any consecrated spot. Therefore he was buried at the foot of the bridge of Benevento, and each soldier of the army threw a stone upon the place until there was a great heap." Some say that by order of the Pope the Bishop of Cosenza had the body removed and sent out of the kingdom, which was sacred ground belonging to the Church, and buried finally in the bed of the river Verde on the confines of Campania. This story, given as hearsay by Villani, is repeated by Dante in a famous passage, in which all the tenderness and pathos evoked by a ruined cause seem concentrated in the one beautiful line describing Manfred—

"Biondo era e bello e di gentil aspetto."

The news of the battle of Benevento caused as much consternation to the Ghibellines as the tidings of the defeat at Mont' Aperti had spread among the Guelphs six years previously. The population of Florence who still mourned their dead—the brothers, the fathers, and sons who had fallen on the fatal field—began to complain openly of the misgovernment of Count Novello, and of the burdens he and his party imposed upon them. The Ghibelline faction, on hearing these first mutterings of the coming storm, tried to avert it by electing two Podestàs instead of one. Both were Bolognese, only one Lotteringo degli Andali was a Ghibelline while his colleague Catalano dei Malavolti was a Guelph. They belonged to the notorious Order of the Knights of St. Mary, called in derision the Jovial Friars, who wore a white dress and a grey mantle, and whose office it was to defend widows and orphans and to interpose in quarrels as peacemakers, but who led such a luxurious and lazy life that they soon fell into disrepute.

The two summoned now to Florence had, however, enjoyed the reputation of governing Bologna well, and the holiness of their habit, if not of their lives, was considered a guarantee that they would administer the finances of the town with honesty. Either they really did disappoint expectations in this respect, or the people of Florence were not in a mood to regard any functionaries chosen by their present rulers with confidence. Any way, the two knights quickly fell into such discredit that Dante placed them in the " Inferno " among the hypocrites.

The first thing the Podestàs had done was to elect a council of thirty-six " Good Men," the best among the citizens, some of whom were Guelphs and others Ghibellines, some of middle class and some of the old governing party (grandi), whose loyalty was above suspicion and who had remained in the town after the battle of Mont' Aperti.

The thirty-six were to meet every day under the portico of the New Market in what was called the Court of the Consols of the Wool Trade. From this portico, from this workshop of the Wool Trade, to quote a well-known phrase, " the Republic of Florence emerged suddenly full-grown."

Long previously the people of the town had been divided into trade guilds, to which the Thirty-six now proceeded to give a definite public organization. To every guild was assigned consuls and captains and a special banner, so that when the city rose in arms the guilds could assemble each under its own standard. The Judges and Notaries had a gold star on a blue ground ; the Guild of the Calimala (a section of the Wool Trade) showed a golden eagle on a red field ; the Money Changers, gold florins on vermilion ; the Wool Merchants, a white sheep on a similar ground ; the Doctors and Apothecaries, a Mother and Child also on a red back-ground ; the Silk Merchants and Mercers had a red gate (the Porta Santa Maria) on white ; while, finally, the Furriers exhibited furs and an Agnus Dei on a blue field.

The Italian communes, as has been seen, sprang from voluntary associations, which, in substance, admitted no higher authority than the necessity of acting for the common weal. But the superstition of Kaiserdom had survived among the Ghibellines, and this public recognition of a purely popular institution, at the very moment when Florence was to be reorganized against the Guelphs, was a bitter blow to chieftains like the Uberti and the Fifanti, the Lamberti and the Scolari. They felt convinced that the Knights of St. Mary intended to favour the Guelphs who had still remained in the city. Count Novello, in his usual state of alarm, sent to Pisa, to Siena, to Arezzo, to Pistoja, to all the towns and places which were now Ghibelline, for reinforcements, and what with these and his six hundred Germans soon had a force of fifteen hundred men at his back. But then arose the question of paying them. The Count's demands seemed exorbitant to the Podestàs, and were resisted by them. This put the crowning touch to the irritation of the Ghibellines, and the

Lamberti with their armed followers streamed out of the Calimala, which was their quarter, crying fiercely, "Where are the Thirty-six? We will cut them in pieces!"

The Council, who were sitting as usual in conclave, no sooner heard these demonstrations than they hastily dispersed. All the workshops were shut; the people armed and crowded into the Via Larga and the Piazza Santa Trinità. Gianni de' Soldanieri, a Ghibelline, abandoned his party on the instant, and placed himself at the head of the Guelphs, earning thereby a place in the "Inferno" among the traitors.

The streets were barricaded: Count Novello appeared with his new army; the fight became general, and the people showed a steady front. Novello began to see that his German cavalry was not much use in the narrow mediæval streets where every house was a fortress, whence, when the arrows gave out, stones descended in showers while the foe remained under shelter. In vain the two knights of St. Mary endeavoured to infuse a little energy into the craven Count; he insisted upon having the keys of the gates, and departed with his Germans and his allies. The next day he would have returned, but he found the gates shut and the Guelphs ascendant. The two knights of St. Mary were driven away, a Podestà was summoned from Orvieto, and another nobleman from the same town appointed Captain of the People. So complete was the triumph of the Guelphs that, on the night preceding Easter, the Ghibellines left the city unopposed to take refuge in Siena or Pisa or their own castles. In this silent confession of defeat they followed the example set by the Guelphs after the battle of Mont' Aperti, and both incidents show how personal rather than political was the spirit of Italian sedition. Neither party fought for a principle, but only for itself.

When the vanquished party were gone the Florentines solemnly conferred on Charles of Anjou the supremacy over their town for ten years. At first the astute prince perhaps divining that he was not likely to get anything more substantial, declared that all he wished for was the good-will of the citizens; but, as they persisted in their offer, he finally accepted it, and agreed to send a vicar every year to govern the town with the assistance of twelve Good Men. This state of things did not constitute any real servitude; the royal delegate was likely to be kept very firmly in hand by his twelve councillors, and Sicily was to give Charles as much to do as he could accomplish. But the French prince was, so to speak, the sword, as the Pope was the soul of the Guelph party, and Florence by placing itself under the protection of Charles only set a seal to the policy it intended to pursue and under cover of which its institutions were to develop and flourish.

The twelve Good Men consequently took the place of the Elders (*Anziani*) who disappeared entirely from the scene. At the same time there was formed a secret or Privy Council of the Captain of the People, the consent of which was necessary for any great expenditure or any important measure. This was a purely popular council, and to it belonged the initiative of all the steps to be taken by the republic.

Its decisions however were to be submitted to a General Council of Ninety, which included also the heads of the seven Major Guilds, and the twelve Good Men, and was convoked by the royal delegate. These two councils were composed of all classes of citizens (except the lowest), being thus distinguished from the real governing Council of the People, on which developed, among other things, the distribution of all offices large and small. Arbiters were appointed for the annual revision of the edicts of the councils and the monks of Badia a Settimo and of Ognissanti were named treasurers of the commune, the duties of which post they discharged by turns for six months.

A question concerning the property of the Ghibellines having arisen, the Pope Clement IV. and King Charles ordered that it should be divided into three parts—one for the commune; one as indemnity to the Guelphs for losses sustained; and the third to remain for a certain time in the hands of the victorious party. When Cardinal Ottaviano degli Ubaldini heard of this order, he exclaimed, "Now, indeed, are the Ghibellines gone for ever!"

The defeat of the faction was in fact complete. Almost all the known and suspected Ghibellines were banished at once, some from all parts of the Florentine territory, some only from the town and neighbourhood. A few were allowed to remain in the city until such time as the Royal Vicar had not pronounced their decree of banishment. The names are extant of some three thousand proscribed in the years 1268 and 1269.

Among the Ghibellines thus driven forth was one Azzo Arrighetti, who established himself in Provence and was the ancestor of the Mirabeaus.

The most important measure of all taken at this time was the creation of a new magistracy, known at first as the consuls of the knights, but destined to be famous as the captains of the Guelph party, whose duty it was to maintain the integrity of its own party and to keep down the Ghibellines. The component members of this magistracy were changed every two months. It was governed by the councils, one a secret council of fourteen, while a larger council consisted of sixty members of the upper and middle class (grandi and popolani) out of which the captains and other officials were chosen by vote. There were further six Rectors, or Priori, three of the upper and three of the middle class, who acted as treasurers, while one kept the seals and another acted as accuser of the Ghibellines. This formidable institution, by consolidating the Guelph party and placing Florence at the head of the league which extended from Bologna to Perugia, assured the greatness, the wealth, and the influence of the republic.

The Ghibellines made one last stand under their principal leaders the Uberti and the Fifanti in the castle of Sant' Ellero, where they were besieged by the Florentines and some French cavalry. The Ghibellines, eight hundred in number, were all taken prisoners or killed, except one of the Uberti, a youth who mounted to the top of a tower, and then seeing that no hope of escape remained but surrender into the hands of the hated Buondelmonti, he threw himself headlong to the ground. The others—bitter fate !—were taken back to Florence and imprisoned with scant mercy, it is to be feared, in the tower of the Bargello.

Pisa and Siena remained firmly Ghibelline: to do so, indeed, was their only chance, and availed if only for a time to save them from the humiliation of sinking beneath the supremacy of Florence. Prato, Pistoja, Lucca, Volterra, San Gimignano, and Colle, renounced the error of their ways and re-entered the Guelph fold.

The memory of Mont' Aperti still rankled, and as soon as possible after the installation of the new government Florence sent an army against Siena, which carried off a complete victory near Colle di Val d'Elsa, and resulted in Provenzano Salvani, who had attained to a position in Siena almost analogous to that of the "tyrants" in other cities, being taken prisoner and losing his head.

In 1273, Gregory, accompanied by Charles of Anjou and the Latin Emperor Baldwin, then a refugee from Constantinople, came to Florence and was splendidly entertained by the Mozzi, wealthy merchants belonging to the *novi homines* whom commerce had enriched. The Pope was distressed at the fierce passions raging in the town, and made an amiable, but necessarily ineffectual, attempt to reconcile the triumphant Guelphs and the exiled Ghibellines. He sent for representatives of the latter, and on the 2nd of July, 1273, held a great meeting at the foot of the Rubaconte Bridge, in the presence of the King and Emperor, and, threatening with excommunication the first to break peace, ordered the deputies on both sides to embrace.

Four days later the Ghibelline representatives departed in great haste, having been informed that if they remained an hour longer, the Royal Vicar, at the request of the Guelph leaders, would have them cut to pieces. The information may have been erroneous, but it is not surprising if the unhappy ambassadors believed it. As soon as the Pope heard of this incident, he expressed the greatest indignation against Charles, and retiring to Mugello laid Florence under an interdict. A few months later, when returning from Lyons, he was forced by an overflow of the Arno to re-enter the excommunicated town, so blessed it again for the occasion, only to renew the ban when himself and his suite were once more outside the walls.

At this time and for some years all Italy was torn by discord. The Ghibellines were a ruined party in Florence, but they were active elsewhere, and the great Guelph republic found itself constantly called upon to interfere in the faction fights now dividing almost all the Romagna and Tuscany. Pisa was chiefly Ghibelline, but a Guelph party, headed for purposes of personal ambition, by Count Ugolino della Gherardesca of Dantesque fame, existed even there, and when driven away by the people, were forcibly restored by the Florentines. In Milan, on the other hand, the Guelphs under the Torriani were expelled by the Marquis of Montferrat, and the Visconti brothers (one of whom was the Archbishop), returned from exile and rose at once to power. The

Romagna was assigned by Pope Nicholas III., an Orsini, to Charles. Meanwhile, Florence itself, although powerful, was not at peace.

The principal Guelphs no sooner found themselves undisturbed, as a party, in the possession of the government, than they began to fall out. The Adimari, and Tosinghi, and Donati were in perpetual feud ; so that the captains of the Guelph party, and the rulers of the commune entreated the good offices of Pope Nicholas with a view to restoring harmony. At the same time the Ghibelline exiles, yearning to return, petitioned him to the effect that the illusory reconciliation ordered by Pope Gregory should cease to be a dead letter. Weary, indeed, must have been their abode in the palaces of strangers, and salt that bread of exile which they, like Dante, had to eat, before such a longing could have found words. The Pope, however, did his best. He sent his nephew, Cardinal Latino Frangipani, accompanied by three hundred knights to Florence where the diplomatic prelate got as far as to reconcile the Uberti with the Buondelmonti.

He then, in the first days of January, 1280, convoked a Parliament of the people in the square of Santa Maria Novella, where he laid the first stone of the lovely church which Michelangelo, later called his bride. The delegates of the two parties were ordered to exchange the usual kiss, and the Cardinal further decreed that the exiled Ghibellines—with the exception of about sixty, including some relatives of Farinata, who were still to remain for a certain time in some place between Orvieto and Rome, under the protection of the Pontiff—should be reinstated in their possessions : also that the Podestà and the Captain of the people during two years should be named by the Pope ; and that the number of the Buonuomini (Good Men), should be increased to fourteen, of whom six were to be Ghibellines and eight Guelph, the term of their office being at the same time reduced to two months. These conditions were agreed to. The Adimari and Tosinghi, the Donati and Pazzi followed the prevailing example and made peace. Various marriages were concluded, and great contentment reigned. Nevertheless the Cardinal's efforts were only apparently successful. The most powerful Ghibellines, the Uberti, the Fifanti, the Lamberti, the Scolari, the Pazzi of Val d'Arno not having been re-admitted, such of the party as did return could have exerted but little influence, and it was easy for the Guelphs to evade the conditions of the peace in the spirit, if not in the letter. There is no sign of any restitution on a large scale having been made to the Ghibellines: and two years after the Cardinal's visit, no member of that party was to be found in high office. But the old distinctions between Guelphs and Ghibellines were now fast vanishing. The Sicilian Vespers followed by the descent on the island of the king of Aragon had broken the might of Charles ; and in Germany the greatest confusion reigned. There was therefore no foreign prince immediately available for the furtherance of political intrigues in Italy, and the Guelphs became Ghibellines, and the Ghibellines Guelphs just as it suited their personal purposes. Some lofty dreamers like Dante may have

BASILICA OF ST. FREDIANO, LUCCA.
(*After a Photograph by Brogi.*)

longed for a world-emperor; some proud despairing spirits like Cino da Pistoja may have fled with words of woe across the Alps from their beloved and bleeding land, but the great mass of the people thought only of their own material prosperity. The Florentines especially were eminently practical and businesslike, and they had two aims which they kept steadily in view—one was the preservation of their communal independence; the other was the extension of their commerce. For the first of these objects they introduced perpetual changes into their internal government, thus keeping it plastic and vital, and adapting it to every fresh need; for the second, they fought, and planned, and plotted, sacrificing Siena, crushing Pisa, keeping their institutions steadily free from the smallest taint of feudalism, and ruthlessly betraying both friend and foe. It was not a high-minded policy, but an eminently successful one. It allowed a small town to play a great part in an age of growing states; it developed some of the strongest characters and keenest intellects the world has ever seen; it trained an unrivalled school of diplomatists, and resulted in a civilisation highly polished, many sided, exquisite, and unique.

In 1282, it was found that the unnatural conjunction in the government of eight Guelphs and six Ghibellines was productive of no special good, and the fourteen Buonuomini were consequently sent away and replaced by three Priors of the Guilds. This change was directly due to the influence and initiative of the great Wool Merchants' Company, known as the Arte di Calimala. They were immensely wealthy, strong adherents of the Church party and imbued with instincts which, if large and splendid, were commercial, as distinguished from aristocratic. Yet it is characteristic of the changes which had now come over the spirit of the factions in Florence, that the guild included some nobles among its number and one of these, Bartolo de' Bardi, was among the three Priors. He represented the Sesto of Oltrarno and the Calimala section of the Wool Trade. The second Prior was Rosso Bacherelli who belonged to the Guild of Money Changers and the Sesto of San Piero Scheraggio; while Salvi Girolami of the Arte della Lana (another division of the Wool Trade), was chosen for the Sesto of San Pancrazio. Their office lasted two months: during which time they lived, like their predecessors the Anziani, and the Fourteen Good Men, in the houses near the Badia and ate and drank at the expense of the commune. In common with the Captain of the People, now called also Defender of the Guilds, they had to administer all the affairs, great and small, of the republic, which thus was ruled by a government of democratic origin and arbitrary aims.

The results in the first two months of the Priors' rule met with so much approbation that their number was increased to six, the guilds of the Doctors and Druggists, the Mercers and Furriers being admitted. As time went on this number was again doubled, and the Minor Arts were given their share of power.

The Priors belonged indifferently to the upper (grandi) and middle (popolani) class of merchants and traders. The election of these rulers was by ballot: the electors being the outgoing Priors, the members of the guilds, and a certain number of persons belonging to each sesto. Under the new government, the Council of the People already described continued in existence, and the Captain of the People was named by it as before.

An administration composed of members of trade guilds, and of which the chief magistrates were elected for only two months, seems to have been consonant to the spirit of the hour, inasmuch as Siena, Pistoja, Lucca, and other towns followed the example set by Florence. Evidently they could imagine no better method of preserving their freedom than this ingenious rotation of individuals, all of whom had an interest in developing the material resources of their town and none of whom remained long enough in power to create a personal party.

XI.

GENOA, PISA, AND LUCCA DURING THE THIRTEENTH CENTURY.

IN Lucca the Podestà was not invariably a foreigner, and as his office encroached on the former power of the consuls, his election frequently gave the signal for a struggle to which private hatreds lent a double intensity.

In 1202, a band of turbulent nobles to whom the new authority was especially obnoxious, fled to Montecatini as a basis of operations against the commune and there entrenched themselves; but Inghirame Porcaresi the Podestà marched against them, and defeated them after a desperate combat in which the nobles fought against great odds.

Peace was then made by the Lord Bishop of Volterra, Ildebrando Pannocchieschi, Duke Philip's Vicar in Tuscany, and the Lucchese in the hope of keeping down disorder created a Council of the People composed of the citizens of the different *contrade* (urban divisions), and commanded by twelve Captains (one for each contrada). At a given signal the contrade were to assemble and form five companies named after the five gates of Lucca. But this device failed to restore peace, the nobles, or consular party proving irreconcilable, and in 1208, frightful cruelties were committed by the Porcaresi who called down on themselves prompt punishment from the Emperor Otho IV., and were despoiled of honours and goods.

Lucca flourished, nevertheless; its wealth increased, more castles surrendered to it, and more fortified villages became tributaries of the industrious and energetic commune. The Garfagnana was a district of which the inhabitants had several times sworn fealty to Lucca and as often again rebelled. Twice had they succeeded in obtaining diplomas of liberty from a German emperor, but only to find that these were dead letters against the overmastering might of Lucca. Finally they appealed to the Pope, and he, on the usual look-out for an opportunity of enforcing the papal claims to the succession of Matilda, sent an officer to take possession of the disputed territory. The Lucchese immediately despatched an armed force, which burned the village of Lupia, respecting neither the churches, the sacred images, nor the priests. They were excommunicated and deprived of their bishop, his diocese being divided among Luni, Pisa, Volterra, and Pistoja. But even these measures could not break the spirit of the Lucchese, who continued to fight and to coerce the people of Garfagnana. But Pisa, quite willing to fight, even for the Pope, against a rival, sent an army to assist the papal officer and the rebels, and inflicted a defeat on Lucca beneath the walls of Barga, which for a time left Garfagnana in the power of the Holy See, until Frederick II., in return for a good sum of money, bestowed it, after more fighting in 1248, on Lucca as a fief. Innocent IV. protested energetically, but in vain, and an end came at last to the quarrel, which is chiefly interesting as showing how little the Italian republics cared for Church or Cæsar where their material interests were concerned.

When allied with the Florentines, the Lucchese had been Guelph, but their ardour in this cause was much cooled by the battle of Mont' Aperti; and in 1264 they recognized Manfred as their sovereign, and were rewarded by getting back some places which had been taken from them by the Ghibellines. The two factions lived together in Lucca in far greater harmony than in Florence, doubtless because neither had any substantial reason for preferring the Pope to the Emperor, or the Emperor to the Pope. In order to satisfy both parties, the government of the town was divided equally between them about this time, the five consuls being abolished and replaced by ten Anziani, whose office, like those of the Priori in Florence, lasted only two months. There were also three Councils in Lucca, a Senate numbering two hundred and fifty, a special Council of one hundred and twenty-five, and a Privy Council (Credenza) of twenty-four chosen by lot. It will thus be seen that there was a general resemblance in the form of government and the process of political evolution in all the Tuscan communes.

In 1266, when Charles of Anjou came to Italy, Lucca returned to Guelph principles, expelled all her Ghibellines, and this time again recovered or acquired various strong places as a result of her accommodating policy.

The history of Genoa formed no exception to that of the other republics during this century. Like Florence and Lucca and Pisa, it was distracted by faction, and, like these, it made good profit out of the Crusades by extending and increasing its commerce. It had alternately resisted and submitted to Frederick II., and by reducing one place after another along the Riviera, was rapidly rising to the wealth and power which were to make it the destroyer of Pisa and the rival of Venice. Within the city the nobles had always been very strong; and from the moment that their predominance began to be disputed by the class whom the commune's growing commerce enriched, they formed a redoubtable party of malcontents, continuously increased by recruits from the coasts in the person of other nobles, whom the republic first subdued and then imported. The first Podestà, Manigoldo del Tettoccio tried to introduce order, and the immediate result of his measures was to provoke a civil war, during which the Grimaldi, Corte, Della Volta, and Spinola families, with their retainers, deluged the streets with blood, and fought from tower to tower. The same scenes recurred under the next Podestà, who reduced all the towers to the height of eighty feet, but failed to restore peace. Nevertheless, the external energy of Genoa seemed quite unaffected by these perpetual feuds. In 1211-12 it faced, undaunted, attacks from Pisa, Venice, Marseilles, Nice, and the ever hostile Marquises of Gavinana and Malespina. The Genoese archers, trained in these external wars, became famous, and were employed, not only by other Italian cities, but also at Crécy by the French.

Between Genoa and Frederick II. open enmity broke out as soon as the Emperor deprived the merchants of the republic of their factory in Messina and seized their goods in Sicily, Tunis, and Syria. The commune prepared for war, while Frederick on his side encouraged rebellion in all the towns along the Riviera which had submitted to Genoa, but were not resigned to her rule. His machinations were furthered by the Ghibelline party within the city whose one overpowering desire was to get rid of the Guelphs at any cost. Pisa, of course, was ready at any time to furnish the Emperor with fleets, and this constituted yet another danger for Genoa, whose priceless Eastern freights might fall at any moment into the power of an enemy. Such peril inspired the whole population with activity. The usual business of the town was suspended, and day and night, by the light of torches when the sun failed, every able-bodied Genoese toiled incessantly, and very soon had fifty new galleys in readiness. Frederick showed equal energy in bringing ships and crews from Pisa, and all that summer and the following the war went on with varying fortunes, but no decisive result on either side. All through the struggle between Rome and the Emperor, Genoa took the side of the Guelphs, and sent a fleet to Civita Vecchia to receive Innocent IV. and convey him to Lyons, where he hoped to hold in safety the council which was to provide for Frederick's eternal damnation.

In the course of 1246, the Guelphs drove away the imperial Podestà from Parma, and at the news Frederick and his son Enzo hurried towards the town, while the Guelphs were reinforced by the troops of the papal legate, by one thousand five hundred men-at-arms raised by Innocent in Lyons, and by four hundred and fifty archers from Genoa. Frederick ordered that twenty-five ships should proceed from Naples to Savona, which was an unwilling tributary of Genoa's; he incited the Marchese de Carretto (the husband of one of his natural daughters) and the hostile people of Luni to fresh efforts against the republic, every enemy of which, inland or along the coast, was assured of his support; while in the south, Andreolo de' Mari, the recalcitrant son of the commune, in command of the imperial fleet, swept the sea for an opportunity to capture Genoese vessels. Thus from every point the enemy gathered; but the undismayed republic provided for defence by equipping calvary, hiring foot-soldiers from Piacenza, and arming thirty ships to protect its commerce. Genoese bowmen helped the troops of Parma to take Vittoria, a town newly built by the Emperor, and on the treasures of which the chroniclers much dilate. It was crammed, they say, with gorgeous stuffs and priceless jewels, and all the strange lovely things of the mysterious East. The streets were full of Jews and Arabs, and eunuchs guarded the seraglios of beautiful women. It was a place at once splendid and iniquitous, a fit abode for a monarch whom the Guelphs named Antichrist.

After Frederick's death, in December, 1250, Savona and Albenga, and the other insurgent towns along the Riviera, repented of their Ghibellinism, and returned beneath the rule of Genoa; and even Pisa seems to have felt a passing wish for peace. One March day a Dominican friar came secretly into Genoa, took aside the Podestà, and explained that he was charged with a message of conciliation. The Podestà replied that his republic desired nothing better than peace, but could consent to no negotiation until the castle of Lerici, now occupied by the Pisans, should have been surrendered. The friar rose; "Rather Chinzica than Lerici," he answered, and departed. The answer was eloquent, Chinzica being a part of Pisa itself.

Nevertheless, a little later peace was concluded, and the castle of Lerici assigned to the Genoese.

At this time four families in Genoa—the Doria (or d'Oria), the Fieschi, the Spinola, and the Grimaldi—had attained to a pitch of overweening influence and authority. The Fieschi and the Grimaldi were uncompromisingly Guelph, while the Spinola and the Doria inclined towards Ghibellinism.

But the town, as has been seen, was now Guelph in its policy, a choice which was determined chiefly by the constant rivalry with Pisa. The steady adherence of the latter commune to the Ghibelline cause finds an obvious explanation in the geographical position of the town, which, by preventing all expansion inland, made commercial advantages in Sicily, Africa, and the Levant a condition of self-preservation; while the ambition, first to equal, and then to surpass, the prosperity of her rival, accounts for the time-serving policy of Genoa.

The power of the Fieschi increased greatly after the assumption of the Papal tiara by their kinsman, Innocent IV., and their tyranny became so insupportable, and was so little resisted by their tool, the Podestà, that a cry arose for a Captain of the People, and Guglielmo Boccanegra was elected to the post.

The new office thus created was made formidable by the decree which fixed its duration at ten years, and Boccanegra very soon suspended the council which had been appointed to assist him, and concentrated the government of the town in his own hands. Such an attitude became quickly intolerable to the Fieschi and Grimaldi, who organized and carried out a conspiracy against him. He sent round the Cintraco (a sort of city watchman) to summon the people to his aid, but the Cintraco was stoned to death. Lanfranco Boccanegra, a brother of Guglielmo, was also killed, and the Captain of the People, finding himself entirely deserted, meekly accepted the inevitable, and took refuge in the house of Pietro Doria.

But the idea of a Captain of the People continued to be dear to the malcontent or Ghibelline party in Genoa, who were assisted in all their risings, or attempts at a rising, by the lower class, who were as hostile as the nobles to the rich and powerful Guelphs; and when a revolt against the Government was got up in 1270, the people seized the opportunity to acclaim Oberto Doria and Oberto Spinola joint Captains. The banishment for three years of the principal Guelphs was demanded, and some changes, fondly called "reforms," were introduced into the machinery of government. A Parliament was to be convoked every month, and the Podestà to be shorn of much of the authority that had still been left to him. A Council of eight Elders—four of one party and four of the other—were appointed to assist them and to authorise an appeal, when necessary, to a Parliament of the People. The duration of the Captain's office was to be twenty-two years, and as this was a very long tenure of power for Italy, a new official, called "Abbot of the People," was appointed to divide absolute authority with the elders and the captains.

Over Pisa the clouds of misfortune were gathering fast. Between the everlasting quarrel about Corsica, where local governors at perpetual war appealed first to one republic and then to the other, and the acute rivalry between Genoa and Pisa in the Levant, there was little chance of peace; and whenever off Sardinia, Corsica, or elsewhere, a Pisan galley met a Genoese war-ship, a long and obstinate battle ensued. In Pisa also faction played its part, and strong as were the imperialist sympathies of the town, there was yet within its walls a Guelph party, headed by Ugolino della Gherardesca, of Dantesque fame.

He commanded a portion of the Pisan fleet in the battle of Meloria, which took place on August 6, 1284, when Genoa struck a blow from which its rival never recovered. Both republics instinctively felt that the issue of the combat would be decisive for their destinies.

The Archbishop of Pisa, in the robes of his sacred office, solemnly blessed his country's fleet, and just as his hands were above the kneeling multitude, the crucifix held between them broke, and the figure of Christ fell into the water. A shudder ran through the assembled crews at this evil omen; but an impious voice was heard to exclaim, "Let God be with Genoa, so long as the wind is with us!"

The battle then commenced, and raged furiously for some hours, when it became evident that the day was going against Pisa, and Ugolino, perceiving this, fled with three galleys, and carried to his fellow-townsmen the news of a defeat which he hoped would provoke a rising in favour of the Guelphs. His defection decided the day against Pisa, which lost thirty-six galleys—more than the half of its armament. The dead were computed at five thousand, while over nine thousand Pisans were taken prisoners, so many of them belonging to conspicuous families that a saying became current to the effect that he who wished to see Pisa must go to Genoa. Ugolino, to serve his own ends, conspired to prevent the surrender of the Pisan prisoners, and thereby eliminating a large Ghibelline element, was able to establish himself in power, and overturning the Anziani (or Elders), had himself appointed governor of the town for ten years. His tyranny gradually made him odious, even to his own Guelph faction, and the gravest sins were laid to his charge. He was accused of having poisoned his nephew, Count Anselino da Capraia, whom he suspected of designs against his government; and of being willing to hand over to Lucca some castles belonging to Pisa; he also intrigued with the Ghibellines, but was not able to win them over to his side. There is a well-known chapter in Villani's chronicles, describing how one day Ugolino had prepared a magnificent festival for his birthday, and gathered round him his children and kinsmen, men and women, all splendidly arrayed. Among those present was a certain Marco Lombardo, whom the Count took by the hand, and, conducting him around, showed him all these signs of pomp and power, then asked him exultantly what he thought. "I think," said Marco grimly, "that only one thing is wanting to you, namely, the wrath of God." And certainly, continues the chronicler, "that was not long delayed," for Ruggiero, Archbishop of Pisa, head of the Ghibellines, succeeded in rousing the people against their tyrant, who was taken bravely fighting, and shut up, with his two sons and two nephews, in the tower of the Ghibelline house of Gualandi. Some months later, in March, 1288, the Pisans, beset once again by the Florentines and Lucchese, elected as their leader, or war captain, Count Guido da Montefeltro, conferring on him very extensive powers; and then, fearing perhaps that defeat in war would lead to liberation of the hated Ugolino, they locked and barred the door of his prison, and cast the key into the Arno, forbidding him and the unhappy boys with him all food. To his despairing cry for a confessor they turned a deaf ear—supremest cruelty in that age of faith—and when all were dead, gave the bodies a base burial.

On the death of Charles of Anjou, and the defeat of his successor at the hands of the Aragonese in 1287, the Ghibellines began to entertain new hopes of repairing their fortunes, and assembled in great force at Arezzo. This town had shared the universal destiny of Tuscan cities in being distracted by the two hostile factions. A popular government had been formed by the Guelphs, but met with so little favour in the eyes of the more powerful members of their party that they joined the Ghibellines in overthrowing it, not without much bloodshed. The Ghibellines then soon got the upper hand so entirely that the Emperor Rudolph sent an imperial vicar to the town with a small force; but his authority must have been nominal in comparison with the power of Guglielmo degli Ubertini, the valiant bishop of Arezzo, who was head of the Ghibelline party in Tuscany, Romagna, and the Marches.

Many of the exiles from Florence being at this time in Arezzo, the Florentines heard of the Ghibelline success with great consternation and alarm, and, calling upon the Guelph towns for aid, assembled a force of two thousand six hundred cavalry and twelve thousand foot. The contingent furnished by Lucca was three hundred, while Siena sent four hundred, Pistoja one hundred and fifty, and Prato, Volterra, San Gimignano, and San Miniato fifty each. The little town of Colle contributed thirty. Florence sent eight hundred of her own citizens and three hundred mercenaries, while the remainder were brought by the Marquises Malespini, Nino Visconti the judge of Gallura (a Pisan Guelph), the Counts Alberti, Maghinardo and others, whose presence on the Guelph side was a proof of the now acknowledged predominance of Florence. The levies were raised in Florence by dividing all the men between fifteen and seventy of each guild into bands of fifty, and then selecting a certain number to fight while the remainder looked after the affairs of the town, and made arrangements for the keep of the army. The Ghibellines in general took no part in the war, but were laid under contribution for horses. On June 11, 1289, a great battle took place at Campaldino, in the Casentino district. One hundred and fifty men lightly armed, called Feditori, were selected to go in front of the Guelph army. Vieri de' Cerchi, although suffering from a bad leg, chose to be of the number, and his example inspired many others. Corso Donati, who led the contingent from Pistoja and Lucca (being at that time Podestà of the former town), showed himself no whit behind in intrepidity, and indeed the battle was waged on both sides with admirable valour. Only Count Guido Novello, Podestà of Arezzo, distinguished himself as usual by fleeing from the field as soon as the likelihood of disaster declared itself;— and in the end the Aretines were thoroughly beaten, their warlike bishop being among the slain. According to Villani the losses on the enemy's side were one thousand seven hundred dead and two thousand prisoners, many of whom, however, were allowed to escape. Among the dead was young Buonconte da Montefeltro, whose body was washed away by a torrent and lost, thus inspiring one of Dante's tenderest passages; and with him fell three Uberti, and many another exile from Florence. Some writers assert that Dante himself, then about twenty-four years, was present at this battle and fought for his own republic, but the story is of doubtful authenticity. Villani, the chronicler, had been left behind in Florence, and relates that the Priors were sleeping after their midday meal, thus resting from a night of anxious watching, when suddenly one of them was awakened by a knocking at the door and a voice which cried, "Arise, for the Aretines are defeated." All then started up, but the mysterious bearer of glad tidings was nowhere to be found, nor had anybody seen him enter or leave the palace. And, strangest of all, it was afterwards discovered that the mystic herald had aroused the Signoria in the very hour that the battle was decided, but confirmation of the news only reached Florence several hours later. The victorious army on its return met with an enthusiastic reception, and the Florentines cheerfully paid the whole expense of the campaign, amounting in all to more than thirty-six thousand gold florins.

After this the republic enjoyed several years of peace and increasing prosperity. Vanished for ever were the days described by Villani, when the citizens of Florence lived soberly on coarse food and with small expense, dressing themselves and their wives in rough woollens. Many, he said, wore no cloth at all, but only skins, and covered their feet with heavy leather shoes. The women were arrayed in a tight skirt of coarse scarlet cloth with no ornaments, and for warmth wore a simple mantle of fur which served also to cover their heads. A hundred lire was the usual dowry of a wife—two or three hundred was considered an extravagant sum—and most of the girls waited till they were twenty or more for a husband. This tradition handed down from the middle of the thirteenth to the fourteenth century is also recorded by Dante in a passage in the "Paradiso" where he embodies all his scorn for his contemporaries in a passionate reminiscence of the time when Bellincione Berti wore a girdle of leather and bone, and his wife came from her glass with unpainted face. Barely half a century had elapsed and now all was changed. Now three hundred cavaliers, accompanied by bands of youths and damsels, spread tables to which all foreigners were bidden and lavishly feasted. Now buffoons and men of pleasure from Lombardy and other parts crowded to Florence, and in May-time there was dancing and music in the streets, and girls went dressed in white with garlands on their heads. Tents were erected in the squares, and for the feast of St. John a thousand men, also arrayed in white and led by one called the Lord of Love, filled the air with the sound of revelry and the rhythm of dances. "Jocund was the intercourse," says the chronicler, "joyous were the meetings, and gracious the songs;" while everybody was engaged in some art or craft by which he made the money which led to these magnificent results.

XII.

FLORENCE IN THE FOURTEENTH CENTURY AFTER GIANO DELLA BELLA'S REIGN OF TERROR.

THE happy state of things above described naturally could not last. Faction soon showed its sinister head above the flowers, and a veritable reign of terror began in Florence against the Ghibellines. This party could neither forgive nor forget the injuries inflicted on it; the Guelphs, on the other hand, saw in every arrogant act or word of the malcontents, in every deed of oppression practised by them in the contado on the lower classes, an assertion of the desire to regain the upper hand. The intense individualism of the commune could and did make great men, but failed to make great institutions, partly because, commerce apart, there were no interests sufficiently wide to divert the public mind from personal matters, and partly also because the government, being founded on the popular will, showed a constant tendency towards oligarchism which could only be checked by the keen, alert, and ever-watchful intelligence of the citizens. The Florentines were hard-headed, practical, slightly pharisaical, like all successful people; they could make no allowance for

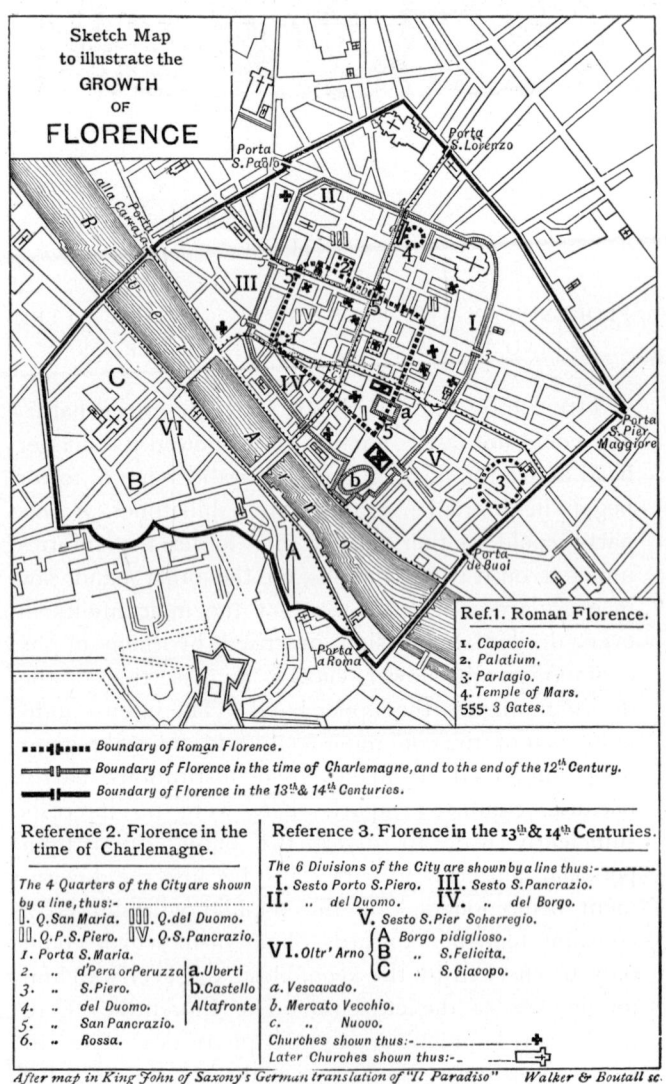

Sketch Map to illustrate the GROWTH OF FLORENCE

Ref. 1. Roman Florence.
1. Capaccio.
2. Palatium.
3. Parlagio.
4. Temple of Mars.
5,5,5. 3 Gates.

▪▪▪◆▪▪▪ Boundary of Roman Florence.
━━◆━━ Boundary of Florence in the time of Charlemagne, and to the end of the 12th Century.
━━◆━━ Boundary of Florence in the 13th & 14th Centuries.

Reference 2. Florence in the time of Charlemagne.

The 4 Quarters of the City are shown by a line, thus: ·········

I. Q. San Maria.   III. Q. del Duomo.
II. Q. P. S. Piero. IV. Q. S. Pancrazio.

1. Porta S. Maria.
2. „ d'Pera or Peruzza
3. „ S. Piero.
4. „ del Duomo.
5. „ San Pancrazio.
6. „ Rossa.

a. Uberti
b. Castello Altafronte

Reference 3. Florence in the 13th & 14th Centuries.

The 6 Divisions of the City are shown by a line thus: ·········
I. Sesto Porto S. Piero.   III. Sesto S. Pancrazio.
II. „ del Duomo.   IV. „ del Borgo.
V. Sesto S. Pier Scherregio.
VI. Oltr' Arno { A Borgo pidiglioso.
                B „ S. Felicita.
                C „ S. Giacopo.

a. Vescavado.
b. Mercato Vecchio.
c. „ Nuovo.
Churches shown thus: ━━━ ✚
Later Churches shown thus: ━━━ ⌂

After map in King John of Saxony's German translation of "Il Paradiso"   Walker & Boutall sc.

their enemies, had no philosophical patience at their command, and provided rough-and-ready remedies for every evil just as it presented itself. In the old simple days faction fights had not vexed them: now, more elegant, more luxurious, travelled men of the world, as these merchants had become, they were tired of the constant brawls between the Adimari and the Tosinghi, the Rossi and the Tornaquinci, the Frescobaldi with the Frescobaldi, the Donati with their kinsmen; and in the course of the year 1293 several merchants and manufacturers met together to deliberate on a remedy for all these disorders.

At their head was Giano della Bella, rich, powerful, and an ardent Guelph. He was one of the Priors who entered office on the 15th of February, and he took advantage of his two months' tenure of power to formulate the famous "Ordinances of Justice." These laws made all relatives responsible one for the other, and decreed that the oath of two witnesses should be held sufficient to prove any deed of violence, and could be followed by the demolition of the houses of the accused. Without the consent of the Priors no noble or magnate (*grande*)—in other words, no conspicuous or overbearing citizen, whether Guelph or Ghibelline—could testify against a commoner (*popolano*), although no corresponding disability hampered the popolani. Grandi were not to inhabit any part of the town where they had committed a misdeed, nor to live within a specified distance of the bridges. They were neither to quit their houses nor receive visitors in times of disturbance, nor appear with armed retainers at the funerals, weddings, or receptions into a religious order of any but their own kinsmen. When the Standard-Bearer of Justice proceeded officially along the town no grande was to be seen in his path. Any popolano becoming a grande became subject to all the disabilities and penalties of the higher estate. One witness *de visu*, and two by hearsay, or four of the latter, sufficed to prove any charge against a grande. A box was placed against the wall of the house occupied by the Executor of Justice, to receive secret denunciations. The grandi had to give security for any fines or indemnities which they were condemned to disburse; but they were debarred from borrowing money for such payments, and any person who advanced sums to them for such a purpose was also liable to punishment. Any popolano who failed to denounce the misdeed of a grande was fined; but, on the other hand, it is gratifying to learn that even grandi were allowed to beat their servants within their own walls with impunity, this being the *jus commune*. There were minute provisions against any occupation by grandi (to the prejudice of popolani), of property in churches or convents. Sometimes the grandi were declared sopraggrandi (super magnates), which supreme degree of social exaltation meant, not only that they were to lose every benefit or mitigation formerly allowed to them, but also that they must quit the part of the town or contado where they had hitherto lived. Commoners related by ties of blood to magnates could not dwell in the same part of the town or country which held their kinsmen, nor take any share in their quarrels; and if a grande became a popolano he was obliged to change his arms.

For the purpose of carrying out these penal laws, the office of Standard-bearer of Justice was created. He was given the banner of the people—the red cross on the white ground—and allotted a force of one thousand foot soldiers to send against the grandi whenever required—besides two hundred masons, carpenters, and bearers of pick-axes who were to be employed in the demolition of houses.

The grandi against whom these drastic measures were levelled were not Ghibellines entirely; but simply a number of families who, having formerly enjoyed power on whatever grounds, whether feudal descent, or commercial wealth, or services rendered by a former generation, had shown a desire to obtain the predominance in the town and proportionately to keep down the growing middle class. Indeed, the old distinctions between Guelphs and Ghibellines had long ago vanished, and there remained only a party of determined malcontents and an equally determined democratic class.

At the same time as these Ordinances, somewhat ironically called of Justice, leagues of the people were re-constituted in the contado with a precisely identical purpose. The leagues were formed of groups of small parishes, self-administering, but united, each group under a vicar or captain of the public, with whose consent money and men could be levied for defence. The leagues were to pursue all grandi who were guilty under the ordinances; and could force them to come armed to the help of Florence whenever summoned.

The republic could levy taxes on the mills, wool-presses, and markets of the places composing these leagues, and, in short, played the part of an overlord to these villages and townlets which taxed themselves for all internal needs and were otherwise quite free. Each league had its own standard-bearer and council, and the interference of the republican vicar in its affairs was only for general supervision.

For a time these measures insured tranquillity, especially as the Florentines, to put an end to wars which constantly afforded the nobles an opportunity of distinguishing themselves, at last made peace with unfortunate Pisa, now ever more declining. The conditions imposed by Florence were that Count Guido da Montefeltro should be sent away and the exiled Guelphs recalled to Pisa; also that the Florentines were to trade freely throughout the Pisan district, and be exempt from all payment of duties on their merchandise. The Lucchese and Sienese and representatives of all the Guelph places in Tuscany intervened at the making of this peace; after which Florence was so tranquil for a time that neither by day nor night were the gates of the city closed. The republic obtained the entire jurisdiction over Poggibonsi, once so hotly contested by Siena, and added various other districts to its territory, all of which was well, but could not long suffice to keep down the irritation produced by Giano della Bella's laws.

Naturally there was endless injustice and confusion in the application of measures which by their very construction subserved private spite far more than the public weal. Mutual suspicion and hostility grew daily, and the magnates were determined to be quit of their oppressors. Strange to say, the only office which the grandi were still allowed to fill was the magistracy of the Guelph party, and they strained every nerve to use this one weapon against the middle class.

Giano, fully alive to the danger which threatened him from the party, sought on his side to deprive it of its seal and possessions, and make the latter (which had much increased of late years) common property, and as the captains of the Guelph party were mostly knights, Giano carried a decree excluding families in which there were men of that rank from any share in the government, thus shutting out thirty-three families at one blow. Giano was a Guelph himself in the sense that he belonged to the Pope's party and had the interest of the middle class at heart; but since to become a leader is always to descend from the ideal to the possible, he really came to represent a section of ambitious spirits, against whom were arrayed other men just as ambitious, and invidious to boot. Giano's opposition to the magistracy of the Guelph party furnished colour to an accusation of reactionary views, and as any hint of that sort never failed to inflame the passions and rouse the facile suspicions of the people, the logic of hatred soon ceased to find anything unlikely in the charge of Ghibellinism brought against the author of the Ordinances of Justice.

There were secret meetings in the houses of the powerful, and excited gatherings among the lower classes, led by a butcher called or nicknamed Pecora, who was protected by the Tosinghi. Giano had

STREET IN OLD MARKET, FLORENCE, NOW DESTROYED.

dreamed of violent cures for violent ills, and very soon had to face a combination of all the turbulent spirits in the town.

Street frays prevailed as usual, and just as passion ran highest, a kinsman or retainer of Corso Donati killed a popolano in a brawl where others were wounded. The matter was immediately brought before the Podestà, and the populace, infuriated against Corso Donati, persuaded itself that the Podestà must condemn him. The Standard-bearer of Justice had already been summoned, when, to the general surprise, Corso was acquitted. A cry arose that the Podestà had been bought off; the people rushed to his palace and clamoured for his death. In vain Giano and the Priors exhorted the mob to appeal, as they were entitled to do, to the Standard-bearer of Justice. The palace of the Podestà was sacked, and he and his beautiful wife, a Lombard lady took refuge in the houses of the Cerchi, while Corso Donati, who was also in imminent danger, escaped across the roofs. The next day the Council of the Priors met, and the popular fury being somewhat cooled, they were able to decree that the property of which the Podestà had been deprived should be restored to him, and himself and family allowed to depart in peace. The anger of the upper classes then turned against Giano whom they accused of having stirred up sedition by his general conduct. All his personal enemies, noble and otherwise, joined in the cry against him; and when he had been persuaded by the Magalotti, his kinsmen, to leave Florence for a few days and thus avert the danger of a civil war (a prospect from which he honestly shrank), a decree of banishment was forthwith pronounced against him; his goods were confiscated and his house sacked.

He never saw Florence again, and died eventually in France.

His methods were arbitrary; but his aim, like that of many of his contemporaries, Villani among the rest, was simply to admit all sections of the people, those composing the lesser Guilds equally with those belonging to the larger ones, to a share in the government; and such a project, though destined later to be realized, was premature.

Pecora, the butcher, took zealously to the work of popular agitation, and though really nothing but a noisy demagogue, he managed to establish a sort of influence for a time, and boasted that he held the balance of power in the town and would be able to appoint his adherents to office. The grandi, led by Forese degli Adimari, Vanni de' Mozzi, and Geri Spini were busy with intrigues of their own, and soon to all these elements of confusion and corruption, another was added in the feuds between the Donati and Cerchi or Neri and Bianchi (Blacks and Whites), who had adopted the names in mere imitation, it would seem, of the two factions thus designated in Pistoja.

"I am Vanni Fucci, a wild beast, and Pistoja was my worthy lair," one of the first and most ferocious leaders of the Neri is represented as saying in Hell to Dante. One must read the chronicles of contemporaries to realize even faintly the horror, the cruelty, the fierce hatred, and, with it all, the vivid splendour which prevailed in these mediæval cities where the streets were drenched with the blood of kinsmen. The Cancellieri of Pistoja, who eventually split into the Black and White factions, were rich and powerful above all their fellow citizens, and counted in their family eighteen knights with golden spurs. Some youths of this formidable clan met together in a wineshop and quarrelled over a game; and from this sordid beginning arose, it was said, the savage feud which for years desolated Pistoja. It is more likely, however, that the Cancellieri were too ambitious and too arrogant even to live in harmony among themselves, and dividing into hostile camps, they drew around them all the warring aspirations of the town. The people of Pistoja sent away one Podestà when the mischief became intolerable, and, finding that his successor was equally powerless to restore peace, the chief citizens eventually decided to place themselves under the protection of Florence, and be governed by it. As some of the Bianchi had shown a tendency to ally themselves with the Ghibelline party in Italy, the Florentines, anxious for the Guelph cause, willingly undertook the offered task, but unfortunately could think of no better remedy than to order the leaders of the two factions to the frontier. They transferred themselves and their hatreds to Florence, and there by a process of natural assimilation absorbed into themselves the equally hostile parties led respectively by Viero Cerchi and Corso Donati. The Cerchi were White and the Donati Black, and although the first named were frequently taunted by their adversaries with Ghibellinism, the truth was that Guelphs and

Ghibellines could be found among the Bianchi, and Ghibellines and Guelphs among the Neri.

The Cerchi were *novi homines*, rich merchants with a great and powerful following. The Donati, their neighbours, were gentlemen and soldiers, but neither rich nor powerful, although Corso's great character and high courage made him a conspicuous personage. After the departure of Giano della Bella the middle class and the higher artizans attached themselves to the Cerchi, who also attracted the Ghibellines by the more liberal spirit in which they were disposed to apply the laws. In short, they formed a party of the sort which we perhaps should describe in these days as Moderate Liberals, while the mass of the Donati adherents were haughty Conservatives, narrow Radicals, and uncompromising doctrinaires.

The Cerchi being merchant-princes, magnificent and tolerant, one understands how they attracted such minds as Dino Compagni, Dante, and the sombre, passionate Guido Cavalcanti, patriots yet dreamers, who might sometimes miss the significance of the moment, but had an outlook on wider horizons than those which bounded the world of the Neri. Among the principal families, the Mannelli, Malespini, Rossi, Scali, a portion of the Frescobaldi, Mozzi and Bardi, and the Cavalcanti sided with the Cerchi ; while to the Donati adhered almost all the great merchants, and new magnates, the bulk of the middle class, who, in conjunction with the historical Guelphs, sought to impose their views on the minor manufacturers and to obtain a monopoly of power. Among the great names to be counted in these ranks were the Pazzi Visdomini, Buondelmonti, Gianfigliazzi, Tornaquinci, Brunelleschi, Acciajoli. Between the two leaders there was a picturesque contrast of character. Vieri de' Cerchi was a brave man, but rather dull and with scant faculty for speech, while Corso Donati was witty and handsome and brilliant. When he heard that Vieri had spoken in a meeting of his adherents, he was accustomed to remark: "Now the ass at the gate has brayed" (in allusion to Vieri's place of residence which was near the Porta S. Piero); and witticisms of this sort were generally repeated, and furnished fresh fuel for the ever-inflammable passions of these political sects. Men were in such an excited state that the faintest trifle—a gesture at a funeral, where kinsmen like the Frescobaldi of opposite political opinions met together—sufficed to provoke an explosion. A crowd might assemble for some peaceful purpose, such as to watch a group of white-robed and flower-crowned girls dance the May, and all at once a brawl would burst out, and the festival end in blood. Boniface VIII., fearing least the Bianchi whom he regarded as Ghibellines might get the upper hand, sent his legate, Cardinal Matteo d'Acquasparta, in 1300, to Florence to restore peace if possible. He was received with great ceremony, and, Dante being among the Priori (who were chiefly Bianchi) at the time, was consequently one of the officials who helped to do him honour.

The Cardinal banished some leaders of both sides (among the rest Guido Cavalcanti who went to Sarzana); but this well-worn device only exasperated everybody, and the Cardinal feeling his own life in danger shortly afterwards departed, first laying the town under an interdict. The Bianchi then obtained the upper hand for a time ; and several of the exiles were recalled, including Guido Cavalcanti who returned, however, only to die of a fever contracted at Sarzana.

In 1301 Boniface was so persuaded by his bankers, the Florentine Spini and others of the Neri, that Florence was returning under Ghibelline influence, as to invite the intervention of Charles of Valois.

The Prince obeyed the Pope's summons, but halting at Siena, there received a deputation from Florence charged to obtain from him an engagement in writing not to seek to establish any sovereign authority over the city. He made no difficulty about signing the document, and pocketed seventeen thousand florins from the Neri.

He arrived on the 1st of November, 1301, with so large a following of knights that many citizens armed themselves, and the coming of the peace-maker seemed to promise anything but peace.

The Neri, encouraged by his presence, began to reassert themselves arrogantly; and the first signal of bloodshed was given when the Medici (powerful members of the middle class, who thus made their sinister entry upon the stage of Florentine politics) attacked a popolano as he was leaving church after vespers and mortally wounded him. On this the citizens poured forth armed from all sides ; the Signoria ordered out the city bands ; excited crowds filled the piazzas, and barricades were erected. Next day the news flew that Corso Donati was at the Pinti

Gate. He entered practically unopposed, and conducted his troop to the Church of San Piero Maggiore. Many new adherents flocked to his standard, and thus encouraged, he sacked and burned the houses of the Priori who had been in power when his banishment was decreed, released all the prisoners, and proceeding to the palace of the Podestà, forced the Signoria to quit it and return home. This amounted to a change of government, for, as already stated, the Priors during their term of office remained night and day in the palace.

In vain the Priors caused the tocsin, summoning a parliament, to be sounded, for the respectable citizens were too terrified to show themselves and only the mob had free play, burning and sacking at their will. This state of things lasted six days, during which time Corso is said to have ruthlessly despoiled his enemies while Charles seized the favourable opportunity to levy black-mail from some Bianchi whom he had placed under arrest.

Favoured by him the Neri were triumphant, and the new Signoria consisted entirely of their adherents. In November the Pope again sent Cardinal d'Acquasparta to restore peace. He united some Bianchi and Neri in marriage, but so little did this avail to calm passion that Niccolò de' Cerchi, going to hear a friar preach in the square of Santa Croce, there met Simone Donati, son of Corso, and his own nephew. The savage youth immediately fell upon his uncle, whose followers fled, taking with them Niccolò's young son, "a boy," says the chronicle, "who was riding with uncovered head." Niccolò himself was dragged from his horse and killed by having his veins cut ; but he succeeded first in wounding his assailant, who died in the Church of San Piero. A touch of pathos lightens the horrible story at the last, for Simone with his dying breath begged that there might be peace between the houses—the vainest prayer ever uttered by mortal lips! The report, true or false, of a conspiracy on the part of the Bianchi, to assassinate Charles, caused a wholesale arrest and banishment of conspicuous persons and families. Among the exiles was Dante, although at the time of the pretended conspiracy he was at Siena. It was decreed that if he ever returned to his native city he should be burned alive ; nor was he the only valuable son thus cast forth by " ungrateful Florence." With him went also Ser Petracco di Parenzo dall' Incisa, whose son Francesco Petrarca saw the light in exile.

The Bianchi being thus ejected, the government fell into the hands of leading merchants or of nobles who claimed to be inspired with purely Guelph tendencies. New names of power, such as the Medici, Peruzzi, Rucellai, and Strozzi, are now found among the great merchants, who were, in fact, slowly forming an aristocratic class. These men and their companions regarded Corso Donati as a sort of official leader, but he soon grew disgusted with them and wished to recall the Bianchi.

The Neri were corrupt and cruel or accused of so being, and the charge of peculation brought against them at last became so general that a cry arose for the publication of the accounts of the commune. Corso, "whose soul was equal to great crimes, but shrank from paltry intrigue," headed the malcontents and directed the street frays. The towers bristled with defences as of old, and the dogs of war were as freely unmuzzled as though "Ghibelline" violence and "Bianchi" treason had never been expelled from the town. Things reached such a pitch that in 1304 the commune had to request armed help from Lucca which sent horse and foot. To these friendly strangers full jurisdiction was handed over, but they were only allowed to keep it for sixteen days, at the end of which time the Florentines began to feel offended with them, and one day in the New Market a patriotic citizen struck a Lucchese and told him to take the blow home and offer it to Santa Zita, the patroness of Lucca.

A few Bianchi returned under the pretext of being converted to Guelph principles, but in the houses of the Cavalcanti near the Mercato Nuovo they soon formed a fresh hot-bed of intrigue. The Medici and Giugni determined to attack them, but Corso Donati, who was ill of the gout and displeased with his old party, made no sign. Fighting began, houses were given to the flames, and a north wind aiding and being helped in its turn by the wax candles before the image of the Madonna under the loggia of Orsanmichele, the fire became extensive and destroyed half the wealth of Florence. It was said that more than seventeen hundred houses were burnt down in the narrow mediæval alleys where the great clans dwelt and had added one house after another to the original abode as their sons married and brought home their brides.

Pistoja being in the hands of the Bianchi, Florence and Lucca determinated to besiege it, choosing for their leader Robert Duke of Calabria, son of Charles II. of Naples. Pistoja, although scarce of provisions from the beginning, made an heroic defence, while the cruelties practised by the besiegers, who cut off the heads and ears of the men, and slit the noses of the women, the retaliations practised on war prisoners by the besieged, the sufferings from famine within the beleaguered town, which caused fathers to thrust forth their children and men their wives, constituted daily scenes of horror, and are related by the old chroniclers with a calm and terrible simplicity. Pistoja surrendered at last on the 10th of April, 1306, and Florence divided the government of the town with Lucca, one furnishing the Podestà and the other the captain.

This victory strengthened the position of the Neri in Florence, and rendered them more than ever intolerant of the tergiversation of Corso Donati, who had just married a daughter of Uguccione della Faggiuola, and had promised the grandi that the severity of the laws against them should be mitigated. One morning the tocsins sounded; the Councils met, and Corso was condemned to death as a rebel. Armed bands led by the Podestà, the Captain of the People and the Executor of Justice, marched with armed city bands against his house. All day the siege lasted, Corso himself incapacitated by gout, being able to encourage his defenders only with his voice. Towards evening a breach was made, and then Corso fled, followed by most of his party. The fugitives were savagely pursued, and Gherardo Bordoni, one of the Donati faction, was barbarously murdered on the Affrica bridge. A youth of the Adimari Cavicciuli house cut off the dead man's hand, then hurried to fasten it on the door of another Adimari, his kinsman and foe. Corso himself was captured by some of the Duke of Calabria's soldiers at Rovezzano, and, for fear of being executed by his enemies in Florence, let himself fall from his mule; but his gouty foot remained in the stirrup, and he was dragged along the ground. The soldiers then either put him to death at once, or wounded him so badly that he lingered but a few moments after, being conveyed to the convent of San Salvi, where he was hastily buried.

In January, 1311, Henry VII. of Germany crossed the Alps. His coming was hailed by the Ghibellines, and in a nobler spirit, also by Dante, who saw in him a prince capable of realizing at last the fond mediæval idea of a universal Emperor and a Universal Church. Far different was the feeling in Florence where the tocsin sounded, the people gathered in arms, the gates were shut and the streets barricaded as soon as it was known that Henry had approached the town. Reinforcements came to the Florentines from Lucca Siena, and Bologna, while Arezzo sent help to Henry. But he, wasted with fever, had little will to contend, and after a short sojourn at the Monastery of San Salvi, proceeded to Pisa, fighting his way through the armed bands sent by Florence to intercept him. Pisa received him gladly, and Genoa sent him galleys and money, and the alarm in the Guelph cities was growing when death came to solve all problems by carrying off the Emperor in the summer of 1313. In his grave were buried the hopes of a ruined party, and the fragments of a noble dream, for all reality departed now from the Holy Roman Empire which survived for some centuries longer only as a majestic fiction.

To Pisa the blow was crushing, and the distracted citizens, not knowing to whom to turn, called on Uguccione della Faggiuola, who was acting as Imperial Vicar in Genoa, to govern them. He showed extraordinary energy, revived the war against the Guelphs, and forcibly occupied Lucca. The Florentines addressed a request to the King for aid, and he sent his younger brother the Duke of Gravina, who, at the head of the Guelph troops, met Uguccione at Montecatini. In the battle which ensued the Ghibellines were completely victorious, Gravina himself and his son being among the slain. But Uguccione was by nature a tyrant, and his conduct soon became insupportable, both to the Pisans and Lucchese. They drove him away and he fled to Verona, there to take service under Can Grande della Scala.

XIII.

EVENTS IN LUCCA AND PISA. FLORENCE IN THE FOURTEENTH CENTURY (*continued*).

AFTER the departure of Uguccione Lucca fell under the rule of Castruccio Castracane degli Interminelli, while at Pisa a popular movement was headed by Coscetto dal Colle, a youth of humble origin, but brave, rich, and handsome. He was speedily betrayed by a friend, and after the usual sanguinary scenes the government of the now fallen and unhappy town was given to Gaddo della Gherardesca.

In Lucca, under Castruccio, a period of temporary prosperity, was partially healing the wounds inflicted by eight years of disorder, during which certain laws had been passed against the nobles in a similar spirit to Giano della Bella's " Ordinances of Justice." Th' soul of the popular party had been Bontura Dati, ar. astute, audacious man, possessed of all the fluency the coarse irony and narrow passions of a demagogue He once formed part of a deputation sent to Pisa to negotiate a peace, one of the conditions of which was that Lucca should restore the castle of Asciano, where in the true spirit of the times the victors had caused mirrors to be placed on a high tower so that, whenever the sun shone, the Pisans might be reminded of their loss. To the request for the restitution of this castle Bontura retorted with an insulting refusal, adding that the ladies of Pisa must do without their mirror; a sneer which filled his fellow citizens with admiration. His rule soon became so insupportable to the nobles of Lucca that they quitted the town *en masse*, and as they took their wealth with them great misery followed on their exodus.

After Uguccione's forcible entry it was the turn of the Guelphs to suffer. One thousand four hundred of their houses are said to have been set on fire, and three hundred families belonging to the guild of silk-weavers were evicted. The pre-eminence which Lucca had hitherto enjoyed in that trade passed to other places, and was especially advantageous to Florence, where the refugees met with an eager welcome.

Castruccio Castracane's tenure of power revived the aspirations of the Ghibellines. His first enterprise was against Pistoja, which he brought under the sway of Lucca, and six years later in 1322 he turned his arms against Florence. Dissensions there had momentarily paralysed the energies of the republic, and every suggestion for a vigorous defence was resisted by the grandi, who sought to take advantage of the situation to obtain a revocation of the "Ordinances." It is plain, therefore, either that the aristocratic faction had never died out in Florence, or was ever being created anew by the tyranny of the governing class. Divided councils consequently prevailed, with the usual result of inaction. Such crises were inevitable at intervals in a political organism so loosely constructed as the commune, and had only not more fatal effects because of the strong individuality, and the perfect freedom of intellectual development which counteracted them.

A Council of Twelve Good Men had recently, as we know, been created in Florence to control the Signoria, but the chronic distrust among the people of their rulers still continued, and yet another new device was imagined to allay it. The Priors and other magistrates put into a bursa the names of those eligible for the Signoria, selecting a sufficient number to last over forty-two months, and including the names of many who had been kept out for some years. The names were then drawn every two months. This system was eventually extended to the election of the Twelve Buonuomini, the Standard-bearers of the Companies, and the leaders of the troops.

Castruccio continued to carry on the war ferociously, but so far with no conspicuous success. Some traitors aiding, he made an attempt to possess himself of the government of Pisa which, already beset with perils, and forced to be equally on its guard against the Lucchese and the Florentines, in December of this year (1325) sustained an additional loss when the king of Aragon finally occupied Sardinia.

In Pistoja things were in a deplorable state. The Lucchese and Florentines had indeed restored jurisdiction over the contado to that town, but the partial liberty thus recovered was completely sterilized by the wild anarchy prevailing within the city. What, for want of a better word, must be called the government, had momentarily passed to a certain Filippo Tedici, who by force and fraud had disposed of his enemies, and was now anxious to dispose of the town to the highest bidder. How he intrigued and plotted, betrayed friends and kinsmen, opened pretended negotiations with Florence, where a keen desire prevailed to keep Castruccio out of Pistoja, and how at the same time he despatched one of the usual ambassadors of the Middle Ages—a monk—to the lord of Lucca; how he poisoned his wife by giving her sweetmeats, and how, he eventually married Castruccio's daughter, all—as related in the "Istorie Pistolesi," a contemporary chronicle—forms a vivid page of Italian history. Eventually Tedici obtained the terms he wished for from Castruccio, who occupied Pistoja, and thus more than ever threatened the liberties and security of the Florentines. The latter strained every nerve to increase the force already at their disposal, and at last got together an army which cost, it was said, three thousand gold florins daily—an incredible sum under the circumstances; but whatever the real expense may have been it is certain that the Florentines paid it with alacrity.

On the 23rd of September, 1325, a battle took place at Altopascia, and resulted in a complete victory for Castruccio. Numbers of Florentines and Tuscan knights were taken prisoners, and the victor made a large sum—estimated at one hundred thousand gold florins—out of the ransom for various illustrious persons, among whom was Raymond of Cardona, the Florentine commander. Castruccio followed up this success by ravaging all the Florentine territory, and on the 2nd of October had pitched his camp at Peretola, only two miles from the gate of Florence. He destroyed a vast quantity of paintings in the churches, and sent off to Lucca all the portable property he could lay hands on. Finally he returned to Lucca to hold a sort of Roman triumph, and for a few weeks the inhabitants of the contado enjoyed a respite from his barbarities.

In the battle of Altopascia the knights on the Florentine side had shown great cowardice, while the city militia had fought very well. Nevertheless from this period the practice of employing mercenaries became more and more common. The interests of the republic were so widespread, the commerce which had to be protected was so extensive, and the influence of the Florentine name so great, that the days were long past when a trained city militia could suffice for military enterprise, or even for purposes of defence. In the "good old times" the merchants and artizans could leave their offices and their workshops, march out a few miles against a neighbouring foe,—inflict a defeat or receive one, take or lose a few castles, and then—such as survived—could return to their business as though nothing of importance had happened. But, as head of the Guelph league, Florence now had weighty responsibilities ; her citizens also were engaged in enterprises which demanded unremitting attention, and could not be abandoned at any moment for the sake of a campaign likely to last months—perhaps, with only a few interruptions, years. Obviously a large army was required which Florence and its contado were numerically too small to furnish, and hence rose the necessity for paid foreign troops. To obtain these and some surcease from mutual suspicion at the same time, the republic agreed to place itself under the protection of Duke Charles of Calabria, Robert of Naples' eldest son, who was to furnish a thousand horsemen on condition of receiving in return for the space of ten years, the annual sum of two hundred thousand gold florins in war, and half the sum in time of peace.

In July, 1326, the Duke, with his suite of knights and barons, and horsemen (four hundred of whom had already been sent to Florence under the command of the Duke of Athens), entered Siena, and was received with much honour. Siena was divided between the two factions of the Tolomei and Salimbeni, and the Florentines were anxious, in the interests of the Guelph party, to re-establish peace there. They despatched ambassadors to Robert, begging him to restore order, which he succeeded in doing by inducing the hostile houses to conclude a truce for five years, and getting himself accepted as governor, in return for which services he wrung another sixteen thousand florins out of the Florentines, and then hastened to present himself in their own town.

Here he and his Duchess, a daughter of Charles of Valois, were welcomed with great splendour, but the humbler-minded or more pharisaical among the citizens were disposed to resent the expense resulting from this magnificence, and to regret the customs which according to them foreign influence destroyed.

Sumptuary laws had been formerly passed to restrain the extravagance of the Florentine women's dress. Now the French, or more probably the women themselves by appealing to the French, caused these laws to be rescinded and went forth crowned with gold and silver garlands, or wearing their hair gathered into nets covered with pearls, while their dresses were of silk adorned with precious stones.

The Florentines had hardly received the Duke inside their walls when they began to find his authority irksome, and were much relieved on his being summoned hastily to Naples by his father who was alarmed at the advance of the Emperor, Louis of Bavaria.

With the help of the last-named sovereign Castruccio had besieged and entered Pisa which had to accept him for its ruler, or rather as Imperial vicar, for Louis kept the income of the commune for his own use and ground down the inhabitants with fresh taxes. He invested Castruccio with the Dukedom of Lucca, and might have helped him in his long meditated attack on Florence, but, fortunately for the latter, had other designs.

In January, 1328, Castruccio having followed his patron to Rome, the troops retained by the Florentines took Pistoja by a night surprise, and for ten days the city was sacked. Castruccio, abandoning every other thought, flew to recover it, but only succeeded in doing this after a two months' siege when the garrison capitulated from hunger. Castruccio being then lord of Pisa, Lucca, Pistoja, the Luigiana and a large portion of the Genoese eastern

Riviera, began at last to prepare for a serious attack on Florence. But before he could carry out his plans he died on the 3rd of September, 1329, at the comparatively early age of forty-seven, having, after all, accomplished nothing grand, but only tried to play the part of a Visconti or a Scaliger without the qualities or the opportunity.

Two months later the Duke of Calabria died, and the Florentines, having thus recovered their independence, set about remodelling their constitution. All former councils were dissolved and two new ones formed, one of three hundred of popolani presided over by the Captain of the People, and one of two hundred and fifty popolani and grandi mixed, headed by the Podestà; the decision of the Signoria being submitted for approval to the larger and smaller council in turn.

The Standard-bearer of Justice, it may be here stated, continued to represent the republic on all great occasions. He presented the wands of office or bâtons to the Captain of the People, the Podestà, the Executor of Justice and the Captains chosen for war.

The Standard-bearer and the Priors ate together with great ceremony, trumpets sounding all the while, and wherever they went they were preceded by trumpeters, guards, and mace-bearers. The cost of the keep of the Signoria and their attendants amounted to ten florins daily. The Priors were not only forbidden to leave the Palace during their time of office for any private business, but if one of them needed to go home at night without the knowledge of the public, he had to ask permission of the colleague who was President of the Government for the day. They were not allowed to have private conversation with anybody, not even a kinsman, but as a compensation could give frequent audiences to clients and petitioners who frittered away a vast amount of public time.

XIV.

GENERAL EVENTS.

By the intervention of Louis (whose services had to be lavishly paid for), Lucca and Pisa got rid of Castruccio's sons and recovered their liberties. Lucca did not keep them long, being occupied by surprise by Marco Visconti, one of those leaders of disbanded mercenaries who henceforth, at brief intervals, are to ravage the Tuscan territory. He put the town up to auction so to speak, and after bids from Florence and Pisa, sold it to Gherardino Spinola, a Ghibelline from Genoa who claimed to govern in the name of the Emperor.

The whole history of the next year is dreary. The republics had lost all the freshness and enthusiasm of youth, and some, like Pisa, in faction and bloodshed, in bitter mutual hatreds and bitterer want were hastening to their fall. Florence was saddened by calamities and disheartening sights. On All Saints Day, 1333, a great flood laid the plain of the Mugello under water, and, extending to the city, penetrated to a great height in the Church of the Baptist, the palace of the Priors and many other buildings. Three of the bridges broke, the statue of Mars at the foot of which young Buondelmonti was murdered fell into the Arno, and so many houses and shops were flooded that the loss in property of all sorts was incalculable.

About the same time Florence witnessed for the first time a lugubrious procession of Flagellants, who entered to the number of ten thousand under the leadership of a Friar from Bergamo. Dressed in white and dripping with blood from their self-inflicted scourgings, they were surely eloquent of a misery so deep that fanaticism alone could give expression to it.

A further cause of depression was the failure of the great bankers the Bardi and Peruzzi, who as is well known, had lent money to Edward III. of England, and being unable to get it back, became bankrupts, and entailed ruin on numerous depositors. For a time the credit of Florence was severely shaken; but nevertheless the Tower (Giotto's) was begun about this time, and the Guild of Wool continued to supply the funds for the building of the Duomo.

A few months after the death of Castruccio, Pistoja was obliged to come to terms with Florence and accept its jurisdiction for a term of two years, renewable at each expiration; and in 1337 the republic also obtained possession of Arezzo by cession from Piero Tarlati. The Florentines agreed to preserve the property and rights of the Ghibellines within that town, but excepted from this favour such families as the Ubertini and Faggiuola. None of these great "irreconcilables" were allowed to intermarry with Florentines, nor could any of their number be called to the bishoprics of Florence and Fiesole. They were also forbidden, under pain of death, to accept imperial fiefs in Tuscany.

The Visconti of Milan now began to influence the destinies of Northern and Central Italy, and one result of their interference was the assignment, at last, of Lucca to Pisa which kept possession of its ancient rival for twenty-seven years.

Passing over other events, we come to those which led in Florence to the tyranny of the Duke of Athens. In spite of their laboriously acquired and jealously guarded liberties, it seems as though the people of Florence were still oppressed by the grandi in many private matters; and apparently what they considered the ill-weed of aristocracy had not been entirely rooted out. Doubtless relatives and retainers of the exiled houses had remained all the time in Florence, and in fact they must have done so, for wholesale as were the prescriptions they could not include everybody, and it is evident that many families returned when the first fury against them had abated. A new generation with revived pretensions had grown up since the death of Corso Donati, and round the nucleus thus formed gathered all the younger, more irreconcilable spirits of the town. Then outside Florence and all over Italy there was still a so-called imperial party with whom the malcontents were united by policy or ties of blood. And certainly some disposition on the part of the grandi to re-acquire supremacy must have manifested itself, for all at once the people apparently finding Podestà, Captain of the People and Executor of Justice insufficient for their needs, created a new officer, a Captain of the Guard or Bargello, who was charged with the administration of justice.

The first of these officials was a certain Gabbrielli from Gubbio, one of an ill-famed house. He pronounced sentence for some slight offence against a Bardi and a Frescobaldi who proceeded to conspire with the Tarlati of Arezzo, the Ubaldini, the Pazzi of Valdarno, and other enemies of the commune. But the plot was discovered; the people rose in arms; and the conspirators were persuaded by the Podestà to leave the town under his escort. About thirty, a small portion of the whole, were condemned to death or spoliation.

There was also a great seething of Ghibellines outside the walls. Probably the hornets' nest expelled from Arezzo helped to keep up the general irritation, and inside Florence the Government was hard pressed. The credit of the republic had been shaken; many depositors, especially at Naples, had called in their funds, and anything which looked like inability on the part of the Guelphs to defend themselves could only increase the general mistrust of the resources of Florence. A special council of twenty citizens, all popolani, had been appointed to carry on operations against Lucca, and continued in office afterwards, charged with the necessity of providing for the public defence. They were empowered to raise any taxes that they liked, and to make war or peace or conclude alliances as seemed well to them. Apparently they thought that the town was insufficiently provided with soldiers, and they seized upon the idea of employing Walter of Brienne, Duke of

COURT OF BARGELLO, FLORENCE.

Athens, a scion of the royal house of France. He was one of the race of military hirelings whom the necessity of the communes had bred : just a condottiere who brought himself and his company to the service of any cause which paid well. He was rich, yet of a grasping disposition ; ugly, small, cunning, disloyal, and seems to have possessed none of the picturesque qualities of some of his titled contemporary bandits. The rulers of Florence made him at first military commander of the town with full powers of executing justice. He was quick to perceive the divisions prevailing among the population, and at once began to intrigue with the malcontents, with whom there had associated themselves a small number of traders who, having failed in their commercial enterprises, were ready to do anything which could restore their fallen fortunes.

On the morning of September 8, 1342, the Duke went with his soldiers and a secret armed following to the Piazza. The Priors came forth and took their place with him on the dais against the palace wall which they occupied on all public occasions, when all at once a cry arose among the crowd, " Let the Duke be our lord for life ! "

The standard of the republic was seized, the Ordinances of Justice torn up, and the Duke's flag hoisted. The election of the new lord received formal confirmation two days later, when the office of Gonfaloniere was abolished.

Walter of Brienne's first unpopular act was to confirm the Pisans in the possession of Lucca ; and he next alienated some of his adherents among the nobles by selecting the Priors from the class of smaller traders with only a slight admixture of genuine old Ghibelline stocks. He ostentatiously protected the popolani against the grandi, and introduced various democratic reforms, such as abolishing the office of Standard-bearer of the Companies, and refusing consuls to all the guilds except those of the butchers, tavern-keepers, and similar humble folk. He also annulled the guild rules about wages in favour of the workmen, thus discontenting the masters; he deprived the State creditors of their share of the customs, annexed a portion of the revenues for his own use, and levied new taxes, besides behaving in many instances with a cruelty which to arbitrary people seemed very arbitrary indeed. He reduced the Priors to a shadow of their former authority, and ruled with the help of the Podestà (one of the Baglioni, magnificent bandits, of Perugia) and two creatures of his own, Guglielmo d'Assisi and Cerrettieri Visdomini. He soon alienated all his former adherents, including the lower orders, who found that trade and industry were languishing under the rule of this new master. The air was full of plots, and the Duke, aware of his danger, appealed to Taddeo Pepoli, tyrant of Bologna, who promised him three hundred horsemen, but these and other reinforcements which he had applied for among his friends were slow in coming. On July 26, 1343, as the workmen were all leaving their shops, a conspiracy which included members of all parties suddenly broke forth; the streets echoed to the cries of "Death to the Duke!" "Long live the People, the

PALACE OF THE PODESTÀ OR BARGELLO, FLORENCE.

Commune and Liberty!" The old banners of the Companies were brought out, barricades erected, while old enemies embraced and made friends. The Duke's followers rushed to the Piazza; but a diversion in favour of the tyrant got up by Uguccione Buondelmonti and his allies the Cavalcanti failed. All day the street fights lasted; the prisons were broken open and the captives set free, and the lists of banished and suspects found in the palace of the Podestà were burnt.

The Duke, besieged in the palace of the Podestà and threatened with starvation, tried some piteous conciliatory measures, such as hauling down his own banner and hoisting that of the people. Reinforcements for the Florentines began to pour in from Siena, San Miniato, and Prato, and were joined by numerous bands of armed peasants. Any follower of the Duke's who was taken found no quarter, and corpses stripped naked were dragged by the lads about the streets. The people persistently demanded the Duke's creatures, Cerrettieri de' Visdomini and Guglielmo d'Assisi—even the latter's young son For a time the wretched tyrant resisted—then gave way. The poor boy, only eighteen years of age, dressed with sorrowful significance in black, was thrust through the heavy portal of the palace by the Burgundian soldiers, and torn limb from limb in the sight of his father, on whom the same fate descended immediately afterwards. The limbs of these victims were paraded on sticks through the town, and some boasted that they had eaten the raw flesh. Cerrettieri escaped, perhaps because the ferocity of the people had been partially satiated; and three days later the Duke himself departed, escorted by the Sienese and some leading Florentine citizens.

When his fall was known, various towns and territories subject to Florence rebelled. Arezzo and Pistoja proclaimed their freedom and destroyed the castles built by the Florentines. Volterra returned under the rule of the Belforti, and Castiglione Aretino surrendered itself once again to the Tarlati. In Florence the magnates, supported by some of the commoners who, or whose predecessors, had formerly enjoyed chief influence and were consequently included under the generic term of the "Families"—tried to re-enter the government, and although the lower classes and minor traders were determined at first to exclude them at any rate from the Signoria (*i.e.*, Priorship) and to prevent their being Standard-bearers of the Companies, they eventually gave way so far as to allow of their becoming Priors. It was decided that there should be twelve of these officers, three for each quarter (a division of the town and contado which had been substituted for the Sestieri)—four out of the total number to be nobles and eight of the middle-class, while associated on all important occasions with this Signoria were to be eight councillors (instead of twelve as before) four being grandi and the rest popolani. This arrangement discontented everybody. The people thought the magnates, who were only one thousand as against twenty thousand, had been invested with too much power, while the magnates naturally thought they had too little. The people became frenzied with the idea that some of the Donati and others of the same sort might once again obtain the upper hand, and the usual conspiracies sprang up like mushrooms. The Priors armed ; the populace assembled in the Piazza, and clamoured for the grandi to be thrown from the windows, unless the Bishop (who was shut up with them) wished to be burnt alive. Fuel was actually brought and heaped up at the door, when at last the Signoria gave way, and the unpopular members returned to their homes in great discomfiture. A few more changes were introduced into the constitution of the government of no special importance beyond the revival of the office of Standard-Bearer of Justice. The whole town continued up in arms, and the grandi sent for reinforcements which the popolani were resolved to prevent their obtaining.

The popular party had possession of all the gates except the Porta San Giorgio, which was held by the Bardi, and an independent assault, headed by the Medici and the Rondinelli, destroyed the houses and barricades of the Adimari Cavicciuli, of the Pazzi, Donati, and Cavalcanti. On the other side of the river, however, in the district known as Oltrarno, there remained the strong and compact party of the Bardi, Rossi, Manelli, Frescobaldi, and Nerli. One after another of these were overborne by the popular onrush ; only the Manelli and Bardi fought long and hard. The street where the powerful Bardi lived, and which bore (as it still bears) their name, was strongly barricaded, and held out for a good while, the assailed throwing showers of arrows and other missiles. But at last even this last stronghold was overcome, and the defenders fled for refuge to their old friends, the Mozzi and Quaratesi, who had espoused the popular side, and were able to use their influence in getting the Bardi hurried safely from the town. Into the fortress-palaces of the great family the very dregs of the population, men, women, and children, now poured, mercilessly sacking and burning, so that Villani says that twenty-two houses were given to the flames, and property to the value of sixty thousand florins was destroyed.

XV.

FLORENCE IN THE FOURTEENTH CENTURY (*continued*); AND AFFAIRS IN LUCCA, PISA, AND SIENA.

THE grandi thus vanquished, the middle and lower classes, or, to call them by the designations in vogue, the popolo and the popolo minuto, became, according to Villani, very overbearing. But every party in Florence was necessarily overbearing in turn, as it was only by a perpetual shifting of the balance that the State was kept going at all.

For the time being the government of the city remained in the hands of the twenty-one Captains of the Guilds, but the Sienese and Perugians intervening, changes were once again introduced, the most important feature being that the Priors were elected from the three parties now recognized as the Upper Middle Class (or Grassi), the Middle Proper (Mediani), and the Lower Class (Minuti): in the proportion of two of the first named, three of the second, and three of the third; while it was decreed that the Standard-bearer of Justice should be elected in turn from each of these three contingents.

Thus in little more than one year Florence had undergone four changes of government, the final result of which was to strengthen the power of the two lower classes at the expense of those rich and powerful members of the community who, whenever the grandi succumbed, had remained the dominant faction.

Under the new order of things the grandi were excluded from everything except the Council of the Commune, the Consulate of Trade, and the Sea-Consulate, this latter office however being still in the future. But whenever a Balià or special commission was formed, it was the custom to admit one of the grandi to membership; and they were also still admitted to the magistracy of the Guelph party, and were allowed to act as ambassadors to foreign powers. The Ordinances of Justice were however revived in almost unmitigated force, and property which had been bestowed upon Pazzi and others of their class, in recognition of old services, was taken from them.

New lists of rebels were drawn up to replace those which had been burnt, and the grandi were altogether so discouraged that they retired in great numbers to the country districts, and it was calculated that no less than five hundred of their number renounced their position and were enrolled in the ranks of the popolo, either because they were in favour with the actual rulers, or because they applied for the privilege on the ground of being weak and impotent (*debiles et impotentes*). But they could only remain in the refuge thus afforded to them on condition of committing no misdeed against the popolo for a space of ten years: otherwise the punishment meted out to them would be restoration to the ranks of their former party.

And in a similar spirit a probationary period of five years was fixed before they could serve their country as members of the Signoria or of the Council of Twelve, or as Standard-bearers of the Companies or Captains of the Leagues in the contado.

After these events four years of quiet followed, saddened by the second outbreak of plague in 1348, during which, in Florence and its district, one hundred thousand persons are said to have perished, one of them being Giovanni Villani. A general demoralization was consequent on this calamity, and as the artizans and agricultural labourers, being reduced in numbers, would only work for very high wages, many fields remained untilled, and scarcity followed on the plague.

It has been mentioned that on the departure of the Duke of Athens several towns had revolted from the rule of Florence; but by degrees they returned to it. In 1349 Colle di Val d'Elsa and San Gimignano re-entered the fold. Prato was bought back from Joan of Naples, the Duke's daughter, for seventeen thousand five hundred gold florins, and Pistoja was alternately coerced and persuaded into surrendering itself and allowing the Guelph Cancellieri to be installed as holders of the chief offices in the town. Seven members of the Guazzalatri family of Prato began to give trouble, but they were enticed to Florence and decapitated; and having thus settled their minor difficulties, the Signoria had time to consider the danger now threatening the republic in the growing power of the Visconti at Milan. Bologna had just been sold by Giovanni Pepoli, its tyrant, to Giovanni Visconti, Archbishop of Milan, who already held sway over twenty-two towns in Lombardy and Piedmont. Such a dominion constituted a grave peril to all the communes which valued their independence, and Florence no sooner learnt that the Pope, Clement VI., had confirmed Visconti in all his recent acquisitions, than it decided publicly to proclaim an alliance with the Emperor, Charles IV. of Bohemia, which all through the winter of 1351-52 had formed the subject of private negotiations.

The agreement was that Florence, Siena, and Perugia should acknowledge Charles as Sovereign lord of Italy; that the Priors of Florence and the Nine of Siena were to be denominated Imperial vicars during their term of office; and that all three republics should pay tribute in proportion to their means. On the other hand, the liberties and privileges of the communes were to be preserved intact. These singular negotiations fell through for the moment, Charles being grasping and the Florentines incurably suspicious. It was said also that the Emperor was offended by the free and easy ways of the republican ambassadors. "You split hairs," one of them observed to him coolly. The whole incident is only of value to show how little the old distinctions between Guelph and Ghibelline now counted for in Florence.

But soon there was a change. Genoa gave itself and all the towns on the Riviera, except three, to the Visconti; the three exceptions being Monaco, Mentone, and Roccabruna, which were held fast by the Grimaldi. Venice concluded an alliance against the common enemy with the Estensi of Ferarra, the

Carraresi of Padua, the Gonzaga of Mantua, and the Scaligeri of Verona. With the Pope's approval the allies summoned the Emperor, and Florence, thus confronted with a double danger, began hastily to fortify, while Pisa sent an ardent greeting to Charles, who proceeded to that ever Ghibelline city, and there met the ambassadors of the various Tuscan towns.

Siena and Pistoja alone gave themselves unconditionally. Lucca wanted back its liberty, but failed to get it, as Charles had no wish to offend Pisa. Florence bribed freely and astutely, thus procuring friends among the Emperor's following; but declined to revoke the statutes against the nobles. Charles, surrounded as he was with hungry Ghibellines and exiles, would have liked to make better terms, but had to give way. He was not even allowed to see Florence, although he expressed a wish to do so. He had to promise never even to approach within ten miles of the town, and in return was assured that an annual tribute would be paid to him, and the Priors denominated Imperial vicars. Charles proceeded by Siena and Volterra to Rome, where he was crowned, but could remain but a very short time, owing to the excited state of public feeling.

Siena at that time was oppressed by the government of the Nove, an oligarchy which, imitating the foremost methods of the government of Florence, and while calling itself popular, had succeeded in obtaining complete possession of the offices and emoluments of State. The whole city, with the exception of the partizans of the governing few, looked to the coming of Charles for deliverance. The instant he appeared outside the walls of the town an excited crowd met him clamouring for the overthrow of the government. The third day after the Emperor's arrival he was conducted by the mob to the palace of the Signoria, and the Nove were forced to resign. The prisons were broken open, the houses of the hated party were sacked and burned, several people were killed, and anarchy reigned for some days. The Emperor, being then empowered to reform the Government, named a committee of eighteen popolani and twelve nobles, set his brother, the Archbishop of Prague and Patriarch of Aquileia, over them, and ordered peace. This was more easily said than done. The Balià appointed by Charles did form a government or Signoria consisting of twelve popolani, but this soon proved itself to be as purely oligarchical as its predecessors. The Archbishop of Prague was left in charge, and Charles went to Pisa. He had hardly arrived there when the news was brought him that the Sienese, detecting despotic intentions in the Archbishop, had deposed and imprisoned him. Charles interceded with the angry commune for his brother, but only obtained his liberty by promising for his own part not again to interfere in the affairs of Siena.

At Pisa, finding that the chief authority had been assumed by the Gambacorti family, who were merchants and Guelphs, he proceeded to destroy their power, and ordered three of them to be decapitated, thereby calling down upon himself great odium among the Florentines, who, in virtue of their principles, were allies of the Gambacorti. For a time he had raised hopes in the Lucchese by showing a disposition to free them, in return for a sum of money, from the hated yoke of Pisa and to convert Lucca into a perpetual fief, which the people were to hold as Vicars of the Empire. The Florentines had also given him money to keep him quiet, and as soon as he had received his imperial crown, and as much treasure as he could wring out of everybody, he recognized how really impotent he was against the Visconti, and returned amid general contempt to Germany.

The next question to agitate Florence was the growing conflict between the Minor Guilds and the magistracy of the Guelph party. As already explained, this was not an office of the commune, but an appanage of the Florentine people. It was a state within a state, having its own Priors, councils, notaries, clerks, and treasury.

In the eyes of this magistracy the increasing pretensions of the Minor Guilds were not to be tolerated, but must be put down by the formation of an oligarchy which should coerce every other party in the State. With this object the Guelph party passed arbitrary laws against Ghibelline suspects, and encouraged secret anonymous denunciations which, while professedly political, really served the purpose of personal enmity. It also invented a famous system of "admonitions" by which every suspect was branded, and went about his daily work with the knowledge that hundreds of invisible eyes were fixed upon him.

About this time the affairs of Bologna complicated the general situation. The commune (which had gone originally through the usual stages of consuls,

Podestà, and tyrant) had been sold by Pepoli to the Visconti of Milan, but shortly afterwards was ceded by them to Giovanni Visconti of Oleggio, who in his turn sold it to Cardinal Albornoz, the Papal legate. Bernabò Visconti, however, besieged Bologna, and was excommunicated by the Pope Innocent IV., who also sent troops commanded by the famous Count Lando.

The war was still raging when Urban V. mounted the chair of St. Peter, and pompously announced the intention of restoring the Papacy of Rome. For this purpose Urban sought the various alliances mentioned; among others, that of Charles who was to aid, as a preliminary, in destroying the power of the Visconti. Florence was invited to join the League, but prudently declined, feeling that the authority of the great Milanese was not likely to be overturned by an alliance of so uncertain a character as that between the Pope and Emperor. And Charles very soon justified all their previsions by allowing himself to be bought off with much money and a few concessions from the Visconti almost as soon as he had descended into Italy. He had arrived with a numerous army which was soon increased by the paid troops of the allies. Italy was inundated with German, Hungarian, English, Burgundian, French, Spanish, and other mercenaries, who, however, failed ignominiously in their first onslaught upon the forces of the Visconti commanded by the famous John Hawkwood. This check being promptly followed up by the offer of a bribe to the venal Emperor, Charles calmly deserted his allies, made peace with the Visconti, disbanded his army, and made his way to Tuscany.

Here he was again appealed to by the Sienese who were in their usual hopeless condition of discord. The Nine, whom thirteen years before he had overturned, had been succeeded by another oligarchy, the Twelve, against whom all classes of citizens were arrayed. On the 2nd of September, 1368, an insurrection broke out, and the Twelve were driven from power. Charles on being requested by a section of the population to interfere, sent eight hundred horse under Malatesta, who, by the treachery of one of the consuls (five had been named after the insurrection), entered the town against the wish of the nobles, and in spite of their strenuous resistance. Once again was a Signoria of Twelve citizens named: three of whom were to be chosen from the party of the Nine, four from that of the Twelve, and five from a new party which called itself the Company of Reformers, or Monte dei Riformatori. The nobles were totally excluded from office.

Charles went to Rome and made his peace with the Pope by promising to sell him several Tuscan cities, among others Siena. He consequently arrived there in December, and conspired with the malcontents against the new government. But the Sienese fought bravely against the Imperial soldiers and so completely defeated them, that Charles had to seek for safety in the houses of the Salimbeni, his chief partizans. They urged him to leave, but for some reason, probably because the distracted state of the town, paralysed all parties, they had to procure him twenty thousand florins from the commune before he could be finally induced to go.

VIEW OF SIENA.

He went to Lucca, and from thence despatched his troops against the Pisans by whom they were defeated. After this fresh reverse, Charles began to think of returning to Germany, but first solemnly declared the Lucchese released from the domination of the Pisans, and presented the Senate of Lucca with a diploma to that effect duly furnished with the Imperial seal. He also gave to the Lucchese all the Val di Nievole which had been annexed to the Florentine territory; and received three hundred thousand florins in return from the impoverished but grateful town, which was no sooner liberated than it restored its communal government, with two Councils, and a Signoria of Ten members, the chief of whom received the title of Standard-bearer of Justice.

Florence and Pisa might have resisted these high-handed proceedings of the Emperor, but both were tired of fighting for the moment; and to get rid of Charles and his mercenaries who were devastating their respective territories, each republic paid fifty thousand florins to the grasping monarch who used his Holy Roman pretensions as a lever to extract as much money as possible from every Tuscan city.

A more dangerous foe for Pisa and Lucca was Bernabò, who had determined, if possible, to obtain possession of both. It was with this ulterior aim that he undertook the protection of the inhabitants of San Miniato, an old stronghold of Ghibellinism, which now revived its pretensions to be governed by an Imperial Vicar. Bernabò, in support of this claim, sent the Company of Sir John Hawkwood, who inflicted a defeat on the Florentines at Cascina. But the Count of Battifolle who was besieging San Miniato got admitted into the citadel by treachery before the victorious mercenaries could arrive on the scene. The nobles of San Miniato who had led the revolt were ruthlessly beheaded, and the chief families of the little town dispersed all over Italy.

Florence next despatched troops against the forces of the Visconti at Bologna, and Bernabò's difficulties were thickening when the death of the Pope or general exhaustion took all spirit out of the League, which shortly dissolved, leaving all the members in much the same condition as when the war began.

The internal state of Florence meanwhile was anything but peaceful. An allusion had already been made to the *ammonizioni*—the new, vexatious weapon of the Guelph party who, as represented by their captains, were straining every nerve to possess and keep chief authority in the commune.

The "admonition" consisted in this, that every citizen suspected, or accused by his enemies of Ghibellinism, was warned that if he accepted any office in the state he would be punished, not only with a heavy fine, but in some cases by death. An "admonition" only needed to be approved by a majority of two-thirds among the Captains of the Guelph party, who consequently possessed an almost unlimited faculty of excluding anybody they liked from public life.

It is easy to imagine the endless intrigues and shameless machinations caused by such a state of things, and how gradually all power came to be concentrated in the hands of the richest, ablest, and most unscrupulous citizens. In 1371, the supremacy, thus obtained, of the Ricci and Albizzi, was felt to be so intolerable that the people named a commission, or Balià of fifty-six members, for the express purpose of excluding those two families entirely from office, and after this was done there was quiet in the city for a little time.

About the same period as the Ricci and Albizzi were pronounced unfit to govern, a new magistracy was formed, named the Ten of Liberty, whose functions were to defend the laws and guard the threatened freedom of the citizens: a significant creation showing how the foundations of freedom and republican security were threatened.

Between 1375–78, the Florentines, faithful Guelphs though they were, went to war with Pope Gregory XI.

During the long sojourn of the Popes at Avignon, many towns included in the territories of the Church had either set up a popular form of government, or fallen under the sway of tyrants. The efforts made by Cardinal Albornoz and other legates, to reconquer these lapsed dominions with the help of foreign arms, were regarded by Florence with uneasiness, and when its allies, Bologna and Perugia, were finally subdued by the pontifical troops, and this success was welcomed by the strongly papal Guelph party, as likely to strengthen its own cause, the Florentine government prepared to fight. For the Guelph oligarchy with its papal supporters everywhere constituted precisely the same menace to popular liberties in the communes as Imperial interference had done formerly; and the great Tuscan republic although the fact was perhaps hardly realized, had really now entered upon its last struggle for the institutions to which it owed its greatness.

The legate in Bologna made peace with the Visconti, and then no longer needing Hawkwood's Company, let it loose on the Tuscan territory. Hawkwood got as far as the gates of Prato, but was then bought off with one hundred and thirty thousand gold florins. Later, as is well known, he entered the service of Florence, and there remained until his death. He was buried at first in the Duomo, but his bones were afterwards claimed by the English king and transferred to his native place in Essex.

About the year 1375, the Florentines created a new magistracy—the Eight of War—to whom full powers were given in all matters relating to the struggle against the Pope. Fully alive to the dangers threatening the republic from the intrigues of the French prelates who represented the Papal Court, the Eight summoned a council composed of the most conspicuous citizens, and it was agreed, after but little discussion, to prosecute the war with the utmost vigour, and to conclude alliances on all sides, not excluding even Bernabò Visconti who, although an iniquitous despot, had the merit of detesting the Pope and his Gallic following. A league was consequently concluded by Florence with Milan, Lucca, Arezzo, and Pisa: and messengers were despatched to the Papal subjects in the Romagna, the Marches, and Umbria urging them to revolt.

The first to obey the summons was Città di Castello,

and this example was quickly followed by Viterbo, Foligno, Spoleto, Orvieto, and many other places.

The news of this general revolt, to which Rimini under Galeotto Malatesta alone remained a stranger, no sooner reached Avignon than the Florentines were ordered by the Pontiff to account for their conduct. They despatched as ambassadors to Avignon Donato Barbadori, Domenico di Silvestro and Alessandro dell' Antella, but also sent sent troops to Bologna to aid the population there in driving out the Papal legate.

On arriving at Avignon the ambassadors of the republic made stately orations, in which they recalled the old devotion of Florence to the Church, and declared that danger to the liberties of the commune had alone dictated the conduct of the Eight of War. The Pope, after a brief interval of consideration, laid the republic under an interdict, and ordered all Florentines to be ejected from their settlements throughout the Christian world and to suffer confiscation of their property. In case of disobedience, they were to be reduced to slavery, so that "their tears might come down as a tradition of terror to their descendants." On leaving the Papal presence, after listening to the recital of this Brief, Barbadori is said to have turned to a crucifix on the wall and appealed to it against the sentence of Christ's vicar.

Six hundred Florentines, doing business as merchants and bankers, were expelled from Avignon, and the sentence was carried into effect also in France, England, and Hungary.

The Pope retained the services of a company of

Breton mercenaries, led by Jean Malestroit, and sent them into Italy accompanied by the Cardinal Robert of Geneva, the most ruthless member of the Sacred College. He induced Galeazzo Visconti to make peace with the Pope, who ruthlessly abandoned to the vengeance of the Lombard tyrant all the Guelphs whom the Church had induced to rebel against his rule.

Bernabò remained apparently faithful to the league, but his whole attitude was such as to inspire little confidence among his allies.

The Cardinal of Geneva, on arriving at Bologna, offered a general pardon to the citizens, together with the right of maintaining their communal form of government, on the sole condition that they would recognize the sovereignty of the Church. The Bolognese, however, unconvinced of the sincerity of these offers, replied that they would never tolerate the presence in their town of a papal legate invested with any sort of authority.

The Eight in Florence meanwhile continued their good work, sending troops to support the Bolognese and to guard the passes of the Alps, and either reducing the lords in Romagna to order or taking the free towns there under their protection. Bologna was held for the Florentines by Ridolfo da Varano di Camerino, and after a while, Hawkwood, who had been languidly fighting for the Church, engaged himself under the banner of the republic; and the Papal troops, discouraged by the prospect of meeting the redoubtable English Company, avoided any pitched battles, and contented themselves with over-running and devastating the lands of the unhappy Romagna.

The Tarlati made an effort to re-enter Arezzo with the help of their Ghibelline supporters and an armed force furnished by the Church (so much was everything now reversed), but the Eight sent reinforcements, a few heads were cut off, and everything settled down. In the March, the Florentine arms, conducted by Count Luzzo, met with good success, and were triumphant also in the Romagna, which Hawkwood ravaged as far as Perugia.

On the 17th of January, 1377, Gregory II., much to the disgust of the French ecclesiastics, had finally returned to Italy, and taken up his abode at Anagni.

The Florentines, previously to his arrival, had done their best, though in vain, to induce the Romans to defend their communal liberties, offering them troops and money for the purpose, and urging on them to consider that the return of the Pope meant a return of political servitude. When all these efforts failed, and Gregory had been conducted to the Vatican amid the acclamations of the mob, the Florentines felt that the days of the league were numbered, and sent ambassadors to the Papal Court to negotiate peace.

Gregory, concluding too hastily that the republic was at last humbled, demanded the dissolution of the league and an indemnity of over one million of florins; also that one hundred citizens of Florence and one hundred representatives of Tuscany should proceed to the Vatican and solicit pardon for the misdeeds of their fellow-countrymen.

These demands were indignantly rejected. The Eight became more popular than ever, and were confirmed in their office for a whole year instead of only for six months as previously. Encouraged by these signs of popular favour, the Eight took council with the Doctors of Canon Law, with the result that it was decided to disregard the interdict just renewed by the Pope, and to order the reopening of all the churches. The measure was a political one, for there had been signs of religious terror among the excommunicated population with a consequent leaning towards the Guelph party. St. Catherine of Siena, whose three friends, Niccolò Soderini, Piero Canigiani, and Stoldo Altoviti, belonged to the extreme Guelphs, had come to Florence, and used the great influence she had lately acquired to stir up the latent fanaticism of the Florentine people. Processions had been organized in the street, the laudi of the Flagellants had been sung at night in the churches, rich youths had joined the ranks of the Disciplinanti, or gone into retreat at Fiesole, or formed societies for the performance of good works, and the redemption of fallen women. The Eight had taken alarm at these significant signs, and after a few tentative measures, such as forbidding the chanting of the laudi, adroitly arrested the current by treating the interdict as null.

They also prepared to continue the war against the Pope as long as necessary, when the news came that Gregory, profiting by the divisions of the Bolognese, had induced them to make peace.

Various other cities of the league followed this example, and all began to show symptoms of weariness in the struggle. The Florentines were rich, powerful, and determined, but they were not quixotic, and they consequently soon recognized the advisability of coming to terms on their own account. Negotiations with the Papal Court were begun, but brought to a standstill all at once by the death of Gregory in March, 1378.

In Florence itself events were taking an unfavourable turn for the lovers of popular liberty. The Eight had been in favour a long while, and the subtle, invisible forces working against them began at last to be felt. They had also sustained a great loss in the death of one of their members, Giovanni Magalotti, whose influence had been immense. In spite of the interdict he was buried at Santa Croce, where the stone marking his last resting-place may still be seen, with the word *Libertas* inscribed above his arms by permission of the republic.

His place was filled by Simone Peruzzi, which was a triumph for the Guelph party, whom the new member of the Eight was more than suspected of favouring. The Albizzi had risen again to all their old power, and for the moment overbalanced the popular faction and its leading adherents, the Scali, Alberti, and Medici families, all of whom fervently supported the Eight. The latter presently received another blow in an "admonition" pronounced against Giovanni Dini, a rich merchant belonging to the corporation of the Druggists, and an enemy of the Guelph party. The prestige of the Eight now declined steadily, being undermined, as was believed, persistently by Peruzzi; and very soon the city was divided as completely as in the times of the Buondelmonti and Donati.

Peace with the new Pope, Urban VI., was finally obtained by payment on the part of the Florentines of from one hundred and fifty thousand to two hundred thousand florins; and the interest in external politics thus diminishing for a while, the internal condition of the republic became all the more exasperated.

XVI.

FLORENCE IN THE FOURTEENTH CENTURY (*continued*). THE CIOMPI RIOTS.

THE Guelph party were now able to inaugurate a reign of terror. They manipulated the drawing of the lots in such a way that only those whom they pleased were called to power. Lapo da Castiglionchio was the soul of the cabal, which, by the simple phrase, "I have seen him go to the country," pronounced by an informer, succeeded in eliminating every name declared until one which met its own approval was reached. The leaders and even the subordinates of the party were treated by the terrified people with more outward signs of respect than even the Signoria.

The timid bribed freely to purchase immunity from denunciation, and hundreds were enrolled as kinsmen, or rather clansmen, of the families whom the party favoured. To realize the effect produced by the constant *ammonizioni* one must remember that for a Florentine under the republic not to form part of the state was to seem to himself and others a person of no account. Moreover, justice was not equal for all, and those who were excluded from a share in the government had to pay a heavier burden of taxation. It may be imagined under all these circumstances how the secret discontent among the population grew, until at last it found a voice in Salvestro de' Medici. He was the Standard-bearer of Justice in June, 1378, and hated by the Guelph party, not for his principles, of which he perhaps had none, but for his slipperiness. Lapo di Castiglionchio, Piero degli Albizzi, and Carlo degli Strozzi, with others of the party, determined that on the Feast of St. John, when the Priors would be at the house of the Alessandri looking at the fêtes, they would enter the palace and occupy all the government posts.

But Salvestro upset this plan by an action of his own. It had been proposed to revoke the Ordinances of Justice, but the predominant influence of the Guelph party, five of whom were Priors, had caused the rejection of this measure, in consequence of which Salvestro bursting in theatrically upon a Council of the People, exclaimed, " I had aspired to free the city from a malignant tyranny, but my colleagues turn a deaf ear ; therefore let me go home, and choose one in my place who can better command obedience." This caused a great sensation, and two days before the Feast of St. John the people rose *en masse* under the standard-bearers of the companies, and burned the houses of Lapo (who had fled), of Carlo Strozzi, of Piero Albizzi, and extended their ravages to the Oltrarno quarter, where they wreaked their vengeance and their greed on the Canigiani, the Soderini, and the Serragli families. For the moment the disturbances went no further,

GATE OF ST GEORGE, FLORENCE, IN THE OLTRARNO QUARTER. CONSTRUCTED IN 1324. (*After a Photograph by Brogi.*)

but after the 1st of July, when a new Signoria came into office, further action was taken against the Guelph cabal, Piero degli Albizzi and others being banished to within thirty miles of the city, while many were declared rebels, and relegated in consequence to the ranks of the grandi.

The Minor Guilds, however, were discontented with these measures, which they considered insufficient, and secret armed gatherings were held in the workshops.

On the 18th of July, peace with the Pope was proclaimed, but the Eight of War still remained in office. The town was in fact now dominated by two oligarchies—the ostensible government and the Guelph party. Between the two, who were opposed to each other, but equally hostile also to the remainder of the population, there floated, alternately compressed and expanding, a vast mass of malcontents — artizans, "suspects" actual grandi, casuals and semi-criminals, besides respectable order-loving people, to whom the state of affairs was unendurable. Attached to the great and wealthy Wool Guild was a powerful minority, comprised of all the associations of workers, combers, beaters, dyers, and so on, to whom the guild gave occupation. In the time of the Duke of Athens these associations had been encouraged to assert themselves, to elect consuls of their own, and to aspire to civic importance. To them generally was given the popular appellation of Ciompi, a corruption of the French *compère*. These workers now formed a secret conspiracy for the overthrow of the government and the Signoria, getting wind of the danger, summoned a certain Simoncino, who was in the confidence of the conspirators, and questioned him as to what he knew. The interrogation, to give it greater solemnity, took place before the altar in the palace chapel. Asked as to the aims of the malcontents, Simoncino replied that they wanted to form official unions of their own, independent of the guild by whose representatives they were perpetually tormented and underpaid; also that they aspired to a share in the government of the town, and not to be held any longer solely responsible for the robberies and burnings that marked every revolt. Simoncino, under torture, revealed the names of two who, he said, knew more than himself, and the same treatment being applied to them, they declared their leader to be Salvestro de' Medici.

It is said that a certain Niccolò degli Orivoli happened to be mending the clock of the palace while the torture was going on, and hearing the cries of the victims hurried to his house in San Frediano, armed himself, and rushed forth crying, " Arise! our masters are butchering." The toscin of the church of the Carmine was rung, and echoed by the bells of every church in Florence. From all the workmen's quarters the people gathered, and no blow was struck in the Priors' favour. Distracted, they turned to Salvestro de' Medici himself, accompanied by Guerriante Marignolle, a member of the Signoria, and some other delegates to know what the popolo minuto might be wanting.

These messengers found the popolo engaged in burning the houses of their enemies, and especially the palace of the Wool Guild, but anxious not to be accused of robbery they had decreed that nothing, costly or cheap, should be saved. In the evening some thousands of artizans and workers encamped at San Barnaba, and from thence issued orders to the Arti to come out under their banners and to assist in drawing up petitions to be addressed to the Signoria. This call not being responded to, the insurgents betook themselves to the palace of the Signoria, and there formulated their requests which were to the effect that all the small traders and workmen, more especially those dependent on the wool trade, should have separate consuls, and be represented altogether by two Priors ; that an estimate should be drawn up of the property of the commune ; that the Public Bank or Monte should cease to pay interest ; and that its creditors should be reimbursed their capital within a period of twelve years, the order of the payments to be determined by a drawing of lots. Loans, they further insisted, should cease for six months, and when resumed, the taxation imposed in connection with them should be graduated according to income—a system, it may be remarked, which was later adopted by the Medici. For a space of two years, no person belonging to the popolo minuto should be compelled to pay any debt of less than fifty florins. All the "suspects" should be requalified, and all the exiles, rebels alone excepted, recalled. Every excess committed since the 18th of June should be condoned, and for ten years at least, if not for ever, anybody whose unpopularity among the rioters had been proved by the destruction of his house, should be excluded from office. With this exception, all ranks of the population should be eligible for the Signoria, for the Council of Twelve, and for the positions of Standard-bearers of the companies and Standard-bearers of Justice. Rewards in money were to be given to certain favourites of the rioters, and Salvestro de' Medici was to receive the six hundred florins yearly yielded by the rents of the shops on the old bridge, for the equipment and support of his troops.

There were various other demands, but these are sufficient to show the temper of the insurgents, and their happy indifference to any claims but their own. It proves the utter demoralization of the government that the demands were acceded to almost at once, and on the day following this last act of its existence the Council of the People dissolved ; and as soon as a determined and threatening crowd gathered again in the Piazza, the Signoria followed the example of the Council. The palace being thus empty of its late tenants, the populace thronged in, the standard of the insurgents being held aloft by Michele di Lando, a wool-comber, whose wife and mother sold pipkins and vegetables.

His appearance with the banner in his hand hit the popular fancy, and when he was half-way up the staircase he found himself suddenly proclaimed Standard-bearer of Justice.

He immediately rose to the occasion, took the direction of everything, and revealed great capacity and boldness.

The following morning he summoned a Parliament

OLD MARKET PLACE, FLORENCE.

of the people into the Piazza, and by this was confirmed in his new functions. Of the old government the Eight had alone been left in power, and they now, with the assistance of Michele and the syndics of all the guilds proceeded to the nomination of the Signoria, the Council of Twelve, and the Standard bearer of the Companies. Three new guilds with respective consuls were created, one containing such folk as tailors, wool-staplers, and barbers; another, carders and dyers; and the third "Ciompi," or the lowest populace generally. This gave the signal for revolt among the dependents of all the larger guilds, including apprentices who rose against their masters.

The Signoria, it was decreed, should consist of nine members, chosen equally from all the guilds, major, minor, and new: while the Standard-bearer of Justice was to be chosen in turn out of each of these three divisions. Nevertheless, when the government came to be formed and all the offices filled up, it appeared that the members of the major guilds had for the most part either held disdainfully aloof, or been eliminated by dexterous wire-pulling.

To relieve the misery of the artizans to whom, as a necessary result of the revolution, all work was closed, a distribution of grain took place, and forced loans of from twenty-five thousand to forty thousand florins were raised.

For the defence of the city a thousand bowmen were equipped, but the majority of the citizens were forbidden to carry arms even in times of disturbance. No murmuring against the government or the popolo minuto was allowed, in this, as in all respects, the example of their social superiors being closely followed by the new masters of the town. For the rest an honest, if ill-judged, effort seems to have been made, both to settle the public finances and to restore order generally ; but, as a matter of course, there had already arisen a party of irreconcilables, and these, two thousand strong, marched in the last days of August to the Piazza in company with some members of each guild, and there proceeded to formulate a series of wild "laws," some of which had sufficient vitality to survive until the next day when they were ratified.

It must be stated that the insurgents had appointed a sort of revolutionary Committee of Eight, who sat in the Piazza Santa Maria Novella, and invited delegates from the guilds to appear before them and deliberate as to the formation of a new government. But the very next day, 30th August, the patience necessary for such proceedings abandoned the Eight, who with the rabble in their train betook themselves to the Piazza in front of the Palazzo Pubblico, and there assisted in a very tumultuous fashion at the drawing of lots for the nomination of the new government. The Eight of Revolution, as we may call them, were most unruly, and their arrogance annoyed Michele di Lando who, remembering that he was not Standard-bearer of Justice for nothing, fetched his sword and struck one of the messengers from the Eight on the head, then turned upon the other, and was with difficulty prevented from killing both. The Piazza filled with an excited crowd: terror spread through the town, and all the well-to-do, peaceable citizens fled to their villas or their friends in the contado, carrying with them such property as they could easily collect, but were brought back by order of the Priors, who commanded the guilds to assemble under their banners in the square of the Signoria.

The town was now split into two factions, and while the tocsin of the palace summoned the guilds, the bells of San Frediano were ringing for the Ciompi to gather.

Michele di Lando hurried to the Square of Santa Maria Novella, where he expected to meet, and hoped to quell, the Ciompi; but these were already in front of the palace, while the guilds were still marching from every side, and all the streets were blocked. A fight finally ensued, in which the malcontent Ciompi were speedily worsted, swept from the face of things with almost no resistance, and dispersed about the town and contado.

On the morning of the 1st of September the new Signoria was inducted into office with none of the usual solemnities, but with every available display of armed force, consisting in a troop of a hundred hired lancers and the companies of the minor guilds.

Michele di Lando handed over the Standard of Justice to his successor (who was one of the new Guild of Ciompi), and returned quietly to his home. But as the victory over the malcontents was attributed to him he was left in possession of a pennon and shield of honour, and confirmed in the office to which he had appointed himself of Podestà of Barberino.

The first act of the new Signoria was to abolish the

recently-created Guild of the Ciompi while retaining the others, thus making the number of minor guilds sixteen, the major guilds being seven as of old. The new Standard-bearer was promptly disqualified, but a preponderance was given to the minor guilds in the government, five of their number being Priors as against four of the major Arti; and it was settled that the Standard-bearer of Justice should be chosen alternately from the two classes.

The new rules concerning the carrying of arms were cancelled, and a two years' grace, accorded by the Ciompi for payment of debts below a certain sum, followed to the same limbo, while the State Bank was once again empowered to pay interest. It is interesting to remark in passing that Salvestro de' Medici managed to keep his six hundred yearly florins. Some alterations were introduced into the Council of the People, which was also to number one hundred and sixty of all classes, with a small additional infusion of grandi, forty in all, being ten for each quarter. In both Councils the representation of the major and minor guilds was equal.

The number of captains of the Guelph party was fixed at eleven—two being grandi, four members of the major guilds, and five of the minor, the same proportion being observed in all the offices and councils of the party.

The Eight of War at the end of three years finally quitted office. Of the other Eight, the two whom Michele di Lando had attacked were condemned to death as authors of the latest sedition. About thirty other people had the same sentence pronounced against them, but as they were away, all that could be done was to confiscate their property. And thus the Ciompi revolt came to an end, having bred another revolt during its brief existence, and having for net result that the power to govern had now reached all but the very lowest stratum of the population. A reaction lay in the immediate future, and, beyond that, extinction of popular government and the brilliant epoch of the Medici. But before that splendid evening, more gorgeous though less glorious than the dawn, of the republic is reached, some dreary intervals of confusion have to be described, varied by an anxious outlook towards the towns now swayed in all their destinies by the Visconti.

The three hundred who had formerly assisted at the nomination of the Signoria were now raised to one thousand. The populace perpetually penetrated into the Palace, and interfered with the Priors in the discharge of their functions, ordering any name which they did not like to be torn up; and as the ranks of the malcontents were increased by those whom the government had ejected as too democratic, it may be imagined how the restless suspicions of the people were utilized for personal ends. The town was honeycombed with conspiracy, the banished of all classes keeping up communications with their friends and adherents inside the walls. Torture was freely applied, and numerous people decapitated in consequence of "confessions" thus obtained. Every man went about with invisible eyes fixed upon him, and names of "suspects" were found written up at the corners of the streets. A Committee of Eight was formed to effect the sales of confiscated property; and they chose their own buyers and compelled them to make acquisition even when they did not wish to do so. For a time all trade languished in the town; and fines had to be imposed on rich families to prevent their retiring to their villas. The Florentine usurers —always renowned—raised their rates, and gambling and financial speculation increased. Assassination became a commonplace and supplied any deficiency in the way of private vengeance on the part of judicial murders. Tommaso Strozzi and Giorgio Scali, both members of powerful middle-class families, kept a paid following of small artizans for whom they had obtained permission to carry arms, and whose time was past in creating brawls and menacing the public peace.

In 1382 a certain Scatizzo, one of these bravoes, was imprisoned on a charge of false accusation. Finding the Captain of the People unwilling to give him up, Strozzi and Scali attacked the palace of the Podestà at night with their armed following. This was too much for the government to stand, and the arrest of the two leaders was ordered. Strozzi took alarm in time and escaped to Mantua, but Scali, confident in his popularity, went before the Captain with a light heart: then suddenly heard a cry for his destruction among the crowd gathered in the Piazza. He was decapitated, and his naked corpse hung for days in the courtyard of the palace, neglected or forgotten. After this the Signoria plucked up courage to make another change in the administration, which resulted in the upper guilds forming a small majority in all the offices of government, and of the Guelph party, the Council of the commune alone remaining composed of an equal number from the Major and Minor Arti. A certain proportion of recent exiles were recalled, some prisoners set free, and some property restored to its owners. Rather more confusion reigned than before: the Ciompi definitively joined the grandi; and in the beginning of February, 1382, more than eighty citizens were banished, one of them being Salvestro de' Medici, who went to Modena for five years, and was presently followed into exile by Michele di Lando, who eventually died at Chioggia.

Gino Capponi, the historian, remarks how little all the revolutions seem to have affected the general character of the people, which he describes as distinguished by a certain cheerful serenity, and an increasing culture. But the truth was that the wealth of Florence had recently received a new impulse from the development of the silk trade, which passed from Lucca to the neighbouring republic just as the wool trade began to decline in extension and importance. Commerce consequently still constituted the real life of the commune, while home politics were the excitement of the idle and the restless, of demagogues and dreamers. Owing to the nature of the government Florence, once imperial pretensions became a thing of the past, had no constitutional questions to distract it, and socially and politically was, on a small scale, in much the same condition as the United States in the present day. Add to this that the streets, with their beauty, their varied life, their floating population of strangers, of mercenary troops, of foreign merchants, and preaching friars; the warehouses stocked with goods from France, from Flanders, from Africa, from the East; the churches and palaces built by wealthy guilds or princely merchants, and growing under the eyes of citizens to whom artists and architects were familiar kinsmen and neighbours—constituted a manifold education and resulted in a rapid movement of ideas through all classes; and this activity of mind—itself a form of liberty—goes far to account for the indifference with which the mass of the population saw one group of political adventurers succeed to another group of political adventurers in the government of the town. The guilds meanwhile administered their own affairs, and the real business of the State was transacted by the chief of the Florentine banking-houses, which were already to be found everywhere from London to the Levant.

In 1382 Florence bought Arezzo for forty thousand florins, from Coucy, a captain of mercenary troops, who had followed in the track of the Duke of Anjou when the latter was called to Italy to help Queen Joan of Naples. The exiles of Arezzo had appealed to the Duke for help. He entered the town after some fighting, but died shortly afterwards, and Coucy then effected the described sale, in order to be free to return to France.

XVII.

FLORENCE IN THE FOURTEENTH CENTURY (*continued*). THE STRUGGLE WITH GIOVAN GALEAZZO VISCONTI.

WHEN Pope Urban VI. excommunicated Queen Joan of Naples and deprived her of her kingdom in punishment for her support of the Antipope, Charles of Durazzo, the only direct heir to the Neapolitan throne, marched with a force into Italy to defend his rights.

The Florentine exiles immediately addressed themselves to him, hoping that he would pass through Florence and help to restore the fallen popular oligarchy.

They gave him to understand that at the first news of his approach a revolution in the town would take place and render his task an easy one. They promised large sums of money if he restored them to home and power, and Charles, like so many of the princely strangers who in ignoble procession had descended the southern slopes of the Alps, lent a willing ear to assurances which he knew had a real basis in the far-famed wealth of Florence.

Other exiles assembled at Bologna under Giannozzo of Salerno, one of Charles' captains; and altogether the situation was full of danger for the existing government of the republic.

Even if an attack on the part of Charles were averted, there was still peril in the probable fall of Joan, who had always kept up friendly relations with Florence. Ambassadors, carefully selected from the two parties so as to ensure neutrality in their views, were despatched to Charles, but succeeded in obtaining from him nothing but vague promises, which only increased the general uneasiness.

In the meanwhile Giannozzo of Salerno at the head of a company of Italian mercenaries and accompanied by the Tuscan exiles, marched out of Bologna. The Florentines sent Hawkwood against him, but no battle took place; on'y, Giannozzo overran Siena, Lucca, Pisa, and Perugia with their respective territories, and obliged all these towns to pay him large sums of money.

Charles occupied Arezzo, but was bought off by the Florentines with forty thousand florins, and proceeding to Rome where the Pope crowned him, he went from thence to Naples, conquered Joan and put her to death on the 12th of May, 1382.

About this time the Venetians, having made peace after the Chioggian war with Genoa, turned their attention to Francesco da Carrara, whom they were determined to eject from Padua. Not able, at the moment to attack him themselves, they edged on against him Antonio della Scala, tyrant of Verona, who was, however, thoroughly beaten in two battles against the Paduans—one in June, 1386, and another in the following year.

But now a new and sinister figure appeared on the scene of Italian politics, in the person of Gian Galeazzo, Count of Virtù, who by the imprisonment and death it was supposed by poison of his uncle Bernabò had remained sole lord of Lombardy. He concluded an alliance with Venice; drove away Francesco from Padua; extended his dominions to the shores of the Adriatic and began to spin the web of intrigue and corruption in which he soon involved all Italy. His design was to possess himself by force or fraud of the whole peninsula. The condition of the country on all sides was favourable to his intent. Venice and Genoa were exhausted by their recent war; the Count of Savoy was fighting against France; Francesco Gonzago, the lord of Mantua, and Alberto d'Este, Marquis of Ferrara, were creatures of the Visconti; while the Tuscan communes, jealous of the preponderance of Florence and wearied of their own discords, were disposed to welcome the tyrant of Milan as a possible deliverer.

The Pope being hampered by the schism, and the kingdom of Naples reduced by the recent events to impotence, Florence alone remained to defend communal independence, and at first hoped to obtain some advantage for itself by defending and assisting Francesco da Carrara. But when he, after flying for his life from the plots of Gian Galeazzo and undertaking an adventurous journey by way of Marseilles, arrived at Florence, the reception he met with was a disappointment, his friends there having for the moment patched up a peace with Visconti, and being, as usual, much disposed to put prudence before chivalry.

In Siena there had been another revolution which caused the substitution of a party called the Monte del Popolo for that of the Riformatori. The new party was favourable to Florence, and for a little while harmony reigned in consequence between the two communes. A quarrel about Montepulciano soon brought the peace to an end. This little town had factions of its own, and was divided in allegiance between two members of the Pecora family, Giovanni and Gherardo. The latter remained faithful to Siena (of which Montepulciano was a tributary), but Giovanni Pecora and his adherents sought the protection of Florence. The Sienese, indignant with the Florentines for interfering in their concerns, sent secretly to offer themselves to Gian Galeazzo, who, for ends of his own, refused the proffer and even went out of his way to assure Florence, through ambassadors, that he had no design on the liberties of the Tuscan communes. The assurances were false, naturally, but the Florentines were anxious to believe them; did believe them; and consequently were oblivious of the claims of Francesco da Carrara.

Visconti, by the art of which he was past master, initiated conspiracies in Siena, San Miniato, Perugia; and under pretence of succouring Pisa which was surrounded by hostile troops he sent four thousand cavalry in whose faces, however, Pietro Gamabacorti shut the gates of the town.

Subsequently Gambacorti himself, feeling all the

insecurity of the general position, persuaded the Florentines and Gian Galeazzo that they would be unwise to fight, and in October, 1389, there was a great meeting of ambassadors in Pisa, and engagements were entered into by Florence and the tyrant of Milan that neither should interfere in the affairs of the other.

This compact, as might have been foreseen, was of brief duration. Francesco da Carrara by superhuman efforts succeeded in reinstating himself in Padua, where he was welcomed with the liveliest affection. But when Verona also rose against Gian Galeazzo, its attempt at rebellion was promptly suppressed at the cost of much bloodshed; while Jacopo del Verme, one of the Visconti's condottieri (small tyrants) of the Romagna, who were Gian Galeazzo's slaves, surrounded Bologna—that old bulwark of the Guelphs against the Lombard lords.

Alarmed, the Florentines recalled Hawkwood (who had entered the service of Charles of Durazzo's widow), and promised eighty thousand florins to Duke Stephen of Bavaria if he yielded to the entreaties of Francesco and came with twelve thousand horse. He came with half the number, succoured Padua, and then returned over the Alps either tired of the enterprise or bought off with Lombard gold.

His pennons had no sooner disappeared than the banner of another foreigner fluttered on the horizon. This belonged to Count John d'Armagnac, whose sister had married a son of the murdered Bernabò and burned to revenge her father-in-law's fate, as well as to put an end to the usurpations of Gian Galeazzo.

This French Count had been engaged by the Florentines at a cost of one hundred and five thousand florins which seemed little in comparison with the dangers they hoped he might avert. For Perugia and Siena had declared for Visconti: the Venetians would not move against the Milanese: Bologna was already half-ruined by the expenses of the war and it was not likely that Francesco, for all his intrepidity, could hold out long alone.

D'Armagnac arrived on the oft-invaded plains of Lombardy, and was ordered to effect a junction with Hawkwood, who intended to march against Pavia and take the town if possible. Fifteen thousand Frenchmen, the scourings of the companies which had long laid waste the provinces of the Rhone and the Loire, descended from the Alps with a lightness of heart and a confidence which are reflected in the pages of Froissart, only to be ignominiously beaten by Jacopo del Verme before Alessandria.

The French captain wounded and taken prisoner, shortly afterwards died either of grief or of a fever caused by drinking water on the burning day in July, 1391, when the battle was fought.

By this disaster Hawkwood found himself unaided in front of an enemy led by one of the most famous condottieri of the time. In order to cut off the English captain's retreat Jacopo destroyed the dams of the Adige and flooded the immense plain of the Veronese valley; then sent exultantly to Gian Galeazzo to ask whether he wished to receive his enemies alive or dead.

Hawkwood, however, and his whole army forded

the waters, rested a while at a castle belonging to the Lord of Padua, and then effected one of the most masterly retreats on record, which extorted admiration from Jacopo himself.

The war was then transferred to the Val di Nievole, and Hawkwood's efforts were all directed to preventing a descent of the enemy upon Siena and Florence. In this he succeeded, and eventually inflicted a thorough defeat upon Jacopo's rearguard.

The danger which had threatened Florence was now reduced to proportions very unsatisfactory for Gian Galeazzo, who had not even destroyed the power of his old enemy, Padua. On the contrary, Francesco's son, Francesco Novello as he was called, was more beloved than his father, and even the Venetians seemed at last inclined to ally themselves with Visconti's foes. Gian Galeazzo consequently lent a willing ear when Antoniotto Adorno, the Doge of Genoa, together with Pietro Gambacorti and Pope Boniface IX. offered their mediation to effect a peace. This was finally concluded in January, 1392, the Milanese and Florentines renewing their mutual promises not to interfere with each other; Francesco Novello da Carrara being confirmed in possession of Padua on condition of an annual tribute to Milan to be continued for fifty years; and Visconti undertaking not to send troops into Tuscany unless his allies the Sienese and Perugians were attacked. Castles were restored on both sides and the Sienese exiles were reinstated in their property, but forbidden to return to their native town.

Lionardo Aretino computes that the war cost

Florence one million two hundred and sixty-six thousand florins, and the republic found itself considerably crippled in its resources. To supply the consequent necessities a variety of devices were resorted to, one of which is worth mentioning.

The officials of the Monte or State Bank were ordered to buy back bonds on the best terms possible from all holders who were willing to sell them, the money for the purchase to be obtained by deducting one quarter of the interest due to the creditors of the State. In this way a number of creditors were bought off at the expense of the rest, and the Monte found itself at once with less interest to pay and fewer people to pay it to.

For more than twenty-seven years Pisa had been governed on the whole wisely and well by Pietro Gambacorti, who, however, for his own misfortune, reposed unlimited confidence in Jacopo d'Appiano, his secretary, whom he loaded with favours. Gian Galeazzo, anxious as ever to possess Pisa, won over Appiano by secret means, and so effectually that in October, 1392, Gambacorti was assassinated in a popular tumult which Jacopo fomented, and the latter then took advantage of the public consternation to have himself proclaimed Captain and Defender of the town. He admitted the troops which Visconti hastened to send, ostensibly to his aid, and thus practically brought Pisa to the feet of the Milanese tyrant.

Florence for ten years past (1382–1392) had again been governed by an oligarchy, called the Ottimati, composed of members of the Arti Maggiori. Their rule, while growing ever narrower and more absolute so as to reduce the drawing of lots for public offices to a farce, was strong and not unintelligent, but it had as usual to contend with the undermining forces of perpetual conspiracies.

The Standard-bearer for September and October, 1393, was Maso degli Albizzi, nephew of Piero, who could not forget the circumstances of his uncle's cruel death. During his term of office a plot was discovered between the exiles at Bologna and their friends inside Florence; and three unhappy wretches, subjected to torture, made a more or less veracious "confession," which implicated Alberto Alberti and others of his family. This furnished the pretext for a terrible persecution of the Alberti house, the chief members of which were banished to long distances and heavily fined if they attempted to set foot again within the forbidden territory, while their property became in point of fact a possession of the State. In this last fact probably lay the key to the whole situation. It is true that the chief instigator of the severities was supposed to have been Maso, ever mindful of how Benedetto Alberti had stood armed in the Piazza while Piero degli Albizzi was done to death; but as Donato, Acciajoli, Alamanno de' Medici, and other conspicuous persons, were treated in the same way as the Alberti it is evident that the Signoria were all either actively or passively quiescent. And the republic being, as we have learnt, in need of money, to an unscrupulous minority no measures were likely to be distasteful which helped to replenish the exhausted coffers of the commune.

Further plots, or pretended plots, coming to light, six Alberti, six Ricci, two Medici, three Scali, Bindo Altoviti, and a number of minor individuals (including some survivals of the old irreconcilable Uberti) were summarily ejected, and more stringent laws than ever were passed against the Alberti. None of the name, over sixteen years of age, was at any time to remain in Florence; and none under pain of death were to approach within two hundred miles of the city. Their palaces were all sold: their loggias razed to the ground, and a fine of one thousand florins was to be inflicted on anybody who married an Alberti woman, or gave his daughter to a son of that house. Every loyal subject of the republic was forbidden to associate himself in business with an Alberti at any place nearer to Florence than two hundred miles. As might be expected, we find the Medici similarly, if not so sweepingly disqualified ere long, and in short the Ottimati spared no efforts, and knew no hesitations, in carrying out a policy which should preserve themselves in power with as little material loss as possible to the State.

The republic continued to keep Gian Galeazzo in anxious observation, and had spies everywhere who reported on his movements and his supposed intentions. The Florentine merchants in Lombardy assisted zealously in the work, and such distinguished men as Bonaccorso Pitti and Niccolò d'Uzzano were despatched to various courts, such as France and Naples (where Ladislaus son of Charles of Durazzo now reigned) as well as to the Vatican with instructions ever to fan the flame of animosity against

Visconti. The Duke of Milan was indeed daily growing to a power which threatened the prompt extinction of all smaller States. Pisa and Siena were now quite under his control, and Lucca was harassed by the troops which he sent under Alberico and Giovanni da Barbiano into her territory. Florence was now on good terms with Lucca which after a fresh period of civil discord had settled down peaceably under the rule of Lazzaro Guinigi, and forgotten all rivalries in the presence of a menace which threatened herself and all her neighbours.

The Florentines sent a force to the help of Lucca, and another consisting of two hundred horse and a thousand foot under Bartolommeo Boccanera, of Prato, into the Pisan territory, with secret instructions (very characteristic of the period) to the general to feign independence of Florence, and pretend to be fighting on his own account for the purpose of restoring the expelled Gambacorti.

Visconti immediately despatched a counter force to resist Boccanera, and, at the request of Jacopo d'Appiano, now an old man and badly seconded by his sons, three hundred lancers also arrived from Milan and entered Pisa, led by Pagolo Savelli. Three ambassadors from the Duke arrived at the same time, ostensibly to comfort and encourage Appiano, but in reality, to extract from him the keys of the fortresses of Leghorn, Piombino, and Cascina.

Jacopo put them off with an excuse, then hastily assembled his armed followers, and intrepidly assaulting the house where Pagolo Savelli lodged, took him prisoner and partly killed, partly dispersed his soldiers. The Florentines hearing this news sent ambassadors to congratulate the Pisans, and to offer their help whenever the latter were threatened by the Duke of Milan. The two communes were on the point of concluding an alliance, when Gian Galeazzo's inconceivable astuteness once again triumphed, and Jacopo deserted the Florentines. Nine months latter he died, after having caused his son Gherardo to be recognized as Captain of the people.

Gherardo, a man without energy, sold Pisa to Visconti for two hundred thousand florins, and received in exchange Piombino and the island of Elba. Gian Galeazzo now gained ground everywhere. Siena, worn out with wars and factions, and nearly depleted of inhabitants, of its own accord crawled to the feet of the Duke; Perugia and Assisi, undeterred by the representations of Florence, also acknowledged his authority, and their example was followed by the Lord of Cortona, the Counts of Poppi, and the Ubertini of the Casentino. At Lucca, Lazzaro Guinigi, who, thanks to his powerful family connections, had risen on the ruins of faction to the head of the State, was assassinated by his own brother at the instigation of Gian Galeazzo, and Paolo, the last of the Guinigi family, who succeeded to him, was too wary to join openly in any struggle against Milan.

Bologna had been governed jointly for a year or two by Nanni Gozzadini and Giovanni Bentivoglio, but as one ruler sided with the popular faction, and the other with the nobles, they soon ceased to work in harmony, and Bentivoglio concluded a secret treaty with the Duke, by which he was allowed to become sole apparent master of the commune, after a rising which he got up himself, and in which the Gozzadini adherents were all either killed or taken prisoners.

The Florentines thus found themselves with no ally but Francesco da Carrara, and in their despair sent an embassy to the new Emperor (Robert Count Palatine of Bavaria) with the usual offers of money in return for armed men.

He responded, somewhat insufficiently, however, to the appeal, and in October, 1401, a battle was fought near Brescia, in which the Milanese troops were victorious.

The next disaster was the complete surrender of Bologna to Gian Galeazzo. He had, in his usual manner, played off Nanni Gozzadini and his exiled following against Bentivoglio, provoked a popular revolt in which Bentivoglio was taken prisoner (to be afterwards beheaded), then betrayed Gozzadini, and caused himself to be proclaimed lord of Bologna, where the populace, distracted and overawed, could only follow the lead given by Alberico da Barbiano, the commander of Visconti's troops.

After his defeat at Brescia, the Emperor had retired to Padua, and then fell to quarrelling with the Florentines over money. The dispute ended in the latter having to pay the greedy monarch to remain at Padua until the spring, with the promise of a vigorous renewal of the war then. In the prospect of this promise being kept lay the republic's only hope. It now saw itself surrounded by the power of Gian Galeazzo as by a charmed circle wrought with diabolic spells. Wherever it looked there was danger; the smaller towns, under its sway, were restless from terror; towards Pisa the outlet for its commerce was closed; Tuscany was infested with paid hordes, commanded by Visconti's terrible condottieri. Every route seemed closed to wealth as to friendship. Vague disquieting reports filled the air. Gian Galeazzo meant to be proclaimed King of Italy, and would have himself crowned in Florence. The prospect of such humiliation was intolerable to the proud republic.

Then all at once the spell was broken, for on September 3rd, 1402, Gian Galeazzo died of the plague.

The kingdom of Milan (for such it may be called) was left by the deceased tyrant to his three sons. Giovanni Maria had Milan, Parma, Piacenza, Bologna, Perugia; Filippo Maria inherited Pavia with all the cities alongside of Lombardy in the direction of Piedmont and Venetia; while Pisa and Crema were left to the bastard Gabriele Maria.

The death of Gian Galeazzo, however, was the signal for a general revolt, but our chief concern being with Tuscany, it is sufficient to mention the effect of the Visconti partition upon the destinies of that province.

The Florentines, just before the death of their foe, had engaged the services of Alberico da Barbiano, one of the most redoubtable of the fearless and unscrupulous condottieri whom Gian Galeazzo had gathered round him, or had, one might almost say, created. Every state in Italy, whether threatened or aggressive, whether principality or republic, was now powerless without these soldiers of fortune, whose picturesque figures and striking deeds fill pages of mediæval history. Themselves, dispossessed barons, descendants of impoverished nobles, or bastard sons of illustrious houses, they combined all the qualities of warriors, freebooters, and statesmen. The communes were too small for standing armies; and although their citizens had shown themselves warlike enough in old days, when Florence marched out against Lucca, or Lucca against Pisa, such a militia as they formed themselves into then would have been obviously insufficient to carry on the prolonged wars which Florence and the other communes now had to wage whenever their political existence was threatened by the ambition of a neighbouring or foreign prince. But it may be remarked that this political existence itself had now come to interest only a class in Florence, the class which composed the Arti Maggiori. The question had become too complicated for comprehension by the lower orders of Minor Guilds, whose interests also, obvious but narrow, were sharply divided from those of the middle class; while the aristocratic party, through tradition, or a memory of injuries, or a consciousness of defeat, could only form a party at all by disdaining the aims and methods of the Major Guilds. The men composing the latter were always ready, even anxious, to undertake wars for the maintenance of Florentine commercial supremacy, or Florentine influence at foreign courts. But these things were of no importance to the blacksmith or mason whom a "spirited foreign policy" even injured.

They desired a rich, aristocratic city population, who

would build fine houses, and live on wealth already accumulated or derived from agricultural sources; and they could only grumble when expenditure at home was restricted by the necessity of hiring troops to fight, for instance, against the Visconti.

Up to the end of the fourteenth century, the Florentine forces had been composed of citizens, foot soldiers from Florence and allied towns. But at the battle of Montaperti these foot were routed by the shock of a small force of German cavalry. The uses of horse soldiers were then appreciated; but the expense of cavalry, and the necessity for keeping it in constant training, rendered any army of which it formed a large part evidently impossible for a working population, and the republics in general had consequently to fall back for their defence upon mercenaries.

This state of things lasted until the invention of gunpowder and guns. The Italians, quick in everything, were quick also to learn the art of war; and although the first condottieri were foreigners their successors were such men as Attendolo Sforza, Braccio da Montone, Alberico da Barbiano, and others, whose, very names are a sufficient answer to the oft-repeated parrot cry of Italian pusillanimity.

The Florentines hastened to form a league against the Visconti family, and drew into it Pope Boniface IX., who, however, in his anxiety to reacquire territory, betrayed his allies by a secret treaty with the Visconti by which he obtained Perugia and Bologna. The Sienese, in the spring of 1404, quietly threw off the yoke of the Milanese, and concluded peace and alliance with the Florentines. Pisa had received Gabriele Maria and his mother, Agnese Mentegatti, very coldly, and though not willing to place itself in the power of Florence, was by no means loth to accept help which would enable it to expel the new tyrant. Gabriele Maria, aware of the danger which threatened him from the Florentines, appealed for protection to France as represented by Boucicault, the governor of Genoa, and thus became the vassal of the French king, with the obligation of sending him yearly a war-horse and a falcon. After this endless intrigues were set on foot, Boucicault being urged by the Duke of Orleans, husband of Valentina Visconti, to take possession of Pisa in the name of France, but hesitating from fear of the effect which might be produced on the Ghibelline party in Genoa by union with the Ghibelline Pisa; the Pope Benedict XIII. being anxious to conciliate Florence by promising to give it Pisa; and the Florentines, finally, having a wary game to play between the conflicting views of the Duke of Orleans, of Boucicault, of Benedict, the Pisans, and Gabriele Maria.

Boucicault himself at last came round to the idea of selling Pisa, brought Gabriele Maria to the same way of thinking, and offered the town to Florence for four hundred thousand florins, part of which he promised to spend in defence of Francesco da Carrara now hard pressed by the Venetians. All these negotiations were carried on with an elaborate diplomacy very characteristic of the period. Gino Capponi having received private advices from certain

Florentine merchants in Genoa, went thither, held long conversations with Boucicault, and committed them all solemnly to paper, but concluded nothing. Meanwhile Gabriele Maria sent word to Maso degli Albizzi that he would like a private conference, in consequence of which Maso departed one day, "for amusement," to his villa at Montefalcone, went fishing down the Arno as far as Vico Pisano, and there had an interview with Gabriele Maria, whose hesitations were, however, fatal for the moment to a decision. In spite of these elaborate precautions, perhaps because of them, the Pisans got wind of the intended bargain, and rose in revolt. Visconti was away at Sarzana, but Boucicault managed to place a hundred French soldiers in the citadel, and afterwards attempted to send reinforcements and provisions in a ship which the Pisans with all their old prowess captured, taking prisoner a nephew of Boucicault at the same time. But this effort availed them little, and, eventually, the town and citadel of Pisa were sold for two hundred thousand florins to Florence, Gabriele Maria keeping Sarzana, and Boucicault, Leghorn. The unfortunate Pisans made a desperate effort to procure assistance from King Ladislaus of Naples, who declined to interfere. Then they resolved to stand a siege, and sent for provisions to Sicily, but the ships containing these were overtaken and burnt by galleys which the Florentines had hired from Genoa and Provence. Efforts to obtain supplies by land were equally defeated by the vigilant Florentine commissioners, Maso degli Albizzi and Gino Capponi, who had been sent to the camp now beleaguering

Pisa. Inside that unhappy town, Giovanni Gambacorti (a resurgent member of the old family) had taken the direction of affairs, and ordered all nonfighters to be evicted.

Incredible to relate, the Florentines ordered that of those thus expelled the men should be hanged, and the women sent back with the lily of the republic branded on their cheeks.

This ferocious command proving ineffectual, some of the men actually were hanged and their bodies left swinging in view of the besieged town, while the women had their noses slit. As for the remainder, they starved to death, or kept soul and body together for a time by eating grass "like the beasts of the field," said the eye-witness, Gino Capponi.

Giovanni Gambacorti finally made up his mind to surrender, and entered for the purpose into secret negotiations, of which the object he chiefly had in view was to obtain from the Florentines terms as advantageous as possible for himself.

He demanded the citizenship of Florence, the countship of Bagno, possession of the islands of Gorgona, Capraja and Giglio, and thirty thousand florins. All this being agreed to on the 8th and 9th of October, 1406, in the night the gate of St. Mark was opened, and the Florentines entered.

The next morning they marched through the town preceded by carts filled with bread and provisions, which the soldiers themselves distributed to the starving population. The Pisans had exhausted all their provisions; a little sugar and cassia and three wasted cows were all that the victors found. Yet, although reduced to eating roots which they had plucked from the roadside and the walls, they had never thought of yielding, were very angry with Gambacorti for betraying them, and in this, the darkest hour of their history, were true to the traditions of their glorious prime.

Gino Capponi was appointed governor of the town, and wishing if possible to reassure the citizens, he summoned all the notables to his presence in the great hall of the Communal Palace, and there addressed to them a weighty oration in the best style of the period.

He reminded them that their town had been guilty of grave misdemeanours in the past, when it was the refuge for every stranger who wished to invade Tuscany; when the English companies in its pay had burnt and devastated all the country side; when it had come to an understanding with the Visconti of Milan, and afforded them every facility for injuring and enslaving Florence; even going the lengths of allowing itself to be sold to Giovanni Gambacorti in order to spite its sister republic. Florence had been forced in self-defence to buy Pisa now, but the intention of its representatives was to govern with justice, and severely to repress all disorder on the part of the army of occupation.

It was a very fine speech, abundantly furnished with the best official arguments, but the only reply it got was from a certain Bartolo of Piombino—every native-born Pisan sitting mute.

In Florence the news that the long-coveted city with all its commercial advantages had at last been won was received with the utmost rejoicing, and celebrated with three days of festival. Fortresses, destined to render the possession of Pisa more secure, were begun without loss of time, and until they were completed it was the policy of the Florentines to keep Pisa as depleted of inhabitants as possible. But, indeed, no laws were necessary to complete the decay of the doomed town; and soon it became advisable to accord special privileges to foreign merchants, such as Germans, who still went there to trade. On the other hand, Florence, feeling itself at last commercially secure, increased in wealth and importance, thus fully justifying all the motives for annexing Pisa which had inspired the measure, but had not appeared in Gino Capponi's oration.

Not very long after the purchase of Pisa, Florence, so lately recovered from its alarm at the Visconti, was exposed to a fresh danger in the person of King Ladislaus of Naples.

This valorous and aspiring prince saw, in the confusion which still prevailed in Rome, an opportunity for interfering in the affairs of Italy generally with prospective advantages to himself. He ostensibly took the side of Pope Gregory XII., who had been elected in Rome against Benedict XIII., who was supported by the French Cardinals, and advanced against the Eternal City to restore order there by force of arms. In the year 1409 he had already reduced Rome, Ascoli, Fermo, Perugia, Todi, Assisi, and by way of keeping up the pretence of protecting Gregory, agreed to give him twenty thousand florins annually, in return for the territory of which he had deprived him.

He required of the Florentines that they should recognize him as sovereign of the States of the Church, and at this price offered them his alliance ; and when this proposal was rejected, he insolently asked the ambassadors of the republic with what troops they intended to oppose him. "With yours," calmly replied Bartolommeo Valori. "We have only to pay them better."

As a point of fact, the Florentines immediately engaged the services of the famous Braccio da Montone, and concluded an alliance with Siena. The adherents of the Twelve in that unhappy little town were suspected of favouring Ladislaus, but the faction which governed for the moment attached itself to Florence.

The war began, and the King of Naples ravaged the country round Siena, then marched against Arezzo, by way of the Val di Chiana ; failed, however, to take it, and directed his attention next to Cortona, then governed by a small tyrant, Luigi da Casale, who was so unpopular, that his subjects promptly opened their gates to Ladislaus.

But this was the only success, if such it deserves to be called, which the king achieved in Tuscany, where he was so harassed by the skilful skirmishing of Braccio da Montone that he finally withdrew with his army to Rome, leaving Cortona and Perugia strongly garrisoned.

This was the occasion on which the Florentines called into Italy Louis II. of Anjou, whom Queen

LIGURIA

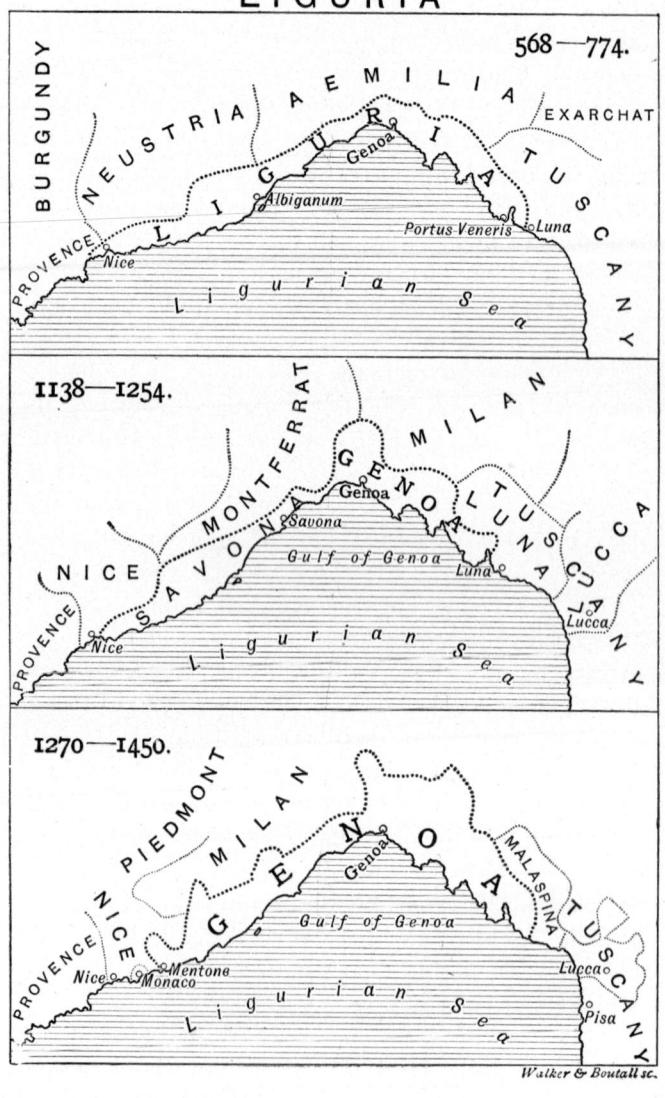

Joan had adopted, and who consequently laid claim to the throne of Naples. He engaged the services of Sforza Attendola, but the expense of this famous condottiere and his army fell, like the cost of their own war, entirely upon Florence, and brought great discredit upon the government of the republic. So unpopular did the latter feel itself, that when the astute Ladislaus made overtures of peace, coupled with the offer of ceding Cortona for sixty thousand florins, both propositions were accepted, and the negotiations brought to a favourable end at Naples, at the beginning of the year 1411.

But the King of Naples was little to be trusted either in peace or in war, and as he continued his campaign against the Church and the new pope, John XXIII., the Florentines were far from feeling themselves secure. They kept quiet as long as they could, even pushing prudence to the unchivalrous extent of refusing to open their gates to the Pope when he fled from Ladislaus' invading army to Florence.

For three months he was not allowed any nearer to the town than the monastery of Sant' Antonio outside the Porta San Gallo, and although more hospitable councils eventually prevailed, the Pontiff did not stay long in Florence, but eventually took himself to Bologna. Before his translation to the Holy See, when he was Cardinal Cossa, he had usurped the chief power in that town, which had, however, gone through one of its usual revolutions as soon as his presence was removed. The populace shook off the yoke of the Church, courageously resisted the forces under Carlo Malatesta, and took and demolished the fortress which Cossa had garrisoned.

The Florentines intervened and effected an understanding by which the Bolognese were to remain in submission to the Church, while the Pope on his side promised to respect their liberties. Barely a year passed before the people found their new masters as insupportable as their old ones; and they were also afflicted by an unendurable weight of taxation. On the 14th of August, 1412, the nobles rose in their turn, took possession of the Communal Palace, hoisted anew the standard of the Church, and requested the Pope to appoint a vicar to govern them.

Ladislaus continued his attacks upon the States of the Church, and pretended that they and they alone formed the object of his enterprise. But it was generally felt, in spite of all his assurances to the contrary, that his intention was to subdue Tuscany and the great republic itself. Among the Florentines the utmost uneasiness prevailed, and then suddenly death came to the rescue, as it had previously done in the case of Henry VII., of Castruccio Castracane and of Gian Galeazzo. Ladislaus fell a prey to a cruel malady, and expired at the age of thirty-seven in Naples, on the 6th of August, 1414.

Three years later the great schism came at last to an end, and there was once again only one Pope, Martin V., and only one Papal Court, the Roman.

XVIII.

GENOA FROM 1288 TO 1410.

THE fifty years following on the battle of Meloria marked the rise of Genoa to her highest power and prosperity, and, yet during the whole period, faction held sway in her streets, and bloodshed stained the record of her noblest families. It has been seen that this state of things was normal in the Italian communes; but in Pisa it was to some extent redeemed or at least adorned by the early splendour which broke like a star through the darkness of the eleventh century; while Florence in art, in literature, in the highest achievements of civilization, brought gifts to humanity that outweigh all her sins. But Genoa appeals to the imagination by few such claims; her successes were chiefly commercial, and beyond the sturdy determination to be free which she shared with all her sister republics, there is little to relieve the dreary monotony of her annals.

The drama is always the same: it is only the actors in it who are different. When it is not the expelled Fieschi and Grimaldi who are organizing a vast conspiracy against the Doria and Spinola, it is the two latter who are conspiring against one another, and embroiling the whole city. Endless partial changes of government took place, sometimes one, at other times two, captains being at the head of affairs: and the Abbot being assisted now by sixteen, now by twelve councillors.

For a time Uguccione della Faggiuola was Imperial Vicar (having been named to the office by Henry VII.), but as soon as he went to Pisa the old faction fights began again, and the Doria with the help of the populace drove out the Spinola.

Occasionally Doria and Spinola being alike expelled, swore a truce and fortifying themselves in Savona practically ruled the western coast, their galleys harassing the Genoese traders and sometimes pursuing their prey into the very harbour of the mother town.

Similarly the Grimaldi secured themselves in Monaco, and from that eerie constantly threatened the safety of the republic.

Even the trade of Genoa was divided between two parties—the Ghibellines having the upper hand in Sicily and Constantinople, and the Guelphs in Armenia, Syria, Flanders, France, and Naples.

The factions united temporarily in attempting to recover Sardinia from King Alfonso of Aragon. That sovereign, however, remained in possession of the island after ten years' fighting, which concluded in 1336. Nearly fifty years previously, Genoa had wrested Elba from Pisa, and in 1299 at last obtained full authority over Corsica: so with Alfonso's triumph the question of the islands was finally settled, although not entirely to Genoa's satisfaction.

After the peace with the King of Aragon, the Ghibellines grew more and more domineering. They prolonged the Captains' tenure of office to three years, deposed the Podestà (who had, indeed, by this time become a person of visionary authority), and deprived the popular party of the right of choosing the Abbot who, they decreed, should henceforth be named by the Captains (now again two). On their side the Guelphs in Monaco also increased so much in power that they were not only able to send out large armaments against the Ghibellines, but began a war with Venice, and through their privateers endangered the trade of that great republic with Flanders. For the rest both factions were equally alive to any prospect of gain, and both cheerfully hired out galleys to the King of France against England.

A constant aim of the nobles was to deprive the people of the right of electing their representative, the Abbot; and for a time the efforts in this direction had been successful: but in 1339 a popular rising forced the two Captains to restore the power of which the populace had been deprived. The day of the election, September 23rd, came, and a deputation from the people were deliberating over the choice in the Abbot's palace, when the crowd waiting outside grew impatient, and a silver foil-worker suddenly cried aloud, "Simone Boccanera shall be our Abbot." The name was caught up and re-echoed by the multitude; and Simone, who happened to be present was detected and lifted on the shoulders of the bystanders. The Abbot's was a popular office, and Simone being of noble family wished to decline the dignity thus thrust upon him; but the Captains themselves, anxious to allay the tumult, begged him to accept. So he called out, "Signori, when you wish I will be not only your Abbot, but your Lord." "Yes, yes, our Lord, not Abbot, but Lord," shouted the crowd. Boccanera replied: "How can I be your Lord when you have two Captains?" Then with one accord the answer burst forth, "He shall be our Doge!" He was borne to the Church of San Siro and the people flew to arms. The Captains barely escaped with their lives: the air resounded with cries of "Long live the people, the merchants and the Doge!" and the houses of the Doria and Salvagi were plundered. The next day, in San Lorenzo, Simone was solemnly proclaimed Doge for life. It seemed a sudden revolution, born of a breath; but it had long been seething among the populace who were tired of tyrannical nobles, of oligarchies and divided authority, and knew of no better remedy than the one they had chosen. Fifteen councillors of the popular, *i.e.*, non-noble, party were appointed to assist the Doge; the office of the Podestà was revived, but invested with no increased authority: and a number of the Doria and Spinola adherents besides all the noble Guelphs were expelled from the town. The non-noble inhabitants were divided into bands analogous to the old Campagne, and at the head of each division a constable was placed who represented his subordinates on all official occasions. The Doge was proclaimed all along the coast, and acknowledged from Ventimiglia to the Magra, with only one exception—Lerici; while the exiled nobility made the best of its

altered circumstances and took definitively to piracy.
In 1340 Lerici was bought over, and then the only
difficulty which Genoa had to contend with consisted
in the persistent efforts of the nobles to return, and
the constant conspiracies which they stirred up among
their friends in the town, including one to murder the
Doge, which was discovered in time to avert the blow.

Simone governed very well, but soon grew dismayed
at the difficulties of his position, and resigned his
post in which he was replaced by Giovanni di Murta.
His term of office was signalized by popular risings
and street fights, followed by fresh futile attempts to
come to a permanent understanding with the banditti
nobles, now securely established all along the western
coast which had entirely submitted to their rule.
After a brief interregnum of government by the
Archbishop of Milan (Giovanni Visconti) who came
to Genoa in September, 1353, Simone Boccanera was
made Doge for the second time, and remained peaceably in the office until 1362, when he was poisoned.
In 1378 a war broke out between the eternal rivals
Genoa and Venice, and in the following year the
Genoese took Chioggia, and placed a galley from
Savona as vanguard at Malamocco. For a moment
the might of Venice seemed eclipsed, but an heroic
rally was crowned with a brilliant triumph.

On the night of the 23rd of December, 1379, a
Venetian fleet fell by surprise on the Genoese ships
off Chioggia, and shut them in on all sides. A
desperate defence lasted till the end of February,
when the Genoese as a last resource abandoned the
water and prepared to stand a siege in Chioggia

itself. They expelled all the women, children, and non-combatants from the island, but were nevertheless soon pressed by hunger, and could receive but little help.

At last, on the 21st of June, 1380, the gallant garrison of Chioggia, five thousand strong, surrendered to famine, and peace was concluded shortly afterwards.

Between 1384 and 1393 Genoa was unceasingly convulsed by the action of Antoniotto Adorno, who, alternately proclaimed Doge and deposed by a fresh revolution, was constantly marching against the town with an armed force composed of all his own adherents, of the exiled malcontents, and of the troops of some such potentate as the Marquis of Carreto—Genoa's irreconcilable foe. On Antoniotto being overturned for the second time, a mere youth, Antonio Montaldo, was proclaimed Doge in his stead. He had but a brief tenure of power and after some vicissitudes with the usual appointments of first twelve and then ten people to settle the government Francesco Giustiniani was made Doge for a year. But Antoniotto Adorno and Antonio Montaldo, with their armed followers outside the town and their adherents within, gave him no peace, and he retired in six weeks into private life. A fight in the streets ensued between Antonio and Antoniotto, who had now both obtained entrance. Adorno had mercenary troops, Montaldo but a small band of followers, but he and all of his performed such prodigies of valour that Antoniotto ignominiously fled in the fashion habitual to him. Antonio was reinstated as Doge, and for four months there was some appearance of tranquillity. Then the dwellers in the valley of the Bisagno revolted, and the young Doge had to march against them. The whole territory round Genoa was indeed in a deplorable condition all this time: overrun with disbanded mercenaries, with organized robbers, and desperate outlaws, made desperate by want of bread and home and hope. Plunder and devastation had become commonplaces—the fairest harvests were ruined and the coast was threatened incessantly by Tunisian pirates. Meanwhile in Genoa the old round of conspiracies had begun again: Antonio beheaded several people; then in May, 1394, threw up the sponge, and, like so many dukes before him, sought safety in secret flight. Of course he came back, and so did Antoniotto, and other pretenders to the dukedom arose, and the streets rang again with the clash of arms.

In 1395 Antoniotto was again Doge, but his position was threatened on all sides—by the Grimaldi from Monaco, by Antonio da Montaldo and his force at Gavi, by a band of Guelphs at Porto Venere, by Antonio Guarco (who had been one of the candidates for the dukedom), from the nearest valleys where he had concentrated Lombard mercenaries. Antoniotto made desperate efforts at defence, and banished eight hundred citizens, but finally arrived at the conclusion that the situation was unendurable, and, rather than cede the place to his enemies, decided to offer the town to a stranger.

The proposition when made to the Genoese found

some adherents, and Dagnano de Malloni, of the noble family of the Cattanei, and Pietro da Persio, a people's delegate, went to the French Court to offer the government of their town to King Charles. The latter lent a favourable ear to the ambassadors, and Antoniotto, on learning this, summoned two hundred Ghibellines of the popular party to his presence, and explained to them that either money for the now overwhelming necessities of the town must be procured, or they must throw themselves into the arms of France. The latter alternative was chosen and accepted also by the Guelphs: the nobles of both parties being, for a wonder, agreed, the preliminaries were speedily settled, and on the 27th of November, 1396, Antoniotto resigned his functions as Doge, but was named governor of Genoa by the French.

This occupation by a foreign power lasted twelve years, but it brought no permanent peace to the distracted town. The greater part of the coast submitted, indeed, at once to the French rule, with the exception of some places to the east of Levanto, which were held by the Ghibelline family of Bertoloti. The latter, with Antonio Montaldo and Antonio Guarco, entered Genoa by surprise one night in July, 1398, and caused one of the usual tumults. For a long while following on this attempt there were daily street fights, to which were added all the horrors of the plague. Among the victims of the fell disease was Antonio Montaldo, whose party, however, survived him.

In 1399 the lowest guilds began to give trouble, but after some stormy months succeeded in obtaining a special government of their own. They chose four priors out of their own class, who were assisted by a council of twelve, and whose election, like that of the council, was to be renewed every four months with formal recognition on the part of the governor of the town and his council of elders (*anziani*). In this way the artizan class in Genoa came at last to possess a constitution of its own.

In the beginning of the year 1400, the Governor, Colard de Calleville, who was unpopular, had to take flight: anarchy reigned again, bloody battles ensued, and Battista Boccanera was made rector, or captain, of the town. A provincial government, composed of the popular party, with three delegates from the valleys (*i.e.*, representatives of the popular party outside the walls) was formed, and the street-fights went on again. Battista Boccanera had retired, and another Battista of the Franchi family was chosen in his stead, and governed in the name of the French with some amount of peace for about twelve months, by which time his power, though the renewed anarchy which prevailed was so discredited that a new authority had to be created in the shape of eight citizens, called Ufficiali di Balìa, and invested with special powers for the repression of disorder.

At last, in October, 1401, came Marshal Boucicault, the best, the firmest, and most able of the French representatives. He brought a thousand horse and foot with him, hired two hundred more foreigners, and garrisoned the fortress entirely with his own men. Then he arrested the two Battistas for having had themselves appointed governors

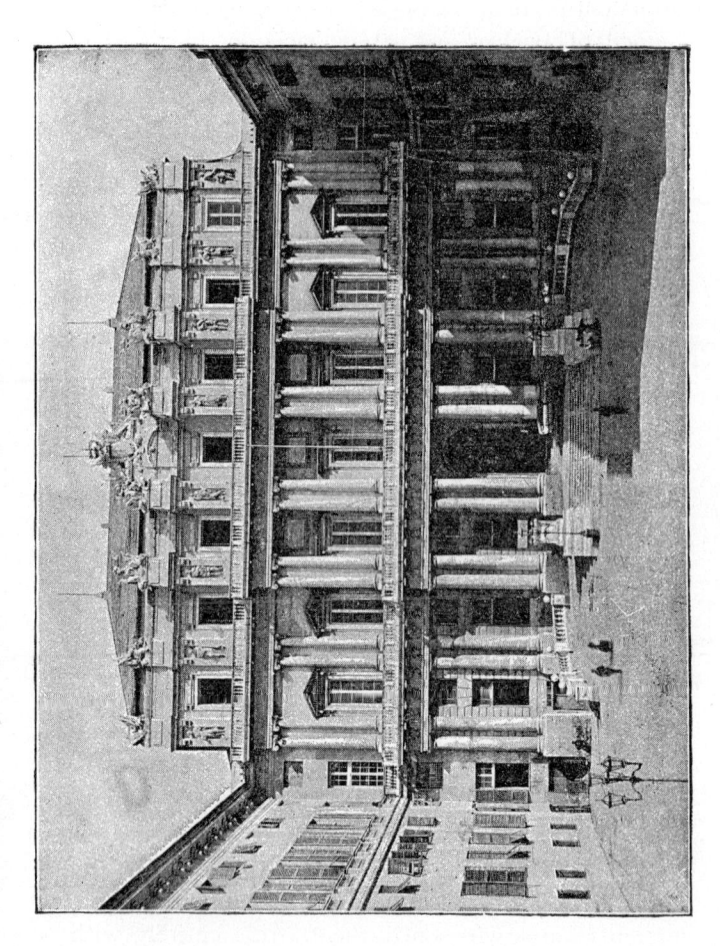

DUCAL PALACE, GENOA.
(*From a Photograph by Borgi.*)

without previous authority from the French king. By evening the square in front of the Doge's Palace was occupied by the foreign troops, and the two prisoners were brought out to execution. Battista Boccanera's head was cut off, but in the midst of the awful tumult which arose Battista Franchi managed to escape, in spite of having his arms bound. Boucicault was so enraged at this evasion that he ordered the knight who had charge of the prisoner to be executed in his stead. This somewhat oriental command was duly obeyed, and for a whole day the petrified citizens had an opportunity of gazing at the two ghastly heads which were exposed in the Piazza. The novelty of such an absolute authority so ruthlessly exercised appears to have startled the Genoese into temporary submission, and for several years there was peace. Again the surrounding territory, with its castles, was brought under Genoese sway, the principal exceptions being Monaco, held by the Grimaldi, Arcola, which belonged to the Malaspina, and another fortified place where the Carretos had established themselves.

But in 1402 even Monaco was taken: the Carretos were beaten, and Boucicault was named governor for life. He broke up the old unions under constables, and divided the citizens into fresh combinations for military purposes; defended Famagosta against the King of Cyprus; deprived the guilds of their consuls (doubtless with the object of eventually effacing old distinctions); created new indirect taxes in the hope of readjusting the crippled finances; and finally attacked Gherardo d'Appiano, the lord of

Piombino and Elba, who had constantly irritated the republic by his steady protection of pirates.

Under Rafaele Montaldo, whom Boucicault sent as governor to Corsica, even this island was brought to a condition of peace which had long been unknown to it. In 1403 a large fleet proceeded against Cyprus, under the command of Boucicault himself, who by this time was so much respected by the Genoese that they had raised his salary from 8,500 to 18,625 lire. The King of Cyprus was forced to conclude a peace and to pay a war indemnity; but after this the Marshal began to make descents upon the Syrian coast, and thus brought on a war with Venice. Carlo Zeno, the Venetian admiral, met him off Modon in October, 1403, and a battle ensued, in which the Genoese lost six galleys, three being taken by the enemy, and three sinking with all hands aboard. Fortunately the Duke of Savoy interposed, hostilities were brought to an end, and Boucicault returned to Genoa, there to carry out what was evidently his intention from the first—namely, a total revision of the constitution. Sarzana, in 1407, passed to the possession of Genoa, and Boucicault, who had obtained Leghorn by negotiation from Pisa, bestowed that also upon the republic. His influence was for a long time so supreme that he even induced his subjects—for such they really were—to transfer their allegiance from the Pope in Rome to the rival Holy Father in Avignon: factions seemed quelled and the sound of street-fights was almost forgotton. This state of things lasted until 1408, when Boucicault, being absent on the north side of the Alps, his irreconcilable foe, Battisti Franchi, persuaded the Marquis of Montferrat and Facino Cane, the condottiere, to march against Genoa, or rather, in reality, against the power of the Marshal there, he having brought their hostility upon himself by acts which belong to the history of Milan. The authority of the French vanished like morning dew, and on the 4th of September, 1409, were elected twelve councillors or elders (*anziani*), half of whom were of the noble and half of the popular party, while as regards their Guelph and Ghibelline tendencies, a similar distribution was carefully observed. They took over the government of the town, and called in the Marquis, who was proclaimed captain for a year. Boucicault came with an army as far as Gavi, but went away again on convincing himself that there was nothing to be done, thus leaving Montferrat in possession, but confronted by a formidable combination of Guelphs, who would have preferred the French to this Ghibelline leader.

XIX.

COMMERCE, MANUFACTURES, AND FINANCE.

The seven Major Guilds of Florence were as follows :—

1. Judges and Notaries.
2. The Calimala, or Cloth Merchants, who procured their cloth from abroad.
3. The Wool Guild.
4. The Silk Guild, called also the Guild of St. Mary's Gate.
5. The Money-changers.
6. The Doctors and Druggists (which included also grocers as vendors of spices and other products).
7. The Furriers.

If the judges and notaries cannot be considered as commercial, they at least contributed immensely to commercial progress ; for they presided with the consuls of the guilds over the chambers of commerce, gave judgment in all suits therein discussed, pronounced sentence on defaulters, and discharged other functions of the same sort. They also reformed the statutes of the guilds, superintended their application, drew up contracts, and habitually addressed the councils of the guilds in the name of their consuls, performing all these offices not only for the major, but for the minor guilds as well. The latter were eventually fourteen in number, and comprised such trades as flax-spinners, shoemakers, smiths, pork-butchers, butchers, innkeepers, vintners, tanners, locksmiths, masons, carpenters, bakers, &c.

The oldest and first to progress of all the guilds were those of the cloth merchants and cloth manufacturers, or, as they were called in Florence, Arte di Calimala and Arte della Lana. Both sold, and eventually both manufactured, woollen goods, but, owing to a difference in their origin, they remained always quite distinct.

The old Florentines, as we have already learnt from the observations of Villani and Dante, clothed themselves in leather, the Venetians alone being already so far advanced in the thirteenth century in trade and wealth as to import rich stuffs for their garments from the Orient. Woollen cloths, however, soon began to be generally in demand, only their manufacture was very difficult, owing to the bad quality of the wool. To improve this meant to have valuable flocks, and such were not possible without two things in which Tuscany especially was lacking—good agriculture and sufficient pasturage. The Italian burgher, so intelligent in all matters relating to manufacture, strangely overlooked and even oppressed agriculture, perhaps because of the frequent raids and devastations to which rural property was so long exposed, and for which retaliation was beyond the power of the communes. The coarse material which the Florentine weaver succeeded in producing very soon ceased to satisfy his customers, but the importation of finer wool, on the other hand, entailed expenses far beyond the capacity of a nascent industry. The Florentines, consequently, had but one course open to them, namely, to import undyed cloths from Flanders, Holland, and Brabant, where the arts of refining and colouring were but little understood, and to prepare them in Italian workshops for the markets of the world. Hence arose the Guild of Calimala, or Foreign-cloth Merchants, which grew in a very short time to immense renown. The superior but ill-dyed materials from Flanders and Holland arrived in Florence to be carded, dressed, and cut, and were subsequently exchanged in Asia for drugs, dyes, spices, precious stones, and other products of the East, while very soon they were found also in the markets of France and England, and even went back to the very countries which had orginally exported them.

In the first half of the twelfth century a company of Lombard weavers who were prisoners in Germany formed themselves into a devout lay community under the name of Umiliati. They returned to their own country after five years of captivity, bringing with them improved methods which they had learned from fellow-craftsmen beyond the Alps. In 1140 they definitely constituted themselves into a religious order, eventually receiving formal recognition as such in a Bull of Innocent III., and, while ceasing then to weave with their own hands, they continued to superintend the work of their lay brethren. Very soon their cloth attracted general attention by its excellence, and out of the industry thus founded arose the Guild of Wool, which soon rivalled the Calimala in wealth and importance—more especially as the old difficulty of importing foreign products now no longer existed and the Florentines obtained wool from Tunis, Barbary, Spain, Portugal, and England.

Giovanni Villani, in the statistics he has given of Florence in the year 1338, says that the wool manufactories numbered three hundred, and sent out from seventy to eighty thousand pieces of the value of one million two hundred thousand florins, while the Guild of Calimala possessed twenty workshops which among them imported cloth to the value of three hundred thousand florins, which was all sold in Florence alone, and may by analogy give an idea of the amount imported to be afterwards despatched to foreign markets. The two guilds divided labour between them in such a way as not to interfere with one another. This is proved by a statute restraining the Calimala from dyeing any but foreign cloths, the other guild having dyers of its own who made one of the subordinate associations already mentioned in connection with the Ciompi riots. For the rest Florentine dyes, especially a particular red one, soon became famous, and were protected by most minute and stringent regulations which, it was hoped, would preserve the branch from all deterioration.

For a time the Florentines were undisputed masters in the art of manfacturing and preparing cloth, and it is interesting to read that, like the merchants of the Steelyard, they had a great contempt for the English,

Dutch, and French, as poor creatures with no business faculty. But intercourse soon produced competition, the poor creatures became good manufacturers in their turn, and the woollen industry of Florence began to decline. Fortunately, however, silk weaving, as has already been mentioned, was introduced by Lucchese exiles; the Florentines diverted their capital and energy into the new channel thus opened; and when Gino Capponi at the beginning of the fifteenth century taught them how to spin gold for themselves instead of procuring it as hitherto ready spun from Cyprus or Cologne, they soon produced silver and gold brocades of unsurpassed and unsurpassable beauty.

The art of banking flourished in Florence from the beginning of the thirteenth to the end of the fifteenth century, and by some writers is claimed as an invention of the Guelphs, who, when exiled, spread the discovery over Europe.

Others attribute it to the Jews, who were more ubiquitous, and had been so for a longer period than the Guelphs. Both these explanations seem rather far-fetched, for, inasmuch as the art of banking, with its system of cheques, &c., was practised by the Romans, and had probably lingered on through the Dark Ages, its flourishing revival in the mediæval commune can excite no surprise.

The Florentine merchants had correspondents, agents, and counting-houses everywhere, and it was quite natural, consequently, that a merchant of Antwerp or Bruges, when having to send money to Italy or the East, should seek a Florentine colleague who had come to Flanders to buy wool or undyed cloth, and should make him the channel of communication between himself and the creditor dwelling at Naples or Novgorod, at Siena or Constantinople, more especially as by this arrangement the Flemish merchant received an agio on his money, and thereby made a profit on the transaction.

The same thing, only reversed, took place in Florence, where a trader, desirous of transmitting one hundred florins to London, had but to visit a workshop belonging to either of the two wool guilds, and there found an urbane person who carried out his wishes by the simple expedient of writing to a correspondent in Lombard Street.

No operation of modern banking was unknown to the Florentine money-changer, and when the republic wanted a loan, it addressed itself to its bankers, just as we turn to our Rothschilds. The Public Debt thus formed gave rise to the institution known as the Monte Commune, of which the luoghi, or coupons, were negotiated in precisely the same way as now; and under the graceful colonnades of the Mercato Nuovo, where visitors to Florence now go to buy their flowers and admire the bronze Boar, the merchants of the fourteenth and fifteenth centuries speculated in the rise and fall of rentes.

Florentine traders are said to have ranked high for integrity and punctuality, but the town had an evil reputation for usury. Legal interest was fixed at from 10 to 20 per cent., but these profits, though large, seemed insufficient to greedy money-lenders, who, by various astute devices, managed to send legal interest up constantly to 40 per cent., or perhaps more.

All operations were much assisted by the good quality of the Florentine coinage. The first gold florin was issued in 1252. It contained twenty-four carats of gold, and was stamped with the image of St. John on one side, and the lily of the republic on the other. Eight florins weighed one ounce, and were worth about eleven lire of the present day. The Florentines did their accounts in lire, soldi, and denari (whence it is doubtless superfluous to remark we derive our £ s. d.). The silver lira had orginally been intended to weigh a pound, its name, in fact, being a corruption of libra ; but its value was purely conventional, often varying from town to town and year to year. It was divided into twenty soldi (from solidi, which were equivalent to the Langobardic schilling) and twelve denari, thereby exactly reproducing the proportions of our pound with its twenty shillings and twelve pence.

The florin never altered in value, although the lira, as has been said, did so perpetually. In 1252, for instance, the florin was equal to one lira; in 1331 its value was as three lire ; and in 1464, as four lire, eight soldi. But the original florin had come now to be replaced by a larger coin worth five lire, six soldi, called fiorino di galea (galley-florin). The object of this change was to compete in the markets of the East with the Venetian gold coin ; and the name "galley-florin" signified that the new form of money was intended to go on the galleys to those ports in the Levant, where long files of caravans from

India and Persia and Central Asia now awaited the unloading of Italian cargoes.

The smaller florin lasted in Europe till 1471, and the large one only survived it by sixty years.

It is necessarily very difficult to estimate the value of money in the fourteenth and fifteenth centuries as compared to the present day, more especially as writers are not agreed upon the subject. According to Sismondi, gold during those two hundred years was worth four times as much as now; and as the small florin had the same value as the sequin and represented eleven lire of the present day, by multiplying by forty-four, the number of the florins mentioned in any case the exact sum in modern lire may be obtained.

In the year 1260 the Salimbeni firm lent Siena twenty-two thousand florins, and failed in consequence some years later. In 1377 one of the Albertis of Florence died worth three hundred thousand florins, got by commerce: while the celebrated loans made by Bardi and Peruzzi to Edward III. of England, and which eventually reduced them to bankruptcy, amounted to 1,500,000 florins. The English kings borrowed largely of Florentine bankers, and Comines asserts that Edward IV. owed his throne to the help thus afforded him.

It has already been mentioned how Florence gradually ousted Siena from its position as chief banker of the Holy See. The importance of the financial connection between the Papal Court and the Republic of Florence can never be too much insisted upon; it is, in point of fact, the key to

Florentine history; the unavowed explanation of the fidelity of the Florentine government to the Guelph cause.

Doubtless the public was not definitely conscious of this, but its wire-pullers were. Doubtless, the sober, thrifty, pious, rather pharisaical Florentine citizen, from the days of Giovanni Villani to those of Luca Landucci, had the liveliest aversion to Ghibellines as free-thinking, free-living, godless folk, and regarded them pretty much as the Roundheads did the Cavaliers. But the men at the head of affairs knew that when defending Mother Church they were fighting for their money-bags, and in their appeals to the passions and prejudices of the multitudes they were careful to foster illusions which served their own ends. These ends were, for the rest, quite legitimate; for the power of the republic was based upon money: existed through money; and received its death blow when the discovery of America introduced a revolution into the monetary affairs of the world.

It was natural that Rome should excite the greed of the mediæval financier, for to the Eternal City converged all the moral and material interests of Christendom. From the rich benefices of cardinals and prelates in Europe, Asia, and Africa, the obolus of the faithful found its way to the coffers of the Holy See. To be the bankers of such wealth, estimated at the death of Pope John XXII. at twenty-four millions of gold, was to enjoy an incalculable advantage, and when the Papal Court removed from Rome to Avignon and from Avignon back to Rome, the great displacement of capital which ensued, and the enormous remittances that had to be made, offered opportunities for profit of which the long-headed Florentines did not fail to avail themselves.

The Money-changers Guild was of ancient origin in Florence. The offices of the guild and the Exchange of the period were, as already stated, under the colonnade of the New Market. In 1338 these counting-houses numbered about eighty, and every year the Mint of Florence coined from three hundred and fifty to four hundred thousand florins. In 1422 the circulating capital of Florence was calculated at two millions of florins, exclusive of the value of existent merchandize. Fifty years later, partly on account of the decadence of commerce, partly owing to the inevitable accumulation of money in a few hands, the number of banks was reduced to thirty-three, which still did a flourishing business throughout Eastern and Western Europe.

The remaining major guilds, that of the doctors and druggists and the furriers, were of less importance than those already described, but were nevertheless very flourishing. It was estimated that no less than twenty-two different sorts of rare furs were brought to Italy by Italian traders; while as to the drugs and spices of the East, they were such a source of wealth, that the Florentines could not rest as long as this prolific branch which had enriched the Amalfitans, the Pisans, and the Genoese remained out of their possession.

Great was the excitement among the citizens of the republic when the first galleys were despatched from Porto Pisano or Leghorn; eager crowds gathered under the colonnades of the Mercato to read the dates of the departure and return of the ships; and sturdy indeed was the spirit of those traders who, departing, for instance, for Pekin, knew that they must be absent three years.

Florence, in the words of a modern writer, may be considered "as one huge, commercial establishment, placed in the centre of Tuscany, and surrounded by competitors. Her external history is a history of wars which always ended with some advantageous treaty of commerce." The wars with Pisa were dictated by a desire to reach the sea. Rivalry with Pisa was the secret of friendship with Lucca; and until after the battle of Meloria the alliance with Genoa was sedulously cultivated, that the ruin of Pisa might be compassed. Once the Genoese were no longer needed by the Florentines, the ardour of the latter perceptibly cooled.

The ordinary expenditure of Florence between 1336 and 1338, according to the celebrated statistics of Giovanni Villani, was only 4,000 florins; while the income of the State amounted to 300,000 florins, obtained chiefly by custom and excise duties and fines. The population of the town alone, calculated, probably very imperfectly, by the consumption of bread, was put down at 90,000 souls; while that of the State amounted to about 110,000, or 200,000 in all. The chief paid officials were the Podestà, the Captain of the People, and the Executor of the Ordinances of Justice, who received respectively 15,240 lire, 5,880 lire, and 4,900 lire (the florin at that time being worth 3 lire 2 soldi). The Priors' food cost the State 3,600 lire; under the head of charity to religious orders and to hospitals, 2,600 lire figure; the night watchmen, cost 10,800 lire; spies and messengers in the service of the commune 1,200, and ambassadors to foreign powers, or other towns, 15,500 lire. All these sums were annual. From 8,000 to 10,000 children learnt to read; there were six arithmetic schools attended by 1,000 to 1,200 pupils; and 4 large schools for Latin, grammar, and logic, counted from 550 to 600 students; 30 hospitals, containing in all more than 1,000 beds, attest to Florentine care of the sick, whose wants, however, must have made themselves imperiously felt in a town which received such a steady influx of wandering friars, pilgrims, soldiers and merchants, Jews, Christians, and heathens with all their attendant diseases.

One of the most interesting institutions of the Middle Ages in Italy were the pawnbrokers' shops or Monti di Pietà, founded, it was said, but not correctly, by Bernardino di Feltre as a make-weight to the ever-growing usury of the Jews. Bernardino was inspired with a hatred of the race of Israel worthy of our Drumonts and Stöckers, and preached a crusade against them as vampires who sucked the life-blood of the people, and whose establishments of credit were to be found not only in Pisa, in Florence, in Siena, but almost in every village in Tuscany. They exacted 30 and 40 per cent. interest, and as the Christian Florentines were also famous usurers, the misery of the unhappy people reduced to borrow can be imagined. In the beginning the Monti di Pietà were hailed with an enthusiasm worthy of institutions where everything was managed free of charge, and the sums required were advanced without interest. But it was very soon found that the promise of a better era for the needy was a delusion: the formalities to be observed at the Monti, the delays in touching the money, the necessity of proving legitimate possession of the deposited object, and the obligation imposed on every applicant of giving his name, drove noble and plebeian alike back into the offices of the discreet Hebrew, whose credit grew eventually to such proportions that a later Tuscan proverb said, "Better beat the Grand Duke than a Jew."

Genoa was quite the equal of Venice in trade for a time, although the Ligurian Republic, hampered until after the battle of Meloria, developed much later than the Adriatic state.

While the home-staying Genoese were deluging their native streets with blood, and proving themselves apparently ungovernable, Genoese merchants, cautious, able, and bold, were to be found in Pera, in Caffa, in Constantinople, on the coast of Africa, and the shores of the Black Sea. The galleys which cast anchor in the Gulf of Genoa were laden with ginger, pepper, indigo, skins, and coloured leather embroidered in gold and silver, from Gujerat; spices, copper, and pearls from Malabar, where all trade was one continual struggle with Corsairs, and where, according to Marco Polo, the priests enchained sharks and other monsters of the deep by magic during the day, and set them free at night, so that they might guard the pearls until the return of the fishers. From Ceylon the Genoese brought rubies, sapphires, topazes, amethysts; from Sumatra, gold, spices, aloes, ebony; from Java, camphor, cloves, and spices.

From Central Asia the caravans started, and swelling with merchandize as they passed through China and Tartary, they diverged through Syria and Egypt, and *viâ* the Black Sea and Constantinople, till they reached the depôts of Italian merchants, who despatched the goods to remotest parts of Europe. The return caravans, which left Syria and Egypt for India, reached that country *viâ* Ormuz and Aden, and skirting both sides of the Ganges, proceeded to Cape Comorin and the Coast of Coromandel, whence, by way of Ava, Malacca, Sumatra, and Java, their contents finally arrived at the interior of China. Yet another way to India was by the Black Sea and China. And thus to every known land, however distant, which fancy painted, and travellers' tales represented, as inhabited by terrific monsters, by accursed spirits and evil magicians, and whence the objects brought—the gold, the silver, the rare and gorgeous stuffs, the birds of strange plumage, the black slaves, the monkeys, the dwarfs—seemed a confirmation of every fantastic dream—did the long arm of Italian commerce reach, or the undaunted spirit of Italian enterprise penetrate.

Cairo was the principal emporium of the merchandize brought from the interior of Africa; and as Egypt produced neither wood nor metals, the Italians followed the earlier examples of the Greeks in carrying these things thither at the same time as wine, oil, soap, saffron, coral, silk, and woollen fabrics—all of which goods—or, at any rate, such as there was a demand for—were carried across the desert to the banks of the Niger. The Genoese did a large trade with Alexandria, where, as in all their commercial settlements, they had established a consulate, and were governed by their own laws.

Indian merchandize found its way on Genoese ships to Alexandria, and until the discovery of the Cape of Good Hope, Aden was one of the most flourishing ports at which the Italians touched. The European produce exchanged for Eastern wares consisted in wine, oil, cloths, brocades, linen (from the looms of Genoa and Rouen), alum, hardware, arms, wood for building, and naval utensils. Similar articles were carried to Tunis and Tripoli, and bartered for corn, wool, ostrich feathers, skins, and dried fruits. It may be remarked in passing, that wherever the Genoese established consulates—but especially on the coast of Africa—they obtained concessions from the ruler of the country, which concessions were afterwards farmed out by the republic to wealthy individuals, who in their turn made them a source of profit, and, doubtless, also of corruption. For instance, in May, 1243, the State of Genoa, as represented by the Podestà and Councils sold the revenues of Ceuta for two years to Niccolò Silvagni for $133\frac{1}{3}$ ounces of gold, worth in that year, according to Canale, five times as much as at present.

Besides the various places already mentioned, Genoa had commercial establishments in the Chersonese and in the Crimea, at places now as familiar to English ears as Sebastopol, Inkerman, Balaclava, where the settlements were, for the most part, in dependence on the great and powerful consulate of Caffa, in which the Genoese sway, though based on trade only, resembled the authority exercised by the British at present in Bombay or Madras.

Skins and wool from the Crimea were briskly exchanged for the wines of Greece and Roumania, and a profitable trade in Caucasian slaves was also carried on by private individuals, being sometimes prohibited, sometimes winked at, and sometimes even regulated by the republic, which could not always afford to close any source of gain to its richer or more active citizens.

The Bank of St. George in Genoa, was a renowned institution, worthy to rank with the Bank of Venice, and, like that, a forerunner of the still more famous Bank of Amsterdam. It was founded in 1407, but its origin must be sought for in 1371, when the first attempt at a state sinking fund was made at Genoa. It had always been the practice there to assign the revenues of certain portions of territory, or particular taxes, to the creditors of the State, who in 1371 formed a society which they called the Chapter, and which met in a Chapter-house, where a staff of administrators resided and the books were kept. The largest part of the State revenues were by this time assigned to these creditors, who divided the debts of the republic into sums of 100 lire each, to which the name of luoghi were given, and which could be sold by one creditor to another. The holders of the luoghi were *ipso facto* members of the Chapter.

It was found, after a time, that a large share of the

income of the Chapter went to the administration of the same; also that interest on the luoghi was not only affected by the wars, famines, and impoverishment of individuals brought about by the political condition of the State, but rendered additionally uncertain by the varying expenses of the society. With a view to economy, a managing committee of eight was formed in 1407, and substituted for the numerous employés who up to that time had administered the different branches of the revenue. This committee received the name of the Bank of St. George, and through its hands passed all the income which was assigned to the creditors of the republic, and served to pay the interest on the luoghi. The Bank of St. George, when once formed, became absolutely independent of State interference; it had its own buildings, and had generally to render account of its stewardship to nobody, except on special occasions, when a meeting of one hundred members of the society (or shareholders), chosen by the remainder, were summoned. The governing officers of the republic had to swear to respect the rights and privileges of the Bank, which formed a state within the state, and very soon was richer than the distracted commune from which it had sprung.

XX.

INTELLECTUAL AND ARTISTIC DEVELOPMENT UNTIL THE CLOSE OF THE FIFTEENTH CENTURY.

ALL through the Dark Ages a popular plebeian drama, descended directly from the Latins, appears to have existed in Italy, but its indecency caused it to be vehemently denounced by the Church, which, perhaps with a view of superseding it, gradually allowed dramatic forms to be introduced into the liturgy.

At certain seasons, such as Easter, plastic representations of scenes out of the New Testament took place, to which dialogues were added later, the interlocutors being, for instance, Mary and Joseph, or the angel and the women at the sepulchre.

These dialogues were in Latin, but presently a more popular form was given to dramatic religious composition in Tuscany by the *laudi*, or penitential chants, of the Flagellants, which, being recited in Italian, appealed, by their eloquent simplicity, to the general imagination.

The company of the Flagellants, or "postulants for the discipline of Christ," was founded in 1258 by the old Umbrian hermit, Raniero Fasani. It was composed of laymen of all classes and ages, who owed their descriptive title to the cruel habit of unceasingly

MEDAL SHOWING DANTE.

Obverse. Reverse.

(From *Die Italienischen Schaumünzen des Fünfzehnten Jahrhunderts.* (1430-1530.) Von Julius Friedlaender. Berlin, 1882.)

flogging themselves until blood stained their footprints. Not even at night did they rest, but wandered continuously in the wildest weather, carrying lighted tapers, and filling the streets of towns, the hillsides, and valleys, with the sound of their despairing supplications to God for mercy. "And all this time," says a Latin chronicle, "the music of instruments and the songs of love were silenced."

To the first mere monotonous chant of these penitents a scenic apparatus with appropriate costumes was soon added, and this gradually grew into the Sacra Rappresentazione, which became one of the street shows of Italian towns, exercising, there is no doubt, a peculiar influence on Tuscan art. The strange anachronisms of Fra Filippo Lippi, for instance, might easily be traced to these spectacles.

Popular poetry first in rustic Latin, then in the various rude dialects out of which Italian was to be moulded, doubtless existed throughout the Dark Ages; but the first poetical impulse of the cultured classes came to Italy from Provence.

The troubadours driven from their own land by the religious wars found safety and welcome at the courts of Azzo VII., of Este, of Gherardo da Canino, Lord of Treviso, and of Bonifazio III., Marquis of Montferrat. The most famous of all these singers was the great Sordello, who, romantic, ardent, patriotic, and dissolute, stands out in picturesque relief from among his crowd of brother-rhymers. Apparently he had great merit as a writer, and did not compose in Provençal alone; for Dante included him among those who wrote in native dialect, and praised his eloquence.

The exact date when Italian arose can naturally not be fixed, but the earliest known singer is Ciullo d'Alcano, a Sicilian, who wrote about 1190. The composition of sonnets was a fashionable occupation at the court of Frederick II. That brilliant monarch himself wrote Sicilian verses, as did his unhappy son Enzo, and his Chancellor Pier delle Vigne. And Manfred carried on the tradition, as we learn from Matteo Spinelli the chronicler, who relates that the Prince, always "dressed in green," went forth at night through the streets of Barletta, accompanied by troubadours and players on the lute, who passed the starlit hours in music and song.

The early Sicilian imitated the Provençal poets servilely, but when poetry passed from the courts of Frederick and Manfred to the streets of Florence and Siena it soared at once on a stronger wing. The language also changed and gradually all local lyrics took a Tuscan form. Guido Guinicelli, a Bolognese who flourished about 1250, enjoyed the honour of Dante's praise. He wrote a literary Tuscan, and his style joined to the philosophical tone of his love-poems which struck quite a new note, one to be heard in full swell in the "Vita Nuova," sufficiently account for the name of "father" by which the great Florentine saluted him (Purg. XXVI.).

There is a strain of originality, of grave and solemn feeling, in Guittone d'Arezzo, who deserted a charming wife and three children to become a knight of Santa Maria, and embodied his cult of the Virgin in some lofty hymns. He was exiled from Arezzo for political reasons, and died at Florence in 1294.

Passing by the sweet singer, Lapo Gianni, and disregarding Dino Frescobaldi and Gianni Alfani, in whose verse there is yet a certain ring of genuine feeling, we come to two really great names in Guido Cavalcanti and Cino da Pistoja. The first named was Dante's great friend for many years, until political differences divided them. Guido was an interesting historical figure, " handsome, courteous, bold, but studious, proud, and of a solitary spirit." That is how Dino Compagni describes him. Boccaccio accused him of epicureanism and free-thinking, like his haughty old father whom Dante saw in a burning tomb in Hell ; and the accusation accords very well with all we know of his disdainful and lonely nature. His sonnets have nearly all a philosophical colouring which sometimes deforms their poetical quality ; but many of his Ballate are instinct with movement and grace.

A jurist of immense learning for his age, a strong-souled patriot, a lover whose manly fervour of expression recalls our own Elizabethans, Cino dei Sinibaldi, better known as Cino da Pistoja, is one of the most attractive and characteristic of all the great Tuscans whose bitter fate it was to eat the bread of exile. His verse is modern in tone beyond that of any of his immediate predecessors, beyond Lapo Gianni's or Guido Cavalcanti's even, simply because it succeeds in expressing moods which belong to all time, which are as old as the hills, and as young as the dawn.

While all these Tuscan lyrics were being poured out, Latin compositions in verse and prose still continued fashionable. The tongue of ancient Rome lingered on in Italy long after the various forms of

Romance had replaced it in France and Spain, being spoken in a corrupt form, which had doubtless resulted from the efforts of successive barbarians to speak the idiom of Virgil. This composite idiom died hard in Italy, and strange to say even after the birth of true Italian, the writers of the Peninsula preferred French for prose composition. To Paris, with its school of theology, the students of Europe flocked, the university there responding better to the wants of the age than could either Bologna or Padua, famous though both were in their different lines, as schools of law. And the Italians who went thither preferred to write French rather than undertake the task of forming out of chaos a language of their own. French was the language used in composing "Il Tesoro," by Brunetto Latini, the philosopher and friend, if not actually the master, of Dante.

The work is a sort of encyclopædia, not the first of its kind in the Middle Ages, by any means; and is chiefly interesting as a literary curiosity. More cannot honestly be said for Brunetto's poem "Il Tesoretto." This describes an imaginary journey of the sort which had delighted mediæval minds before Dante raised the impossible conception to sublimity. The poet of "Il Tesoretto" discourses with Nature, personified as a stately dame, on science; seeks philosophy; goes to Montpelier to make a confession of moral theology, and is last seen on Olympus in the company of Ptolemy the astronomer. In spite of the lofty ideals which he appeared in this composition to entertain, when Brunetto died after some years of exile, in Florence in 1294, he left a very mixed reputation as a great philosopher and a still greater sinner.

The vices of this dry old pedant were seemingly of the furtive order, but a singularly frank pleasure-seeker was the Sienese poet, Folgore da San Gemignano. He abandoned the beaten path of chivalrous love to celebrate the delights of good living, of banquets, hunts, riding parties and dances, all of which took place at splendid villas, or within the frescoed walls of still more splendid palaces, and formed the favourite diversions at the end of the thirteenth century of a certain "joyous company" of Sienese, to whom there is a disdainful allusion in the twenty-ninth canto of the "Inferno." This "joyous company" consisted in twelve noble youths who, having heard in a sermon the announcement that the end of the world was near, retired, perhaps in ironical imitation of friars, to a common dwelling, each one carrying with him a sum of eighteen thousand florins which was to be spent for the general enjoyment, any instance of purely personal expenditure being punished with instant expulsion. They passed their days in feasting and merriment, affording a theme for Folgore's muse, and to posterity a glimpse of those early times when Italian nobles already ate off gold and silver plate, and slept on silken couches beneath coverings of fur.

Another poet who sang the life of Siena in a very different strain was Cecco Angiolieri, a tragic spirit, generated as he said by grief and trained by melancholy. According to Signor Bartoli, Cecco was a forerunner to some extent of Rabelais and Swift, of all the men in short who laugh that they may not weep. He led a wild unhappy life, and poured out all the bitterness of his soul in cynical, indecent verse, wherein real suffering sometimes breaks through the satire.

One of the earliest of the many delightful and vivid annalists of Italy was Caffaro, the Genoese, who, as has been already mentioned, was an eye-witness of the scene between the Archbishop of Pisa and the Pope, when the latter, about 1120, had summoned a Lateran Council to settle the eternal differences between Genoa and Pisa concerning Corsica.

Caffaro was more of a diplomatist and man of the world than the Florentine, Giovanni Villani, who began his chronicle after the Jubilee of 1300, when, being a visitor to Rome, he had first felt the historical spirit stir within him. His records cease at the year 1346. Two years later he died of the great plague, and his brother Matteo continued the chronicle. He died in turn of the plague, in 1362, and the work was then taken up until 1365, by his son Filippo. Of these three Giovanni is by common consent the greatest.

Dino Compagni's delightful narrative is like a genre picture, being an account of the brief period which embraced the revolution of Giano della Bella and the rise and struggles of the Neri and Bianchi, and although some recent German critics have endeavoured to prove that the work is apocryphal, counter arguments are not wanting.

We left true poetry with Cino da Pistoja, and return to it now to make a brief and necessarily inadequate mention of Dante Alighieri.

THE DIVINE COMMEDIA.

The "Vita Nuova" is generally accepted as the history of the poet's love for Beatrice Portinari, whom he saw first, when he was nine and she a few months younger, at a festa in her father, Folco's house, where she appeared, a flower-crowned, golden-haired child, clad in crimson raiment. How years elapsed before he met her again, and then only casually, how she married and died, are facts related in exquisite verse often obscure in meaning, but of poignant beauty. No description can give any idea of its mysticism, its purity, tenderness, and passion. To be appreciated it must be read.

A long time from these early days had elapsed, and Dante was in exile when he wrote the "Divina Commedia," or, rather, continued it, for the first six cantos are said to have been composed before the year when he was banished from Florence.

The poem begins in March or April, 1300, when in a gloomy forest, supposed to be the tangled path of sin and error, Dante sees the gleaming peak of a mountain, and is about to climb it when deterred by the apparition of three (allegorical) beasts of prey.

He has sadly renounced the enterprise when Virgil, "his voice hoarse through long silence," suddenly appears, and inspires the wanderer with fresh courage by the promise of a future deliverer (the mysterious "Veltro" or greyhound, whose identity is still not established by the commentators), and proposes a journey through Hell, Purgatory, and Paradise.

In the first circle, where are the Elysian Fields, Dante sees the august of old, heroes and noble women of antiquity, with Homer, Horace, and Aristotle, the master of those who know ; in the second, he faints with the pity inspired in him by Francesca and Paolo, driven through the thick black air by a storm that never ceases ; in the sixth, he beholds Farinata degli Uberti and Cavalcante Cavalcanti in the burning tombs of the Heresiarchs, and to Cavalcante's pathetic question, "Where is my son? Why comes he not with thee?" Dante can but answer in words that show his friend, Guido, is dead.

The vision grows ever in intensity as it continues, till the wanderers reach the lake of ice where traitors, like Ugolino of Pisa, are thrust into frozen pits. A piercing blast blows for ever on this lake, caused by the fanning of the wings of Lucifer, sovereign of that dolorous region, a monster with three heads, who unceasingly devours the three great traitors—Judas Iscariot, Brutus, and Cassius.

On emerging from the Inferno, Dante and Virgil behold the stars of morning, and the opening lines of the "Purgatorio" have a peace and a freshness as of dawn. Among the spirits whom the poet meets in the region of expiation and hope is Casella, an early friend, of whom but one insufficient, yet charming, record exists, in a note to a madrigal by Lemmo di Pistoja, to the effect that the words had been set to music by Casella. Him Dante entreats for a song as of old, and he lifts up his voice in a hymn of such sweetness that all his companion souls cannot choose but linger to listen.

Sordello, too, is in Purgatory, and guides the journeyors to the valley of fair colours and sweet odours, where is gathered a company of kings. In the same world of redemption is Forese Donati, brother of the great Corso, who relates in sweet and touching words that Nella, his "little widow," is curtailing his punishment by her unceasing prayers on earth. Dante comes at last, at sunset, to the threshold of a Fiery Furnace, through which he must pass before he can behold Beatrice in Paradise. This purifying trial over, he presently enters the Earthly Paradise and its flower-decked meads where Matilda, a lovely and gracious figure, walks, gathering blossoms and singing evermore. She leads Dante yet further on his way, till he sees Beatrice white veiled and clad in a green mantle over a robe the colour of flame. At this point Virgil vanishes wordless, and Dante ascends to the real Paradise.

This pilgrimage is a journey through the starry heavens as conceived in the Ptolemaic system. The Earth is the centre of the Universe, and there are nine spheres, the Moon, Mercury, Venus, the Sun, Mars, Jupiter, Saturn, the Fixed Stars, and the Primum Mobile. Beyond all these is the Christian Empyrean. As Dante, guided by Beatrice, enters this at last, and his sight is unsealed, he sees the rose of Paradise, whose centre is a crystal lake and whose petals are the ranks rising, one above the other, of the elect. Here Beatrice suddenly leaves Dante, lapsing from his side as Virgil had done, and looking up he beholds her enthroned among the blest. St. Bernard takes her place, and shows the seer the company of the saints and the Mother of God. Beyond is the Ineffable, the Eternal Light, a vision which cannot be rendered by mortal lips.

Petrarca, or Petrarch, was born at Arezzo, in 1304, his father having been exiled from Florence at the same time as Dante. He was brought up partly in Tuscany and partly in Avignon. He was the first of the humanists, and with the prescience of genius foresaw and hailed the future revival of classic learning. He spent years in collecting manuscripts of Cicero, and employed copyists, or went himself, to transcribe any fragments of his favourite author that he could hear of. He was also the first to advocate public libraries, to appreciate the value of coins and inscriptions, and to plead for the preservation of ancient monuments. It has been well said by a modern critic that Dante remained intensely Florentine, while Petrarch was a true Italian. He dreamt of a united Italy and a Roman Republic on the old model. Dante would not be crowned poet except in his native city, but Petrarch eagerly ascended the Capitol, and accepted the laurel wreath from the Roman Senate. As for the "Canzoniere," in which he poured out his love in sonnets to Laura, it cannot be better described than in the words of Shelley, who speaks of these verses as "spells which unseal the inmost enchanted fountains of the delight which is the grief of love."

Petrarch first saw Laura in the church of St. Claire, at Avignon, on April 6, 1327, and adored her for twenty-one years, at the end of which time exactly, that is, on April 6, 1348, she died.

To close this brief and inadequate review of literature there remains now to speak of Giovanni Boccaccio, born in 1313 of a French mother, with whom his father became acquainted when residing in Paris on business.

Giovanni's own early life was passed in commerce at Naples, where he made love to the ladies at the court of the very dissolute Queen Joan. He was a middle-class sensualist, who had one elevating sentiment in his love for literature. A story, quoted by Filippo Villani, was current, that walking alone one day for amusement he came upon the tomb of Virgil, and from this moment vowed to dedicate himself to the Muses. Boccaccio's capability of disinterested admiration for genius is one of his most engaging characteristics. He had the liveliest, warmest appreciation of the genius of both Dante and Petrarch. He transcribed the "Divina Commedia" with his own hand, and lectured on it in public. With Petrarch he enjoyed unbroken friendship for twenty years, and it was by the advice of the lover of Laura, whom he always humbly regarded as his master, that he began the study of Greek. He accumulated stores of miscellaneous learning, and, in spite of his erotic ideals, lived the life of a student, whose quiet-going ways earned for him the nick-name of Giovanni della Tranquillita.

De Sanctis very aptly calls the "Decameron" "The Human Comedy," thus emphasizing the qualities which make it such a direct contrast to Dante's "Divine Comedy."

The plan of the work is well known. It opens with a description of the plague of 1348. To escape from the city where the streets were filled with corpses, seven young ladies, with three men, the youngest of

VIEW OF THE PIAZZA DEL DUOMO, AT PISA.

whom is twenty five, betake themselves to a luxurious villa, and there pass the time in relating stories, beautiful in form, instinct with knowledge of human nature, and very licentious. The " Decameron " was not Boccaccio's only work of imagination, but it is the most perfect and the best known.

Three styles of architecture existed before the Renaissance in Italy—the Lombard, the Tuscan Romanesque, and the Gothic. By " Lombard " must, however, only be understood the style of building which was common during the Langobard occupation. Examples of Tuscan Romanesque are the beautiful church of Samminiato above Florence (about 1013) and the Cathedral of Pisa (begun 1063). They are basilicas with round arches and colonnades of pillars or pilasters. Italian Gothic are the cathedrals of Siena, Bologna, and Florence, and the town-halls of Siena and Florence.

The architect of the Palazzo Pubblico, or town-hall of Florence, was Arnolfo del Cambio, who in 1298 received the order to erect a dwelling for the commonwealth. He had previously designed the cathedral, Santa Maria del Fiore, begun in 1294; the lovely bell-tower owed its creation to Giotto, but the dome is a much later erection, not having been begun (by Brunelleschi) until 1420.

Niccola Pisano was the first great Italian sculptor: and to his distinguished son, Giovanni, the world owes the Camposanto at Pisa and the façade of the Sienese Duomo. The first of the three bronze doors of the Baptistery at Florence was the work of Andrea da Pontedera, called Andrea Pisano, because taught by

WEST GALLERY IN THE CAMPOSANTO AT PISA.

Giovanni. Andrea in his turn trained yet another famous artist in Orcagna, poet, painter, goldsmith, architect, and sculptor.

In the first years of the fifteenth century, the Signoria of Florence determined, with the help of the Guild of Merchants, to complete the bronze gates of the Baptistery, and called upon the sculptors of Italy to compete for the work. Jacopo della Quercia, of Siena (born 1374), Ghiberti (born 1378), and Brunelleschi, of Florence (born 1379), presented their designs. Donatello, younger than any of them, having been born only in 1386, some sixteen years before the competition, was invited, it was said, to be the judge. For a long time the choice remained uncertain between Ghiberti and Brunelleschi, but the latter, feeling himself really inferior to his rival, generously withdrew. Ghiberti began the work in 1403, but finished the second gate only in 1452.

To Jacopo della Quercia, besides some celebrated bas-reliefs on the façade of San Petronio in Bologna and other works, we owe the beautiful recumbent figure of Ilaria del Carretto on her tomb in the Cathedral of Lucca.

Space forbids anything like a complete enumeration of the many works of Donatello. Suffice it to mention his reliefs of dancing boys at Prato; a similar series intended for the organ-loft in the Cathedral of Florence, and now preserved at the Bargello, and the St. George of Orsanmichele, Florence.

It is almost impossible to name Luca della Robbia without being betrayed into enthusiasm,

CHURCH OF SANTA CROCE. MONUMENT TO CARLO MARSUPPINI.

and yet a bare and passing mention of him is all that is possible here. His compositions are entirely in glazed terra-cotta work, white on a pale blue ground ; and in this line he may truly be said to have been unique, as the taste of his followers, Andrea, Giovanni, Luca II., Ambrogio, and Girolamo della Robbia, was far less pure and perfect than the master's own.

There are four sculptors all younger than Luca della Robbia who present themselves to the mind in a group. They are Matteo Civitale (a Lucchese), Mino da Fiesole, Benedetto da Majano, and Antonio Rossellino. The last named built, in 1427, the perfect and pathetic funeral monument to the young Cardinal of Portugal, which is one of the treasures of the Church of Samminiato.

Another famous designer of tombs was Desiderio da Settignano, who may be studied at Santa Croce in the fine sepulchre of Carlo Marsuppini, Chancellor of Florence, who died in 1455.

As well as a sculptor, Benedetto da Majano was an architect. In 1489 he began the magnificent fortress-looking palace of the Strozzi family in Florence. The commission to design the Palazzo Riccardi was given by Cosimo to Michelozzo some sixty years earlier; and in 1425 the basilica of San Lorenzo was designed by Brunelleschi, who also gave the plans for the great Pitti Palace, as well as for the church of Santo Spirito, built in 1470, only when the master was dead. San Lorenzo has been described as "a masterpiece of intelligent Renaissance adaptation."

CHAPEL OF THE MADONNA DELLA SPINA, PISA.

Great among Florentines was Leo Battista Alberti, the versatile and many-sided, who built the lovely Palazzo Rucellai, conspicuous even in a town which is all beautiful.

In these few notes no adequate idea can be given of Tuscan painting. Already in 1267 Cimabue was renowned for his Madonna, which now hangs in the church of Santa Maria Novella, and was hailed as marking a new epoch in art—the emancipation of the painter from the lifeless traditions of an effete school. The next great (and by far the greater) painter, Giotto Bondone, was born at Vespignano in 1276. Specimens of his work are to be met with in almost every Italian city. He painted portraits of Dante, and Brunetto Latini, and Charles of Valois, on the walls of the Bargello, adorned two chapels in Santa Croce with frescoes, and is known to all pilgrims to Assisi by his representations of the life and the allegories of St. Francis.

To Orcagna, who painted the frescoes of Death and Hell, Heaven and the Last Judgment in the Strozzi Chapel of Santa Maria Novella, were long attributed the strong, terrible, dantesque panels in the Camposanto at Pisa, but these are supposed by Crowe and Cavalcaselle to be the work of Ambrogio and Pietro Lorenzetti, who were Sienese.

Siena had an artist even earlier than Cimabue in Guido, whose Madonna in the church of San Domenico was dated 1221. A greater painter in the same bright, lovely, yet unfortunate, little city was Duccio di Buoninsegna, who died about 1320. His Majesty of the Virgin, when completed, was carried in procession to the Duomo, accompanied by all the clergy and prominent citizens of the town, followed by the rest of the population, men, women, and children.

STUDY BY BENOZZO GOZZOLI, IN THE UFFIZI GALLERY, FLORENCE.

Simone Martini, better known as Simone Memmi (born 1283 at Siena, died 1344 at Avignon), painted a portrait of Petrarch's Laura, and, like Giotto, left specimens of his art in many parts of Italy.

The Palazzo Pubblico of Siena has an immense composition of his—The Enthronement of the Virgin.

Returning to Florence at the very beginning of the fifteenth century, we find the wonderful youth Masaccio, who, in his twenty-seven years of life, painted frescoes wherein all succeeding artists, not excepting Raphael, found some lofty inspiration. Born at San Giovanni in 1402, he died at Rome in 1429. The frescoes of the Brancacci Chapel in the church of the Carmine at Florence, painted almost entirely by his hand, prove the existence of a genius far in advance of his greatest contemporaries. We can but enumerate various other Tuscan painters, such as Paolo Uccello, Piero della Francesca, Fra Angelico, Benozzo Gozzoli, Fra Filippo Lippi, Sandro Botticelli, not because there is little to say about them, especially the second and the two last named, but because there is too much. Domenico Ghirlandajo died at the age of forty-nine in 1498, the very year that has been described as the beginning of the Renaissance. His art is vigorous, uninteresting, and, technically speaking, consummate, although deficient in colour and imagination.

Among the great Tuscans was Luca Signorelli, born in Cortona in 1441. Vasari says of him that "even Michaelangelo imitated the manner of Luca, as every one can see." He must be studied, to quote a recent writer, in a "gloomy chapel in the Gothic Cathedral of that forlorn Papal City (Orvieto)— gloomy by reason of bad lighting, but more so because of the terrible shapes with which Signorelli

STUDY FROM THE LIFE, BY LIONARDO DA VINCI, IN THE UFFIZI GALLERY.
(*After a Phototype by Alinari.*)

LEONARDO·
VINCI

From the Original Drawing by Leonardo da Vinci.   Engraved by F. Bartolozzi R.A. Historical Engraver to his Majesty.

IN HIS MAJESTYS COLLECTION.

Published as the Act directs Sep.r 1, 1795 by I. Chamberlaine.

has filled it." Like Giotto, Orcagna, and Michaelangelo, Luca felt the influence of Dante.

Leaving Fra Bartolommeo, Cosimo Rosselli, and Mariotto Albertinelli unnoticed, we come to Lionardo da Vinci, the natural son of a Florentine notary, in whom says Vasari, " extraordinary power was joined to remarkable facility, a mind of regal boldness and magnanimous daring." His greatest works have unfortunately perished: even the Last Supper is a wreck, and when the student has extracted the final fragment of meaning from that, he must turn to the master's studies and sketches.

XXI.

FLORENCE AND GENOA IN THE FIFTEENTH CENTURY.

GOVERNMENT by an intelligent oligarchy had now given the best results of which it was capable in Florence. Founded in 1382 by the victory over the Minor Guilds, consolidated after the exile of the Alberti, further strengthened by Maso degli Albizzi, who increased the proportion of armed citizens in 1393, it had held the power of the Visconti for forty years in check, had conducted two wars to a favourable issue, and had acquired Pisa, Leghorn, Arezzo, and Cortona for cash.

All this had been accomplished by sheer force of will in the governing few, for no abuses had been reformed, and tyranny still reigned triumphant.

The Minor Guilds, although nominally still participant to a small extent in the administration, were shorn of influence, and, in fact, only continued to exist politically by attaching themselves to members of the Major Guilds.

The truth seems, however, to have been that the guilds themselves were rapidly becoming insignificant. In Florence there were now only rich and poor, and the need of capital for wide-reaching commercial enterprises reduced the social status of the smaller traders, and concentrated authority in the hands of a few. Even the Guelph party was rapidly becoming a dead letter. The Ottimati would have liked a form of government similar to the Venetians; but circumstances and the character of the Florentines themselves were equally opposed to such an institution.

The Doge's office in Venice was of old growth. Set above the ambitions of the hour and the aspirations of the populace, it was an incarnate principle of order, while the government of Florence owed all that it had achieved to its elasticity. The nobility of Venice was a patriciate imbued with the sentiment of caste, and associated for a long period with the city's special form of administration, but in Florence, as we have seen, a nobility only existed to be uprooted.

Venice had few home industries, but an extensive carrying trade, and its wars had been on the whole exterior struggles by no means involving the growth or constitution of the republic.

The commerce of Florence, on the contrary, was based on its manufactures, and its wars had been first for self-assertion, and then for self-preservation.

The populace of Venice was chiefly seafaring; peaceable, and docile when on land, and anxious for repose; but even had it been otherwise the waterways of the city were not favourable to popular risings.

In Florence every house was a fortress, and

bristled with armed retainers; every Piazza formed a meeting place into which the populace could pour at the first sound of the tocsin, and the walls made a prison inside which the hostile factions shut up together irritated one another by forced contact. Venice, sea girt, fantastic, mysterious, with the stealthy lapping of water for ever against its walls, suggested secrecy and escape; a blow in the dark, a noiseless flight, and the lagoons for a refuge. Its conditions, therefore, were opposed to revolution, but eminently adapted for a narrow and conservative government founded on monopoly, and upheld by pride and wealth.

The era of government by one man in the Tuscan Communes had now fairly begun.

In Siena Antonio Petrucci commanded, while Paolo Guinigi, the husband of Ilaria del Carretto, had succeeded in establishing himself as tyrant of Lucca, under the title of Captain and Defender of the people. On October 28, 1421, the Doge Tommaso Campofregosi, unable to make head against hostile factions in Genoa, allowed that town to be incorporated by Filippo Maria Visconti with the Milanese dominions; and Florence, alarmed at the prospect of a sovereign prince in North Italy, whose ambition threatened the independence of every commune, engaged troops, under Pandolfo Malatesta, to make war on Visconti. An alliance with Venice and several other towns was also concluded; and, thanks partly to these efforts, the designs of Filippo Maria were checked, and Florence, having picked a quarrel with Lucca, was able to turn her arms against that town, beginning a siege which it was hoped would end in possession, but the Florentine feeble captain, the Count of Urbino, was defeated by Piccinino ostensibly despatched by Genoa, but in reality by Filippo Maria, to the aid of the beleaguered town, and the long-cherished dream of annexation remained a dream still.

Paolo Guinigi had been deposed by a conspiracy in Lucca some little time previously to these events, and died in the fortress of Pavia (where he had been handed over to Visconti's tender mercies), in 1432, at the age of fifty-nine.

Within the walls of Florence meanwhile intrigues were seething and events rapidly concentrating to the point at which Cosimo de' Medici, without sovereign power, was to be practically lord of all.

The head of the Ottimati was Rinaldo degli Albizzi, but he was not a great character, and in any case would have been powerless to free the mass of the Florentine citizens from the far-spreading yet invisible toils which Cosimo, by means of his great wealth, had dexterously gathered round them. As a desperate expedient the government succeeded in exiling him and his brother Lorenzo, but it was a fatal move, which only brought Cosimo's power and influence into stronger relief. With his unfailing astuteness he chose Venice as his place of exile; was welcomed there like a prince; with princely munificence ordered Michelozzo to build the library of the Benedictine monks of St. George; and led a life of ostentatious culture in the midst of humanists and scholars. In vain Rinaldo clung to a power

MEDAL OF COSMO DE' MEDICI.

(*From Die Italienischen Schaumünzen des Fünfzehnten Jahrhunderts.
(1430–1530.) Von Julius Friedlaender. Berlin, 1882.*)

which had never fairly been his, and was now fast slipping from his grasp; he had to bow to the inevitable at last and order the recall of his enemy; and from the year 1434 the history of the Commonwealth of Florence became the history of a house.

There is a positive fascination in watching Casimo's gradual and noiseless monopoly of power. Cool and wary, utterly ruthless when necessary, he recoiled before no measures which could strengthen his own position; and, where his interests were concerned, he seems to have possessed an unique faculty of penetrating to the secret sentiments of men. Against his enemies says Guicciardini, and against those whom he suspected of being his enemies, he used the public taxes as he might have done a dagger. He filled the Borse with the names of his creatures (and all his countless creditors were such), ordered them to assess the taxes, and gratified his own resentments and his own greed while allowing them to gratify theirs.

What is really interesting is not the moral turpitude of himself and his tools, but the complex, refined, and highly evolved environment in which they lived, and where everything in the absence of traditional authority seemed reduced to a fortuitous interaction of human interests and pure intellectual force.

After the revolt against the French domination, the Marquis of Montferrat had been named Captain of Genoa, but he soon met with the same treatment as Boucicault. In vain the best of the Genoese endeavoured to endow the office of their Doge with the same stability as prevailed in Venice; every effort was wrecked on the shifting quicksands of faction.

About 1412 Genoa engaged in a finally successful but exhausting war with Alfonso of Aragon, who had seized Corsica, and on repossessing that suddenly surprised Florence by the offer of the long-coveted port of Leghorn. Florence had galleys now, and longed to be a naval power, so its government lost no time in concluding the bargain, and on the 30th of June, 1421, finally acquired Leghorn for one hundred thousand florins.

It was shortly after this that Campofregosi handed over Genoa to Filippo Maria, who undertook to preserve intact the municipal liberties of the commune, and appointed Carmagnola governor.

On the 5th of August, 1435, Genoa had the immense glory of defeating Alfonso of Aragon in a naval battle off the island of Ponza, where the fleets of the republic were outnumbered by two to one. The fight lasted ten hours, at the end of which time every Aragonese vessel but one had been captured, and Alfonso, after inquiring the names and ranks of the different Genoese commanders, surrendered his sword to Jacopo Giustiniani, whose family ruled over Chios. Filippo Maria Visconti saw this victory of his vassal with an uneasy eye; and in order to defraud Genoa of some visible marks of its triumph, ordered Alfonso to be sent to Milan, where he was received with every mark of respect. He also ordered the Genoese to prepare six battle ships for the purpose of conveying the captive king and his courtiers back to Gaeta; and thereby put the culminating touch to the angry disappointment of the victors.

Francesco Spinola, on the 27th of December, 1435, placed himself at the head of a determined body of insurgents, who, attacking the Milanese garrison, forced it to surrender. Savona followed the example thus set, and with the single exception of Castelletto, which held out for a few months, all the castles occupied by the Duke's forces capitulated. Genoa thus recovered its liberty and appointed a Balià, or provisional government of six to revise its laws and "reform" its constitution. At this point for the moment we must leave it again and return to Florence, where through all the chance and change of critical and varied years Cosimo worked unremittingly and unostentatiously at the consolidation of his power. He had no court or guards; he feigned to live as modestly as the least unpretending of his subjects, and allowed petitions and protestations to be addressed to the Signoria, while himself alone giving effect to them by making the Priori his tools. He tried to appear as conciliating everybody, even upholding with false hopes of return the exiles who, he had determined, should never see Florence again. Very characteristic is the speech he made to Luca Pitti: "You pursue the infinite; I, the finite. You lean your ladders against heaven; I rest mine on earth, so as not to fall in trying to mount too high."

Money had been and remained the root of Cosimo's power. Contemporary statistics are extant which give an approximate idea of the wealth of the Medici. Between 1434 and 1471 they disbursed in alms, public works, and taxes not less than 663,755 gold florins, four hundred thousand of which were paid by Cosimo alone. He lent Edward IV. of England one hundred and twenty thousand florins, and went security for him to the Duke of Burgundy for one hundred and thirty thousand florins more. It has been mentioned in a previous chapter how the lower classes in Florence desired an aristocracy which would build splendid palaces and villas. Cosimo understood this, and founded the convents of San Marco and Santa Verdiana and the church of San Lorenzo. It was by his order also that the Riccardi Palace arose, and in the villas which he built outside the town, at Fiesole, Cafaggiolo, Trebbio, and Careggi, he had, as Machiavelli said, four residences worthy of a king rather than of a private gentleman.

A year hardly passed that he did not spend fifteen thousand to eighteen thousand florins in building alone. The Riccardi Palace cost sixty thousand florins; San Lorenzo seventy thousand; eighty thousand the convent at Fiesole, and half as much went to the construction of San Marco. Naturally such evidences of wealth excited the envy as well as the wonder of contemporaries, and Cosimo was freely accused of peculation in the public treasury; but Cavalcanti makes the remark that "nobody said anything when he supplied the commune with far larger sums than those mentioned (as taken by him)." He was probably just as cool and calculating in his charities and public expenditure as in everything else, and was neither beneficent, lavish, nor pitiless at any time without a purpose. For the rest his far-seeing financial views are proved by the fact that he helped to create and develope many commercial houses which depended more or less upon his own. In this way he improved the position of families like the Sassi, the Portinari, the Benci, and Tornabuoni, and allied himself through his son Piero by marriage with the last named.

All these men became not his rivals, but his coadjutors, and had an interest, only less than his own, in preserving Florence from revolution and consolidating the Medicean power. But the misery of the population was great. "We do nothing but pay," wrote Alessandra Macinghi Strozzi, and goes on to observe that the excessive taxation could no longer be justified by the war budget, since the country was at peace. All who opposed Cosimo soon found that they did so to their cost, for they were ruined by the arbitrary taxes from which the supple and privileged few alone remained exempt. The once wealthy Pazzi were brought to the verge of ruin, and only saved themselves by matrimonial alliances with the powerful house in whose breath Florence now had its being.

The system of the Medici, infamous, but, one is inclined to think, inevitable, made also some noble victims, one of the most interesting among whom is the humanist Giannozzo Nanetti. When twenty-five years of age he quitted commercial life, and establishing himself in the exquisite solitude of his garden in the quarter of Santo Spirito, for nine years never left that umbrageous and perfumed retreat. There he gave himself up to study, and mastered Hebrew, Latin, and Greek. Already the enthusiasm for learning which was to distinguish the Renaissance had begun, and Giannozzo's polished orations won him universal celebrity. Whenever he was sent as ambassador he was received like a prince of royal blood. The brilliant Alfonso listened to him in a statue-like immobility, and Venice was warned by its ambassador that it would be eternally dishonoured by sending a less eloquent representative to congratulate Nicholas V. on his accession. Giannozzo also enjoyed the reputation—difficult to deserve, but still more difficult to acquire in the midst of a cynical, observant, and brilliant society—of being absolutely incorruptible, but because he sympathized neither with the views nor the methods of Cosimo he was ruined by taxation.

He retired to the Court of the Pope, who gave him a salaried post; and eventually, when Nicholas was dead, went to Naples to his admirer, Alfonso, and died there on the 26th of October, 1459.

In 1458 Cosimo's authority was further increased by the renewal for five years of the Balià or Board which when he was recalled had been appointed with special powers to "reform the State."

The ability of Cosimo enabled him to see how all the old institutions were decaying; how the Standard-bearer of Justice had begun to have less and less power over the Podestà; how the Captain of the People had become merely the Commander of the Palace Guard, and the Executor of Justice was reduced to the condition of a mere headsman: and instead of making chivalrous but useless efforts to revive the corpse of communal independence, he erected his own power in the place of that which had vanished.

PITTI PALACE, FLORENCE.

When he and Piero, both ill and generally resident in the country, were absent, their work was done for them by Luca Pitti, a violent, ambitious, commonplace man, who could imitate the methods of the Medici with safety and success, because the Medici after all were there in flesh and blood to back him up.

One of the ways in which he copied his models was to build himself magnificent residences, a villa at Rusciano and the palace which still bears his name.

In 1464 the shadows of death began to close round Cosimo. In the year previous he had lost his favourite son Giovanni; and as Piero was always an invalid, the hopes of the house were centred in the young grandson Lorenzo. Cosimo is said to have been saddened by the stillness and emptiness of these latter years, and great though were his crimes, ignoble though were his ambitions, one cannot refuse to feel the pathos of the remark attributed to him, that his house, the superb Riccardi Palace, was very large for so small a family.

He died at last on the 1st of August, 1464, at Careggi, alone but for that small family, as most of his household feared that he had the plague.

He had left directions that his funeral was to be a simple one and few invitations were issued, but the procession of voluntary assistants was immense.

From Careggi the body was carried first to San Marco and then to San Lorenzo by four slaves for there were many slaves in that brilliant Florence, which brought human as well as other merchandize from the East. Cosimo himself had a son, Carlo, whose mother was a slave, perhaps the very Circassian whom he bought at Venice, in 1427, for sixty-two gold ducats.

The death caused a great commotion all over Italy, and letters of condolence poured in upon the Signoria, and no praise seemed too great to be lavished upon this man who, as somebody said, "dressed like a peasant and lived like a king." His was one of the characters which make us most rebel at the inexorable silence of the grave, and long that it would yield up the enigma of a nature which the very curiosity of contemporaries, by transcribing every visible detail, has enabled to baffle all analysis, and to appear, for ever, irreconcilably commonplace and great.

XXII.

FLORENCE UNDER THE MEDICI *(continued)*.

PIERO'S brief tenure of power, which only lasted from 1464 to 1469, is chiefly interesting through the conspiracy to overthrow him wherein some conspicuous citizens took a part. Chief among these were Luca Pitti, Dietisalvi Neroni, Angelo Acciajoli, and Niccolò Soderini. They were discontented for various reasons: Luca Pitti because he felt himself superior in ability to the mediocre Piero, and was not disposed to play a subordinate part any longer; Niccolò Soderini because he was really honest, while the others joined in the movement for motives which are not so clear. Thanks chiefly to Luca's influence the Balià was suppressed, and the old method of choosing the public officers by lot restored; but this change from which the majority of the population expected much, without exactly knowing what, was hardly effected before an irreconcilable divergence of views among the conspirators themselves rendered it illusory. Of the four leaders the only one who really desired a popular government was Soderini; the others, and Luca especially, simply wished for a transference of power into their own hands. With a view to correcting the financial abuses Soderini, who on the first drawing of lots had become Standard-bearer, tried to see the accounts of the late government, but failed in consequence of Luca's opposition.

It soon became clear that with all his good intentions Soderini was not strong enough for his position, and his brother Tòmmaso said of him—" He has come in like a lion, he will go out like a lamb."

Very soon he found himself alone, while a semi-reconciliation had taken place between Piero and the other malcontents, the principal question still unsettled between them being which of two alliances was preferable, that of Milan (to which Piero inclined) or that of Venice. The old Sforza had died on the 8th of March, 1466, and opinions were divided as to the future of Galeazzo Maria, who was only twenty, and showed little natural talent. He was however supported by France, and Piero in spite of the mediocrity of which he is so freely accused, showed some of the family astuteness in appreciating at its full value the worth of this support. Moreover he and all his party felt that if Florence abandoned Galeazzo he would be powerless against the ambition and intrigues of Venice. The Republic of the Lagoons had of course given great encouragement to the conspirators against Piero, and placed Bartolommeo Colleoni, the last of the great condottieri, at their service. It was arranged also that Borso d'Este, the Duke of Modena, should send his brother Ercole with an army to support the rising in Florence, and become Captain-General of the liberated city. But these projects naturally failed from the moment that the chief conspirators became reconciled to Piero.

When in September (1466) new lots were drawn, the Standard-bearer of the government, Roberto Lioni, himself an adherent of the Medici, was able to bring over to the same side all the Priors who wavered. Francesco Neroni, brother of Dietisalvi, was put to the torture and confessed all he knew, including the secret agreement with Borso d'Este. Great excitement prevailed in the town: the majority were indignant with the conspirators, and pursued those suspected of favouring them with hue and cry through the streets. Several arrests were made, and terror took possession even of the innocent. Not so easily were the Medici to be got rid of; that was what everybody felt, and this sense of the inevitable together with fear of the consequences if it were not accepted, served to strengthen Piero's position. As for Luca Pitti he could no longer even find workmen to finish his great palace, and the obscurity which overtook him at the end of his life was so complete that the historians of Florence do not even record his death.

Piero was wise enough to put an end to the punishments before they could provoke any revulsion of popular feeling, and even went the length in apparent clemency of recalling some of the old proscribed, those whom his father had persistently excluded from grace. Among the men thus reinstated was Filippo Strozzi. Only the recent conspirators met with no mercy, in spite of the humility to which all condescended with the one proud exception of Niccolò

Soderini who went to Venice there to live amongst the Florentines who had been exiled when the Albizzi fell.

These exiles and Dietisalvi Neroni now placed their hopes in Colleoni whom Venice, while remaining ostensibly neutral, had, as already related, made over to them. He with an army composed of the enemies of Piero and the enemies of Florence, such as Ercole d'Este and the lordlings of Carpi, of Mirandola, of Forlì, of Anguillara and Faenza crossed the Po on the 10th of May, 1467, with the avowed intention of invading the Florentine territory. The Signoria had not lost time in taking measures of defence, and the force it had collected was numerically equal to that of the enemy.

But neither Colleoni, nor the Florentine captain, Federigo di Montefeltro, seem to have put much heart into their work; the war dragged on with no decisive result to either party, although Venice took advantage of it to seize the merchant ships of the Florentines and to stir up sedition among the Genoese against Milan.

Piero, however, was anxious for peace, and Venice perhaps perceived that little could be gained by war. The intervention of the Duke of Modena was solicited, and although Pope Paul II. interposed in favour of the exiles, on finding Piero determined to show no further mercy, he abandoned them to their fate. Venice restored the property it had confiscated, and peace was finally made in May, 1468.

A few more small conspiracies, real or feigned, cropped up and were punished by prompt beheadals;

and when on the 2nd of December, 1469, Piero died, he left to his sons, Lorenzo and Giuliano, an inheritance which, in spite of ill-health, supposed mediocrity of mind, and insignificance of character, he had at least done nothing to compromise or impair.

At the time of their father's decease the two Medici were very young, Lorenzo being twenty-one and Giuliano but sixteen. It must not be supposed that they succeeded without question to the lordship of the commune. Although Piero had been addressed by the humbled Dietisalvi Neroni with the title of Signore which up to that time had been reserved for the tyrants of Lombardy or Romagna, the friends of the Medici found it necessary to educate the citizens into acceptance of the predominance of the two young men. For this purpose on the very night of Piero's funeral five or six hundred adherents of the great house met in the church of Saint' Antonio, and Ridolfo Pandolfini opened the proceedings with a speech, in which he recalled all the benefits conferred on the Republic by Cosimo, and exhorted his hearers not to neglect to reap the harvest sprung from such good seed.

Here again the word Signore occurred, and it very soon became evident that the citizens were rapidly growing accustomed to its sound. Two days after the meeting, Lorenzo and Giuliano were formally invited to act as "chiefs of the state." Outside the commune they were universally recognized; every power in Italy, from Venice downwards, vying in protestations of friendship and marks of respect.

Lorenzo, in virtue of his seniority, naturally became

at once the most important of the two brothers, and partly through this circumstance, partly through his striking qualities, speedily concentrated all attention upon himself.

M. Perrens, like Sismondi, seems inclined to think that the title of The Magnificent applied to Lorenzo has less importance than is generally attributed to it, being, in fact, a common appellation in Italy. This is true, as what reader of Materazzo's wonderful chronicle but recalls with a thrill of admiration for the appropriateness of the designation his picture of El Magnifico, Astorre Baglione spurring his charger into the bloodstained Piazza of Perugia on the night of the "great betrayal"?

But if Lorenzo was at first only called The Magnificent in recognition of his supremacy, the instinct for the picturesque of his contemporaries doubtless saw in the adjective one that best described his peculiar characteristics. For he was very magnificent in his tastes, in his lavishness and his love of literature; and there must have been some unique ineffable quality in him which vanquished criticism, or the superlative designation that has clung to his name would have seemed ironical when contrasted with his almost repulsive appearance. His swarthy face, huge mouth, and ill-developed nose, were even suggestive of some insidious hereditary disease, and although he was tall, his movements were awkward, and he had not even the redeeming charm of a melodious voice.

But what fascinated the citizens, whom he helped to enslave, was that passionate appreciation of learning, that enthusiasm for the Greeks which he shared with such men as Giannozzo Manetti, Pico della Mirandola, Niccolò Niccoli, and others, men of the most opposite characters and divergent minds, in whom the new impulse worked the miracle of a faith, ennobling the base among them as far as they were capable of being ennobled, and transfiguring with ideal light the sublimer virtues of the good.

Lorenzo's own gifts as a poet show how cultivated and versatile and sensitive was his mind. And, since the political evolution of Florence was inevitable, the world may at least be thankful that the liberties of the commune did not die in gloom and decay, but were lighted by a refulgent dawn to their rest.

One attraction of the epoch which we are now approaching consists in its strange contrasts. Writers never tire of insisting on the contradictions between the refined culture and violent passions, between the enlightenment and the superstitions of the Renaissance; and of all the dark dramatic stories in which the period abounds none give a more vivid idea of what the Italy of those times was really like, than the great conspiracy which nearly destroyed Lorenzo on the threshold of his power. He had been less prudent than his father and grandfather, perhaps because he felt himself more secure, and at one stroke had created three powerful enemies for himself in Pope Sixtus IV., Girolamo Riario, the pontiff's nephew, and Francesco dei Pazzi, a wealthy Florentine merchant established in Rome. Sixtus wished to buy for Girolamo on his marriage the lordship of Imola, but Lorenzo, who desired to add that region to the territory of Florence, ordered Francesco dei Pazzi not to give security for

Obverse.   Reverse.

MEDAL OF SIXTUS IV.

(From *Die Italienischen Schaumünzen des Fünfzehnten Jahrhunderts.* (1430–1530.) *Von Julius Friedlaender. Berlin, 1882*).

payment by the Pope of the price of the sale. Out of these circumstances a certain bitterness arose which other events helped to increase.

The Pope had ordered another of his nephews, the warlike Giuliano della Rovere, to lay siege to Città di Castello, and reduce it to obedience to the Holy See. Lorenzo thought Città di Castello was too near Borgo San Sepolcro (lately acquired by the Florentines), and had no wish to see the dominions of the Church extended in that direction. Consequently he concluded an alliance with the Vitelli, who were the predominating family in Città di Castello, and secretly promised them help, thus again interfering with the plans of Sixtus, and at the same time creating enmities outside Florence. Also by suppressing the last remains of liberty within the commune he raised up a hostile faction which found its best supporters in the Pazzi.

On July 3, 1471, the Signoria, at the bidding of their new lord, named ten "Accoppiatori," who were empowered to appoint all future priors and the Standard-bearer of Justice, also forty citizens, who in their turn should elect a council of Two Hundred. Lorenzo himself belonged to the number of the Accoppiatori, who were appointed for life, and in this way became virtually masters of the State. The councils of the commune and the people were arbitrarily deprived of all their old authority, the only exception being that they still retained the right of assessing the taxes, and their powers were transferred to the new Council of Two Hundred, of which the members through the Forty were named in reality by the Accoppiatori.

Further revolutionary measures followed on this bold invasion of the rights of the people. The fourteen Minor Guilds were reduced to five, and the property of the suppressed corporations was confiscated for the public service. As none of the seven Major Guilds were suppressed, the object of the new order seemed to be a restoration of what might be called the merchant aristocracy, and this naturally excited a wide-spread dismay.

The Medici were now able, more completely even than before, to manipulate the revenues of the State. They could tax and exempt whom they pleased, fix the rate of interest to be paid by the Monte, raise the duty on wine and other things, and employ the public income for private ends. This state of things, if pleasing or tolerable to the majority, was insupportable to a large minority, which found adherents among the exiles and a friend in the Pope. At Rome there existed a centre of intrigue against Lorenzo, and chief among the exiles there gathered was Franceschino dei Pazzi. He belonged to a family of the old feudal nobility which had consented to descend into the ranks of the people ; and, having engaged in commerce, became renowned for its wealth and the importance of its commercial undertakings throughout Italy.

The Pazzi were essentially the children of their epoch ; they had all the sumptuous habits and cultivated tastes of the men of the Renaissance.

Piero dei Pazzi kept open house, and spent ruinous sums for copies of ancient MSS., books, and miniatures. He had the qualities which charmed the Florentine crowd, and when he returned from France, whither he had been sent in 1461 to congratulate Louis XI. on his accession, all the principal citizens and strangers resident at that moment in Florence crowded to the gate to receive him as he rode in. Perhaps it was this popularity which led Cosimo to ally himself with the Pazzi by giving his granddaughter Bianca to a nephew of Piero, but however this may have been, it eventually happened that the Pazzi, for some unexplained reason, became generally disliked, and this doubtless helped to make them enemies of the Medici. After the Imola business Lorenzo punished Franceschino's disobedience by ordering him to return to Florence ostensibly to answer certain accusations, but in reality to have him within reach. At the same time, a vexatious measure was constructed which especially touched Giovanni dei Pazzi, a brother of Franceschino's. He had married the only daughter of a wealthy Borromei, and expected to be left in sole possession of her riches, when suddenly a law was promulgated to the effect that in the event of intestacy females should be excluded from inheritance in favour of collateral males. And as the decree was perfidiously made retrospective, Carlo Borromei, an adherent of the Medici, found himself sole heir of a man who, dying before the new law was heard of, had naturally made no will in favour of his only child.

These facts were more than sufficient to make a conspirator of Franceschino, who seems to have possessed one of those restless, resentful, energetic natures which are cut out for sedition. He found two uncompromising allies in Girolamo Riario, who feared that at the death of Sixtus, Lorenzo might deprive him of the Romagna, and in Francesco Salviati, Archbishop of Pisa, who hated the Medici apparently for no other reason than that they had prevented his being raised to the archiepiscopal see of Florence. All through the year 1477 these conspirators had meetings, and directed their efforts to winning over the head of the Pazzi family, Jacopo, who was very reluctant to join in the plot. Renato, another brother, declined to have anything to do with it, on the ground that Lorenzo, who had no talent for finance, had already brought his affairs within a measureable distance of bankruptcy which, when it came, would entail his deposition. Renato's unpalatable advice to wait was naturally not listened to by the three men who were drunk with the strong wine of conspiracy, and even Jacopo yielded at last when Gian Battista Montesecco, a condottiere in the pay of Girolamo Riario, consented to join. The Pope, instructed as to the plot, gave his consent on condition of there being no bloodshed. It is difficult to imagine how the Holy Father could have expected this proviso to be observed in an age when men's lives were held so cheap, and there seems to have been some conscious irony in Girolamo's replying that if bloodshed were inevitable the Pope would doubtless forgive it. "You are a fool," answered Sixtus ; " I tell you I will have no murder." After which he dismissed the three conspirators with his blessing, and promised them the support of an army if necessary.

This matter of the Papal consent settled ; the plot proceeded apace. Jacopo dei Pazzi paid all his debts, consigned to their rightful owners all the goods which had been deposited in his warehouses, and, in short, made every preparation just as if he were on his deathbed. Renato retired to his villa, too prudent to join in the conspiracy, but too loyal to his people to denounce it. It was arranged that a pontifical army under colour of attacking Montone should assemble in the territory of Perugia, another force under Gianfrancesco di Tolentino, one of the Papal condottieri, was to await events in the Romagna, while Franceschino Salviati and Montesecco proceeded to Florence. At the moment when Lorenzo and Giuliano fell, the town was to be attacked from two sides at once. Some inferior accomplices were also enrolled ; two Salviati, one a brother and the other a cousin of the archbishop, Giacomo Bracciolini (the son of Poggio) one of those needy adventurers who are never absent from a conspiracy, Bernardo Bandini, Napoleone Franzesi, and finally two priests, Antonio Maffei and Stefano di Bagnoni. These various people met constantly together with their chiefs in the Pazzi villa at Montughi, and considering how many people were now initiated in the plot, and how intense their excitement must have been, it is a marvel that the secret should have been so well kept. Montesecco arrived punctually with the soldiers whom he was conducting ostensibly to Montone, and Lorenzo received him with the utmost cordiality. If he was not, as has been suggested, entirely deceived as to the condottiere's object in coming to Florence, he must at any rate have been far from guessing the truth.

With their chief ally now in their midst the conspirators had no need of further delay. In spite of the difficulties which the project presented, they had been compelled to make up their minds to strike both brothers at once. The chief point then became to find them in some convenient place together. Young Raffaello Sansoni, a nephew of Girolamo Riario, a mere lad, was to pass through Florence on his way to Perugia, of which place he had been appointed Cardinal legate. The occasion would be one of festivity, and Jacopo dei Pazzi invited his intended victims to meet the beardless prelate at Montughi; but Giuliano was laid up with a bad leg, and Lorenzo came alone.

Then a fête was given by Lorenzo himself in his villa at Fiesole, whither the conspirators came, only to find Giuliano again absent. It is thrilling to read of these disappointments, and how one day after another went down unmarked by the accomplishment of the fell intent.

Yet another banquet was to take place at Palazzo Riccardi on Sunday, the 26th of April (1478), but here again it was known that the ailing Giuliano would not be present. But he could not avoid attending high mass in the cathedral, and it was at last decided that the blow must be struck before the altar, at the moment when the priest turning towards the congregation should pronounce the words, "*Ite, missa est.*" At that moment a portion of the congregation always rose to go, and it would be easy for the assassins to advance upon the brothers, unobserved among the crowd. Moreover the bells of the cathedral would ring, and that was to serve as a signal to the Archbishop and to Giacomo Bracciolini to take possession of the Palace of the Priors. Franceschino dei Pazzi and Bernardo Bandini undertook the murder of Giuliano, who was likely not to be so easily despatched as his brother, owing to his habit of wearing a coat of mail beneath his clothes. Montesecco had been told off for the attack on Lorenzo, but at the eleventh hour drew back appalled by the sacrilegious task assigned to him. The want created by this characteristic scruple of the condottiere was supplied in a manner more characteristic still. The two priests were chosen in Montesecco's place because, as it was most cynically said, they were accustomed to holy places, and would feel less awe at them. According to Guicciardini this change of persons saved Lorenzo's life, the priests being bunglers at their unfamiliar task.

The day came and the vast cathedral was crowded. Lorenzo and his guest were already present, and mass had begun, yet still Giuliano tarried. Franceschino and Bernardo, in fear lest he should escape them, went to fetch him on pretence that his presence was necessary.

On their way with their destined victim to the church they passed their arms as though in play around him to discover if he were wearing his cuirass. Because of his suffering leg he had come out quite unarmed, not carrying even his hunting-knife, ordinarily his inseparable weapon, but of which the weight or the pressure would have been irksome. By so much therefore was his murderers' object facilitated.

Mass was sung through, and the words, "*Ite, missa est*," were spoken: Lorenzo and Giuliano had already risen from their knees and were moving freely among the crowd when Bernardo Bandini dealt a blow with a dagger at Giuliano's breast. The hapless young man staggered forward a few steps, then fell, and Franceschino springing upon him finished what the other had begun. At the same instant the two priests attacked Lorenzo, but only succeeded in wounding him slightly in the neck. He made a good defence, and his two assailants lost courage. Franceschino rushed to the rescue of his accomplices, followed by Bandini who killed a man on his way; but Lorenzo had time to take refuge in the sacristy, where his friends closed and barred the door. Antonio Ridolfi sucked the wound in the neck, and bandaged it. The uproar in the church reached their ears; they could hear cries and the clash of arms; but of Giuliano's fate they were still ignorant. Presently there was a knocking at the door and a call to come forth, but before Lorenzo was allowed to leave his retreat a young man mounted by a small stair-way to the organ loft from whence he saw Giuliano lying in his blood, but assured himself also that none but friends were in the church. Then Lorenzo was released, and, surrounded by armed men, traversed the short distance from the cathedral to his home.

That he was safe constituted a bitter disappointment to the conspirators, for they had never doubted of the success of their plot. Salviati, when the bell rung at the conclusion of mass, had gone with about thirty others to the Palazzo. He left some of his followers at the door, and mounting the stairs with the remainder, hid them in a room of which they accidentally closed the door, thus trapping themselves unawares.

The Priors were at table when the Archbishop, already wondering at the stillness of the streets where the tide of revolution should have been mounting, asked to speak with the Standard-bearer. This functionary Cesare Petrucci was a creature of the Medici. On entering the hall of audience to receive his visitor he was struck with his shifty air, with his incoherent words, and the way he coughed as if for a signal. Rushing into the corridor Petrucci called for help, and coming suddenly across Jacopo Bracciolini, had him arrested as a suspicious character.

All the exits of the palace were promptly guarded, and the conspirators seized one by one. They were either put to death within the palace or thrown alive from the windows to meet a ghastly end in their fall.

Already in the Cathedral Square the two priests had been cut to pieces; Bernardo Bandini had escaped outside the town; Franceschino, weak with loss of blood, had taken refuge with his uncle; and although Jacopo dei Pazzi was advancing towards the gate of the Croce with a hundred armed followers the conspiracy was at an end. The apathetic population would not rise to overturn Lorenzo, and such small crowds as did gather in the Piazza cried, "Palle," "Palle" (an allusion to the Medicean balls), as soon as the Standard of the Commune was seen floating on the roof of the Palazzo. "Nobody cried, 'Marzocco,'" says an historian, sadly. That rallying word of old Florentine liberties had died with the lips which uttered it in the ardent days of Campaldino. Even Jacopo soon saw that the game was up, and retreating through the Croce gate while it was still strongly guarded by his own men, he made the best of his way to the Romagna with two hundred adherents. His flight was the signal for a general revulsion of feeling in favour of the Medici, and Lorenzo came forth to show himself with his bandaged neck to an enthusiastic crowd. A terrible vengeance then began. Salviati, his two kinsmen, and Bracciolini, were hung from the windows of the Priors' palace, and with one exception his thirty followers were massacred.

Franceschino was dragged wounded from his bed, hurried just as he was to the palace, and hung up at the same window as the Archbishop. Even Renato, who had tried to escape disguised as a peasant, was arrested, and, in spite of his innocence, hanged, while his brothers were imprisoned in the dungeons of Volterra. Galeotto Pazzi was found in the church of Santa Croce, vainly hiding in the dress of a woman, and conducted to the Stinche. Montesecco, although he had refused at the last to strike Lorenzo and made a full confession, was beheaded. The execution continued until the 18th of May, and a hundred people perished in a few days. According to Luca Landucci, gravely contemplating these scenes from his grocer's shop at the corner of the Via Vigna Nuova, twenty persons were put to death on the very evening of Giuliano's murder.

Jacopo dei Pazzi was captured by some peasants in the Apennines, who brought him to Florence in spite of his prayers that they would kill him. He met an ignominious death upon the gallows, and at first was buried in the family tomb. But a tremendous downpour of rain ensuing immediately afterwards, it was supposed that heaven wished to show its wrath against the impious populace which had defiled consecrated earth with the body of a blasphemer reported to have invoked the power of hell with his dying breath. So on the 16th of May, three weeks after his death, the old man's corpse was disinterred and shovelled hastily into a dishonoured grave dug at the foot of the city wall.

But the next day some lads dug it up again, Landucci relates, and trundled it about the streets at the end of a rope tied round the neck. On reaching the Pazzi Palace where Jacopo had dwelt so long in splendour, they fastened the body to the bell-rope amid ironical cries of "Knock, knock!" Wearying of this amusement after a little, the boys detached it again and threw it into the Arno, where it was seen floating face upwards. Once again it was seized and hawked about, then consigned anew to the stream, under the eyes of the curious crowds assembled on the bridges, and amid a popular song improvised for the occasion. Finally, it was reported to have been seen at Bocca d'Arno still face upwards, thus becoming to the popular imagination a sort of bogey endowed with a horrible life of its own. The demure and peaceful grocer dwells unctuously on all these details, even adding a pleased allusion to the smell of the corpse "after so many weeks."

The Pazzi arms were obliterated from every public or private building which bore them. All the surviving members of the family were ordered to change their names, and it was decreed that anybody contracting a matrimonial alliance with the male descendants of Andrea dei Pazzi, Jacopo's father, should be deprived for ever of all offices and dignities. Insults were not spared to the unhappy family even when dead. It had long been a strange, grotesque yet impressive habit of the Florentines to paint the enemies of the commune upside down, and in strained attitudes on the walls of public buildings, and Sandro Botticelli was commissioned to cover the tower of the Bargello with frescoes, which in such guise commemorated the infamy of the Pazzi.

All possible pomp accompanied the unfortunate Giuliano dei Medici to his grave. His posthumous illegitimate son was brought up with Lorenzo's own children, and is known in history as Pope Clement VII.

In the hope that the conspiracy might have succeeded, the Pope, King Ferdinand of Naples (Alfonso's son), and the Republic of Siena had entered into an alliance against Lorenzo, and declared war for the purpose ostensibly of freeing Florence from his yoke; and on learning the execution of the Archbishop of Pisa, Sixtus immediately launched a Bull of excommunication against the impious persons who had dared to hang an ecclesiastic.

The Florentines recognized their crime, and responded humbly to the Papal denunciations, but nevertheless prepared to defend themselves against the armies of their enemies. In defending Lorenzo they were, by a strange irony of fate, defending their own independence as a State, for the project of Sixtus was to unite Tuscany to Lombardy, while Ferdinand seemed to have nourished the dream which had already haunted his father of annexing the Tuscan Communes to the kingdom of Naples. He therefore assisted the Pope with a view doubtless to some future arrangement.

The Florentines engaged as their captain Duke Ercole of Ferrara, and the campaign began. Various small places surrendered to the Papal and Neapolitan troops, and Ercole d'Este, who was singularly inefficient, did not succeed even in saving Monte Sansovino in the Val di Chiana which was one of the most important positions on the frontier.

Florence all this time was practically without allies, neither Venice nor Milan being sufficiently at leisure to afford any help. The danger which threatened Lorenzo was serious, when the luck which had attended him through life came again to his aid. Lodovico Sforza had usurped supreme power in Milan, and for ends of his own wished to break the alliance between Sixtus and the King of Naples, and by saving Florence to render useless the league between the Tuscan republic and Venice. Consequently he negotiated a truce, and Lorenzo went to Naples to treat for peace with Ferdinand. That sovereign exacted that the members of the Pazzi family who were imprisoned at Volterra should be set free; and that the republic should retain the services as captain of the Duke of Calabria, Ferdinand's son at a salary of sixty thousand florins a year. The object of this last condition was to enable the Duke to obtain possession of Siena, but Lorenzo made no difficulties, and peace was concluded on the 25th of March, 1480.

On returning to Florence, where he was received with enthusiasm, he proceeded to further strengthen his position by the creation of yet another Balià, composed this time of seventy citizens, whose authority was to override that of every other council in the already complicated machinery of the Florentine state. One of its first acts perhaps explains the chief object of its existence, for it employed the State funds in paying the debts of Lorenzo, who, always magnificent and always embarrassed, had much need of this assistance.

XXIII.

GENOA FROM 1435 TO 1488.

GENOA remained an irreconcilable enemy of Alfonso the Magnanimous all through the struggle between him and René of Anjou ; but no sooner was the ruin of the latter irrevocable than the republic, only momentarily diverted by foreign war from its factions, was rent anew by the discords of its citizens. Giovanni Antonio Fieschi entered the town by surprise. Tommaso Campofregoso was deposed, and eight "Captains of Liberty" were substituted for the Doge. This arrangement found favour for a month, at the end of which time the Doge was restored in the person of Raffaele Adorno. Civil war began within and without the town, and lasted on and off for four years, when another Campofregoso (Pietro) was made Doge, and his brother Commandant of the town.

In 1453 the republic sustained a great loss in Pera, the pearl of its colonies, which was taken by the Turks, and fearing that Caffa might meet the same fate, it transferred that settlement to the Bank of St. George, which continued to offer an example of stability and good government in strange contrast to the distracted councils of the State. Alfonso, whose enmity to Genoa became the more bitter the longer it lasted, continued to threaten Corsica and ravage the whole coast of Liguria, till at last the Doge Pietro Campofregoso called in the inevitable stranger, transferring to Charles VII. of France the lordship of Genoa in February, 1458.

The Duke of Calabria (John of Anjou) was appointed governor, but replaced by Louis de la Vallée, when on the death of Alfonso, John set off to Naples to dispute the crown of the Two Sicilies. For this expedition he obtained money from the Genoese, who, however, found the drain on their exhausted exchequer an almost intolerable source of suffering. Discontent, however caused, always reacted on the ruler of the town, and Louis de la Vallée made himself unpopular by favouring the nobles. They had been called upon to relieve the necessities of the republic by renouncing the privileges which exempted them from taxation. They refused and suggested that money should be raised by further duties on provisions. Straightway faction raised its hundred heads and the people clamoured for the Adorni and Fregosi who, surveyed from the flattering distance at which exile had placed them, appeared suddenly in the light of redeemers. The King of France unconsciously fanned the flame of popular anger by requesting the republic to arm some galleys for the war against England. Genoa had no quarrel with the latter country, and was anxious to avoid any step which might injure the many Genoese merchants established in London. Many days passed in discussion and growing bitterness, till one night when, as by a breath from the evil angel of sedition, the whole town sprang up armed. The Fregosi poured in at one gate, the Adorni at another; the French retired to the fortress of Castelletto, and then the Adorni and Fregosi turned upon one another. Two groups of people apparently never could find themselves face to face in Genoa without raising opposite war-cries and coming to blows. The insurgents were presently appeased by the mediation of the Duke of Milan, who desired ardently to drive the French away from Genoa, and furnished the arms and money necessary for dislodging Louis and his garrison from Castelletto. Charles VII., on his side, assembled a large army in haste and despatched it under the command of old King René. A battle took place on the heights above San Pier d'Arena, and ended in a complete victory for the Genoese. Two thousand five hundred dead were found on the field of battle, and many of the flying French, encumbered by their heavy armour, were drowned in trying to reach the fleet from whence King René had watched their disaster.

This really great triumph was celebrated in their own peculiar fashion by the Adorni and Fregosi who, the very same evening, had a battle of their own within the walls of Genoa.

Louis Campofregoso was made Doge, and although Louis de la Vallée still held Savona, the connection between the republic and the French was practically over, and from this year—1461—Genoa ceased to furnish any aid to the Angevins in the Two Sicilies.

For the rest the expulsion of the stranger brought no peace. Four years of anarchy followed in Genoa, culminating in a period of some months during which, murder, pillage, rape, became commonplaces, and everybody whose misery did not keep him chained to the doomed city, fled beyond its walls. The head and front of all these horrors was the infamous Archbishop Paolo Campofregoso, who had carried the Palace of the Commune by assault and had himself named Doge.

He was deposed, only to be restored, and reduced the republic to such impotence that all along the coast the subject towns revolted and raised the standard of the Duke of Milan. Sforza sent an army against Genoa which was joined by all the factions, by the families of Spinola, Adorni, Fieschi, and some malcontent Fregosi themselves. The Archbishop felt that he was not strong enough to resist, but, determined not to yield, he fortified Castelletto, left it in charge of his brother Pandolfo, and Bartolommea, the widow of his brother Pietro, then seizing four vessels which were in the port, he set out upon the seas to live as a pirate until such time as a fresh revolution should restore him to his ducal authority and his archiepiscopal mitre. After this, in April, 1464, Francesco Sforza was solicited to take Genoa under his protection on the same conditions as had been imposed upon the King of France.

In 1475 Genoa lost Caffa, which surrendered to the Turks, who put several senators and magistrates to death; sent fifteen hundred youths to Constantinople to be incorporated in the Janissaries, and drove the remaining Christian population away to Pera.

Caffa had belonged to Genoa for nearly two centuries, and had grown in population and wealth until it nearly rivalled the parent-city. It was the market for all the merchandize from the North—wood, wax, and furs—which were sold to Genoese merchants. Through the hands of this enterprizing race passed also the silks and cottons of Persia, the spices and dyes of Hindostan. The Khan of Tartary treated the Genoese with awe and respect, and consulted their wishes before naming the governor of the province. Now all this power and glory were over, and the domination of the republic in the Black Sea became a memory.

At the time that this misfortune overtook Genoa the town had actually enjoyed eight years of tranquillity. The Milanese still governed the republic, and Paolo Campofregoso was still pirating in the Mediterranean. But as soon as Galeazzo Maria succeeded to his father things changed. He was more careless of his engagements than his father had been, and caused the commune to tremble for its liberties. These fears seemed more than justified when the Duke ordered a line of forts to be built from Castelletto, where the Milanese had their garrison, to the seashore. A double wall was to cut the town in two parts which could be shut off one from the other and occupied separately at the will of the governor.

So grave an infringement of the liberties of the republic was not to be borne, and Lazzaro Doria ordered the works to be stopped. This act of energy met with universal approbation; but Galeazzo Maria at once prepared an army to punish it. Before he could carry out his plans, however, he was assassinated in the Basilica of St. Ambrose on the 26th of December, 1476, and at once all the factions in Genoa welcomed the opportunity of recovering the liberties of the republic with freedom to resume tearing one another to pieces.

Francesco Sforza had taken care to disperse the principal members of the warring families all over Italy, but new leaders were soon found among the Fieschi, who were consequently the first to appear in armed force outside the town, which they scaled by surprise, and where they endeavoured to excite a revolt.

Simoneta, who, together with the Duchess Bona, was ruling Milan during the minority of the young Duke, recognized the fact that the best way of pacifying the Genoese was to give them a native governor, and he offered the post to Prospero Adorno, who undertook to occupy it in the name of the Duke of Milan, and on the same conditions as had been accepted by Francesco Sforza. He was furnished with an army, and succeeded in establishing himself on the 30th of April, 1477.

In 1478 King Ferdinand of Naples, anxious to prevent the Duchess Bona from coming to the help of Lorenzo, suggested to Prospero to get up a revolt against the Milanese. Prospero welcomed the idea with avidity, created six Captains of Liberty, had himself proclaimed Doge, and gave the command of the Genoese insurgents to Roberto di San Severino. Bona sent troops to quell the insurrection, and a battle was fought in the defiles of the Apennines, seven miles outside Genoa on the 7th of August, 1478, when, after several hours of desperate combat, victory remained with the Genoese. But this brought but little satisfaction after all to Prospero who, having taken advantage of the situation to put several of his enemies to death, became suddenly unpopular, and, finding himself abandoned by his partizans, had to quit the town on the 26th of November, 1478, while Battista Campofregoso was proclaimed Doge in his stead. This brought back the Archbishop Paolo who, in spite of his career as a pirate, had been made a cardinal by Sixtus IV. and had not grown more saintly or less ambitious during his exclusion from his native town. He began intriguing again at once, and in five years had so matured his plans that he was able, unopposed, to arrest his nephew and have himself made Doge.

In 1468, Piero dei Medici had bought Sarzana from Luigi di Campofregoso for thirty-seven thousand florins; but Agostino, another member of the same family, had taken advantage of the preoccupations of the Florentine to repossess himself of the town and fortress, which he afterwards ceded to the Bank of St. George. This company also held Pietrasanta as security for a loan made to Lucca, and seemed but little disposed to part with either possession. This was intolerable to the Florentines, who at the first favourable opportunity despatched an army, which after some fighting recaptured both Pietrasanta and Sarzana.

These events cannot have been welcomed in Genoa, but no remedy now, mild or drastic, could cure the republic of its long disease of anarchy.

Some members of the Fieschi and Adorno families joined Battista di Campofregoso, who was panting for revenge, and together they organized an attack, at dawn (August, 1488), on the Doge's palace, and were only prevented killing Paolo by his precipitate flight to the citadel. Twelve citizens were then appointed to govern the town, and the first order they gave was to attack the citadel. The old cardinal with his wonted energy had rallied all the troops in his possession round him, erected barricades in the streets, occupied all the houses adjacent to the fortress with soldiers, and prepared to stand a siege.

The battles which ensued reduced Genoa to a condition of appalling desolation. Every palace in turn was attacked and defended with cannon, and whenever the besieged were beaten, they set fire to the house they were leaving. In the midst of carnage and flames the soldiers pillaged, and the distracted inhabitants, women and children, defended their property as best they could. At last the propositions which, during all this time, Lodovico Sforza had never ceased making, had to be partially accepted by the promoters of the revolution, none of whom were strong enough to stand alone; and it was agreed that Agostino Adorno should discharge the functions of Doge for ten years with the title of Lieutenant of the Duke of Milan. Paolo Fregoso was promised an annual sum of six thousand florins, while his bastard son Fregosino was to receive a pension of one thousand, until such time as the Pope should confer on him ecclesiastical benefices to that amount.

On these terms the old cardinal might have continued to remain in Genoa if he liked, but his fierce spirit would submit to no such humiliation, and on surrendering the citadel he went on board a galley and quitted Genoa for ever.

XXIV.

FLORENCE UNDER LORENZO DEI MEDICI
(continued).

THE dawn of the year 1481 found the Medici in a more exalted position than ever.

Lorenzo, with no statesmanlike views or lofty ambitions, yet possessed the ability peculiar to his family, and in which even the mediocre among them did not seem wanting, of piecing together authority by a system of patient astuteness. He had married his young daughter Maddalena, the "apple of her mother's eye," to Franceschetto Cybo, a middle-aged trifler, and a bastard of Pope Innocent the Eighth. The Pontiff had been forced, by this alliance, to give a Cardinal's hat to Giovanni, Lorenzo's third son, who at seven years of age had been tonsured, and at eight had entered into possession of four abbeys, one of which was the great foundation of Monte Cassino. In spite of these precedents Innocent would have liked to wait a few years before admitting the boy to the Sacred College, but his unsatisfactory son Franceschetto was dear to him, and for his sake he consented at last to a step

By a series of events too long to be related here in detail, Lorenzo had become the protector of Forlì, Imola, and Faenza, which gave him great influence in the Romagna. He had wished to establish Franceschetto Cybo as princeling of some sort, and had cast his eye upon the two first named of these towns, which were ruled over by Girolamo Riario, who, since the death of the Pope Sixtus IV., had lived in prudent retirement within his little state. Naturally, Lorenzo had no cause to love Girolamo, and he was suspected with some probability of being no stranger to the murder which presently removed the obstacle to Franceschetto's aggrandizement from his path. But Girolamo had left a redoubtable widow Caterina Sforza, an illegitimate daughter of the last Duke of Milan. She asserted herself with such vigour as to intimidate all the malcontents who wished to shake off the Riario yoke, and succeeded in having Ottaviano proclaimed in his late father's stead.

As for Faenza, there had been a moment when Florence, with great alarm had seen it offered by its tyrant, Galeotto Manfredi, to Venice. Such proximity of the Republic of the Lagoons to the territory of the Florentines would have been intolerable, but the danger was presently averted by another assassination, that of Galeotto himself, who fell a victim to a conspiracy headed by his wife Francesca Bentivogli, of Bologna.

The Bentivogli then manifested the intention of annexing Faenza, but the people of the town took possession of it in the name of the young Astorre Manfredi, and successfully invoked the protection of Florence.

Thus, partly by luck, partly by cunning, Lorenzo managed to build up a policy of equilibrium in which he lived very comfortably. Lodovico Sforza was indebted to him for a mediation which had prevented the Duke of Calabria from succouring Lodovico's dispossessed nephew. Pope Innocent VIII. and King Ferdinand of Naples, who had a quarrel of their own, had been reconciled by Lorenzo's interposition, and on all sides peace, if not good will, was assured.

Nowhere were princes and foreign ambassadors received with greater sumptuousness than in Florence. Lorenzo loved display as he loved poetry, art, and debauch. His tyranny was incapable of wide efforts for the public good, but it condescended to minute inspection of his subjects' domestic affairs. The alliances, the friendships, and undertakings of his fellow citizens interested him in the highest degree; and he built up secret associations mutually ignorant of one another's existence, and which neutralized the factions in the town without knowing that they did so.

Lorenzo's extravagance and the sums he spent on entertainments as well as more ignoble pleasures reduced him to the verge of bankruptcy, and in order to redeem his position he trafficked shamelessly in the finances of the State. This was the only way in which he could raise money, having inherited none of the commercial genius of the grandfather whom he nevertheless resembled in so many ways.

Lorenzo was indeed still nominally engaged in business, being among other things a partner in the bank of Francesco Sacchetti at Lyons, and having agents for his own house all over Europe. But he left everything to his subordinates, who profited by his negligence to live luxuriously at his expense and that of their creditors. Very soon Lorenzo had to borrow from his relatives, and even from Lodovico Sforza, besides resorting to every device, honest and dishonest, to keep himself afloat. He suppressed numbers of religious foundations, caused his soldiers to be paid by the Bartolini Bank in which he was a partner, but kept back 8 per cent. of the pay for himself, invented fresh arbitrary modes of taxation, and finally laid hands on the public dowries assured to young girls, by which, according to contemporary historians, many of these poor maidens were unable to find husbands and driven to lead immoral lives.

In August, 1490, Lorenzo had recourse to a measure which rendered his already absolute power more undisputed still. The Council of Seventy, although composed of his creatures, seemed to him too numerous to be handled any longer with the speed and dexterity which his embarrassments needed, consequently he suppressed it, and created a Commission of Seventeen of which he was himself a member. This Commission undertook to "reform" the finances. It pronounced that the currency was worn out, and ordered it to be received by the Treasury at one-fifth less than its nominal value. A new coinage was struck containing two ounces of silver to the pound and more valuable by one quarter than the old currency, and it was decreed that all taxes were to be paid in this, while the State continued to make its own payments with the old depreciated money. By this ingenious fraud the public revenues increased by one-fifth and the receipts of the commune rose considerably, but all the necessaries of life became much dearer and the people suffered. They suffered, protested, and did nothing. For, after all, the republic was at peace; no princely French adventurer, no tyrant in the North or South, no rival commune threatened its existence any more. The commercial classes if overburdened with taxes, at least could carry on their operations with a security long unknown, and they were gratified in their dearest, most immediate interests by the lavish expenditure of their master, whose royal hospitalities were "so good for trade." All writers, painters, poets, sculptors, and humanists also had good reason to praise Lorenzo's hospitality, and then there was the graduated income tax to persuade the lower classes that the rich paid far more than themselves, and to enrich the privileged Medicean partizans at the expense of less brilliant, less lucky or more uncompromising members of society.

By the various devices which have been described, Lorenzo succeeded in retrieving his position, and then apparently recognizing the fact that he had no genius for affairs, he withdrew as much as he could from the family business. He applied the sums which had been unscrupulously obtained to the purchase of land and houses in ruined towns and districts like Pisa where such property was cheap. He spent much time in the country (to his love of which his poems testify), devoted himself to agriculture and improvements, and in this way, at the expense of the Florentines, did much good in many places which the selfish policy of the republic had ruined. For instance, he revived the languishing University of Pisa, which perhaps owes such prosperity as smiles on it to-day to this enlightened conduct of a tyrant whose tastes were fortunately less ignoble than his aims.

The Italian Republics were always the scenes of dramatic contrasts, and it only seems a part of the general appropriateness of things that above the bustle of the workshops, the noise of the looms, the disputes of the platonicians, the quarrels of the humanists, the polished verses of Politian and Lorenzo's obscene Carnival lays, a voice should suddenly have resounded which startled like the trumpet note of Doom. Savonarola had come to Florence, and from the pulpit of San Giorgio d' Oltr' Arno was thundering forth his denunciations of a luxurious and perverse generation.

At first he found few hearers among the frivolous, free-thinking Florentines; but superstition and the fear of futurity slumbered beneath their impiety, and the Dominican obtained a hearing as soon as he began to prophesy. His predictions were of elementary simplicity; what insight into the secrets of the universe was needed to announce the approaching deaths of Lorenzo, already stricken with a mortal malady, or of the Pope and the King of Naples, who were both quite old? Nevertheless, the mere announcement that these things were to happen, stimulated the curiosity of a population whose active minds were ever agog for novelty. Then Pico della Mirandola detected the fire and force which broke fitfully through Savonarola's rugged discourse and urged Lorenzo to keep the monk near him in the Convent of St. Mark. Lorenzo himself was half-unwilling and half-fascinated, but he yielded at last and sent for Savonarola, partly perhaps as he might have sent for something rare and strange like a Greek manuscript; partly perhaps because he vaguely felt that the friar would achieve salvation for him.

Savonarola gave voice to the cries of malcontent, despairing souls, and disclosed vistas of consolation, as of vengeance, in his promise that the Church of God on earth should be purified and that Italy should speedily expiate her sins. Moreover, he was one of a long line of fiery preachers whose passionate words had at intervals roused society from an indifference to sacred things which was always partly feigned. Bernardino of Siena, Alberto da Sarteano, Jacopo della Marca, and Giovanni Capistrano, had in turn endeavoured to bring their hearers to a sense of the curse, of the mysterious personal expiation, worse than any torments of hell, which must befall those who lived in defiance of God's law. That was the argument which appealed most strongly to a world too steeped in scepticism and too highly cultured to believe any longer in eternal fires or devils with horns and tails.

Now came Savonarola, and predicted that the expiation should be not only for this man or that, for the fratricide or the robber of orphans or the ravisher of women's honour, but for the whole of the fair and splendid land, and the very grandeur of the prophecy seemed a kind of earnest of its fulfilment.

Nor can Savonarola's conduct in another respect have failed to impress the Florentine population. The majority lived in abject fear of Lorenzo or regarded him with an admiration only one degree less base, but the friar, when made Superior of St. Mark, refused to conform to the usual custom of paying a ceremonial visit to the tyrant in his palace. "I owe my election to God alone," he said; "and to Him I will render obedience." Lorenzo was indignant. "See!" he exclaimed, "a stranger comes to my house and he does not condescend even to visit me." Nevertheless he determined on a conciliatory behaviour; went to hear mass at St. Mark's, and walked afterwards in the garden; but not once did Savonarola leave his cell to bear him company.

Lorenzo sent rich gifts to the community, and these the Superior accepted, but declared in the pulpit that he considered himself under no obligation of gratitude for them. "A good dog," he said, "barks to defend his master's house. Let a thief throw him a bone to silence him, he will still bark, and bite the thief."

These insults did not enrage Lorenzo; on the contrary, they seem to have inspired him with a superstitious veneration, for when he was dying, in the first days of April, 1492, he sent for Savonarola. Three sins, it is related, lay heavy on his conscience— the money of which he had robbed dowerless girls, the vengeance wreaked after the conspiracy of the

Pazzi, and the ruthless sack of Volterra. At the end of the year 1471 that town, which was only in partial dependence on Florence, had chosen Lorenzo as arbitrator in dispute between the commune and the concessionaries of some mines. Lorenzo's decision was considered unjust, and the government of Volterra rejected it. But Lorenzo's own financial interests were at stake, and he sent an army to invade Volterra, which surrendered on condition that persons and property should be respected. The engagement was entered into only to be violated, and the town was sacked by the soldiers, who respected neither men nor women nor sacred things.

Now, as the grave opened before him, Lorenzo is reported to have repented of these great crimes, and to have sought absolution for them from Savonarola. "God is good and merciful," said the friar, "but to obtain His pardon three things are necessary. Firstly, you must have a great and vivid faith in the mercy of the Creator." "This I have," answered the dying Platonician. "Secondly, you must give back, or order your sons to give back, all that you have unjustly acquired." Lorenzo appeared surprised and sorrowful for a moment; then made an affirmative movement of his head. Savonarola rose to his feet, and towering to a height that looked unnatural to his terrified penitent, who seemed to shrink beneath the bedclothes, he said solemnly: "Lastly, you must restore their liberty to the people of Florence."

Lorenzo turned his face in angry silence away, and the friar left him without pronouncing absolution. Alas! what he had exacted was an impossibility.

Lorenzo might have restored his ill-gotten fortune, but he could not revive the dead freedom of Florence.

He died at Careggi on the 8th of April, 1492, in spite of the decoctions of precious stones which his doctors tried as a last resource to save him. He was only forty-four, but was worn out with hereditary disease and dissipation. His faithful friend Angelo Poliziano remained with him to the last, while Pico della Mirandola and Ficino were constant visitors. They admired, and Poliziano really loved, him; yet he died without leaving behind him the record of one truly magnanimous act.

XXV.

THE HUMANISTS IN FLORENCE, AND THE POETS AND HISTORIANS WHO GATHERED ROUND THE MEDICI.

THE first association of humanists in Florence was long anterior to the rule of the Medici, having formed round Luigi Marsili, the learned Augustine friar who lived in the convent of Santo Spirito. He died, aged sixty-four, in 1394, and was consequently a contemporary of Coluccio Salutati, the great collector of codexes and author of Latin treatises, who was the first of a long line of learned Secretaries to the Commonwealth of Florence.

Yet another indefatigable collector of ancient MSS. was Niccolò Niccoli, whose library was open to every student, and who joined Palla Strozzi in reforming and increasing the Florentine University or Studio. He died in 1437, at the age of seventy-three, leaving his books to his native city, a disposition in which he was munificently seconded by Cosimo de' Medici. Thus Niccolò's collection formed the first public library in Europe.

Conspicuous among the learned was Palla Strozzi, mentioned above, who contributed to the expense of bringing the Greek teacher Crisolora from Constantinople. He was arbitrarily exiled by Cosimo when already advanced in years; but found consolation for that misfortune, as for every other, in the study of his beloved ancients, and died, a lonely, patient, benign old man, at Padua, at the age of ninety-two.

The appointment of Crisolora brought about a veritable revelation of the Greek world of old to the Florentines who thronged to his lecture-room. To discover and possess Greek codexes then became the ambition of every cultured person, but the most unwearied explorer in this path was the celebrated Poggio Bracciolini, whose bitter disputes with a brother humanist, Filelfo, are among the most curious and least edifying of professional quarrels. He wandered half over Europe in pursuit of his hobby, even reaching England, where he found himself much out of place at Cardinal Beaufort's in the company of a swinish aristocracy. He had nevertheless the acuteness to note how these same coarse nobles were already far-seeing enough to recruit their ranks from the middle classes. Poggio was very unsparing in his attacks on the immorality of the ecclesiastical order to which, however, he himself belonged, and whose favourite vices he was careful to imitate.

An ardent dispute between two Aristotelians, Giorgio Scolaro and Teodoro Gaza, on one hand, and Giorgio Gemisto Pletone, the Platonician, on the other, awakened such an admiration for the Platonic doctrines in Cosimo de' Medici, that he founded the celebrated academy, first selecting as its future head a youth of eighteen, the son of a doctor in Figline, whom, with his usual penetration, he judged adapted to his purpose, and educated accordingly.

This youth was Marsilio Ficino, who, from the time that Cosimo found him to the end of his life, incessantly studied Plato and the Neoplatonists, on which subjects he wrote original treatises as well as making many translations from the Greek. He was really the soul of the Florentine Platonic academy, which lived and died with him. The meetings at which Lorenzo frequently assisted were held sometimes in summer in the forest glades of Camaldoli, while every year on the 7th of November, which, according to the Alexandrine tradition, was the date of Plato's birth and death, the associates assembled in Florence or at the Medicean Villa at Careggi to celebrate the anniversary with peculiar solemnity. Proceedings opened with dinner, followed by a philosophical dispute that wound up with an apotheosis of the Master. The Pazzi conspiracy disturbed these tranquil meetings, men's minds being too agitated for questions of Platonism; and although the academy met again later in the Oricellari Gardens and Machiavelli was among the members, politics, and not philosophy, formed the real subject of discussion there, and the whole association was a cover for conspiracy.

Among all the Florentine Platonists who gathered round Ficino in the palmy days of the society, only two merit much attention. One was Cristoforo Landino, the commentator of Dante and Petrarch, and a distinguished Grecian; while the other was the extraordinary Leon Battista Alberti, architect, poet, writer, man of science, versatile even in that versatile age and in the land which produced Leonardo da Vinci.

The remainder were men of no note, but the academy remains an interesting, even fascinating, intellectual phenomenon, and Marsilio Ficino, although a man of little original power, was inspired with genuine enthusiasm ; and having had the merit of perceiving, in spite of the general fanaticism for antiquity, that Christianity reposed on a very solid foundation, he made an effort to prove that it was logically derived from Platonism. Hence his adoration of Plato, whom he regarded as a saint, and before whose bust he burnt a taper.

This is the place also to mention Pico della Mirandola, who seemed a miracle of learning to his contemporaries, and was, in fact, remarkable for a prodigious memory. He was generally adored for his personal attractions, his gentle character, and princely munificence ; and being assured by every one around him that his erudition was boundless, he found no difficulty in believing this himself; and, to prove the proposition, drew up nine hundred conclusions and offered to answer all objections to them triumphantly, inviting the learned of Europe to meet him for the purpose in Rome, whither he undertook to pay the journey of those who could not defray their own expenses. This sort of intellectual tournament did not take place eventually, owing to the opposition of the Pope, and is solely worthy of record as showing the real nature of Pico's mind.

He was, without knowing it, a pretender to culture,

and had so little real taste as to prefer the poetry of Lorenzo de' Medici to Dante's. He proved his want of intellectual power by endeavouring to reconcile Scotus and St. Thomas, Plato and Aristotle, and by this process to confound the enemies of the Church. It is not surprising to learn that he wound up by being one of Savonarola's most fervent disciples, and was buried in the convent of St. Mark in the habit of a Dominican, according to his own last wish.

During the revival of learning Italian had been discarded by the erudite for Latin, but the Platonists gave the first example of a return to the mother tongue.

Lorenzo de' Medici himself wrote Italian poems— remarkable for the union of several high qualities. He was a keen observer of human feelings and a lover of nature in an age which did not abound in descriptions of the external world. In his " Beoni " he is a satirist; in his " Canzoni a Ballo " (Dance Songs) he skilfully uses and perfects popular forms of verse ; while in the "Canti Carnascialeschi" he gave a literary stamp to obscenities which were then sung in the public streets, but which now repose for the most part undisturbed on bookshelves.

The best judges are unanimous in numbering the "Stanze" of Angelo Ambrogini of Monte Pulciano, better known as Poliziano, among the immortal works of Italian poets. The poem, which is unfinished, was written to commemorate a tournament of Giuliano de' Medici, and is considered unsurpassable for beauty of form.

The author of the " Morgante Maggiore," Luigi

Pulci, was born at Florence in 1431. His poem was built up out of old materials, the adventures of Orlando and the battle of Roncisvalle, as related by many previous generations of street singers (*cantastorie*) to the crowds in Italian piazzas; but contains, in the words of a modern critic, all "the elements of pagan and Christian culture," all "the scepticism and superstition, the irony and sense of natural beauty,"

MEDAL OF PIUS II.

(*From Die Italienischen Schaumünzen des Fünfzehnten Jahrhunderts.* (1430-1530.) *Von Julius Friedlaender. Berlin,* 1882.)

peculiar to the age. Antiquity, with which he was familiar, gives a special colouring to his work, "but his muse remains essentially popular," so much so as occasionally to become as trivial as his letters, which nevertheless abound in witty and graphic descriptions.

Lionardo Bruni and Carlo Marsuppini died Secretaries of the Republic, the one in 1444, and the other eleven years later. Both were erudite humanists, and

Bruni also wrote a history of Florence in Latin, a work which on his death was continued by Poggio. Florence at no time lacked historians among her citizens, but her two greatest names in this line are Machiavelli and Guicciardini. Born respectively in 1469 and 1482, they felt all the blighting influences of the Medicean rule; but while Guicciardini, with his immense talents, was utterly time-serving, and consulted no interests but his own, Machiavelli's more philosophical mind desired the good of the State. He was the first thinker of his day to conceive the possibility of a strong and united Italy. Besides his history, unapproachable for style, he wrote his notorious "Principe," some "Discorsi," a witty novel "Belphegor," and three comedies, one of which, the "Mandragola," has the highest literary, and the smallest possible moral, merit.

XXVI.

FLORENCE UNDER THE INFLUENCE OF SAVONAROLA.

PIERO DEI MEDICI was a very different person from his father. The blood of his Orsini mother seemed to have obliterated entirely in him all the qualities which had distinguished his ancestors in finance and diplomacy.

He spoke with elegance and improvised verse; was a lover of music, and unsurpassed in riding, jousting, and athletic sports, but he united to these aristocratic tastes such an uncontrollable temper as constantly to shock the urbane Florentines, who regarded the box on the ear, which he once publicly gave his cousin, as more unpardonable than any violation of State laws.

Under his rule Florence speedily lost the influence which Lorenzo's careful cultivation of foreign friendships had achieved for her. Piero showed himself a Medici only in one respect, namely, in the constant effort to concentrate all government in his own hands, and he carried out this purpose with a careless disregard of the appearances by which Lorenzo had contrived to mask his own encroachments.

He was impatient of the influence of Savonarola, and in his youthful ardour and inherited tendency to debauch, he so soon tired of hearing of the doom that was to overtake society, as to forbid the Dominican preaching the Advent Sermons.

Savonarola, hurt, went to Bologna for the Lent of 1493, and the Florentines missing him, and the stimulus which his sermons afforded to their jaded consciences, murmured angrily against Piero.

Outside the state of Florence the position of things in Italy had again become extremely complicated, and demanded greater political genius than was possessed by Lorenzo's son. Between the King of Naples, or rather between the dying king's heir, the Duke of Calabria and Lodovico Sforza, there was enmity, and much depended upon the side taken in the quarrel by Venice, the Pope (Alexander VI.) and Florence. Piero unfortunately decided for Naples, and Lodovico fearing for the safety of Lombardy, which was coveted by the Duke of Calabria, found himself eventually forced to call in the French.

Louis XI. had been too wary to listen to any proposal of invading the Two Sicilies, but Charles VIII., foolish and vain, lent a willing ear to the assurances of the exiled Neapolitan barons, that he had only to appear and the Aragonese dynasty would fall at once.

Lodovico made similar representations, and the French ambassadors whom Charles despatched to Italy, found that if most of the rulers were opposed to the idea of the invasion, with the ruled it was quite the other way. To all the oppressed and discontented, to all who longed for deliverance, or who desired power, as well as to those simply yearning for change, the brilliant, adventurous, uncertain French seemed to promise the realization of their hopes. In Florence especially the population, excited by Savonarola, who, from his pulpit, invited the foreigner to come, were strongly in favour of Charles, and irritated at Piero's contrary policy.

The very delegates whom Piero sent to France to palliate his conduct to Charles were untrue to their mandate, and one of them, Piero Capponi, even went so far as to council the King to expel all the Florentine merchants from his territory, and thus so exasperate the people of Florence, that they would rise against the Medici. Charles shrank before so extreme a measure, although it might have been applauded by a certain portion of his subjects, who hated the usurious Florentines just as in the present day some populations do the Jews. The members of the Medicean bank in Lyons were driven out, and there the persecution stopped.

Lodovico Sforza, now Duke of Milan, advanced two hundred thousand ducats to the impecunious French king for the equipment of his army, and further sums were obtained from the Genoese bankers, who were naturally eager in any cause which threatened the security of the grandson of Alfonso the Magnanimous.

The crown jewels were also pawned; contributions were levied from various nobles, and at last the army was ready. It was a model force for those days, while in Italy military ardour and science were at their very lowest ebb. The race of great condottieri had perished, and there were no Italian captains of adventure now to teach the art of war to Europe. Nevertheless Alfonso of Naples (who had just succeeded to his father), determined on a resolute resistance, and lost no time in sending his brother, Don Federico, in command of an armament to Genoa, where the French fleet was already assembled.

The Duke of Orleans, whose ships far outnumbered the Neapolitan fleet, easily compelled Don Federico to retire; and then sent a Swiss regiment against Rapallo, which was held by a small garrison of Neapolitans. The place was taken, sacked, and burned, and not only the garrison (which surrendered), but every inhabitant, including even forty sick, was massacred. This sickening cruelty was no sooner known than it spread terror over Italy, and the coming of the French began to inspire as much loathing as it had formerly done joy. Only towns like Siena, Lucca, and Pisa, whose motives were political, still looked towards Charles as a deliverer. Piero, when too late, had felt some doubts as to the wisdom of his own policy, and had tried feebly to play a neutral part, which must always, under the circumstances, have been an impossibility. In his vacillation he had refused a free passage and provisions to the French which gave Charles an excuse for demanding two hundred thousand florins of indemnity, and occupying Sarzana, Pietrasanta, Pisa, and Leghorn, as security for the sum. Piero, who had gone to Sarzana to meet Charles, accepted these conditions without any reference to the Florentine government, and thus raised the irritation against himself to fever heat; and the Signoria had recourse to Savonarola to calm a threatened revolt. He succeeded in appeasing the people for a moment, but every hour now added to Piero's unpopularity. So great and evident was the storm he had provoked that he feared to return to Florence. He remained with Charles, who, on the 8th of November, 1494, made his entrance into Pisa with an escort of three thousand men. He was received with enthusiasm. The houses were covered with flowers, a carpet of verdure was spread along his path, and the population crowded round him with cries of "Liberty, liberty, dear Prince!"

Poor Pisans, enslaved but unsubdued, generous, ardent, deluded, who can fail to pity them? Charles promised them their freedom, which was a bad preparation for his entry into Florence, and on the strength of this careless assurance, the people drove away the Florentine officials, and cast the marble marzocchi into the Arno.

After a few days Piero ventured to return to Florence, and endeavoured to conciliate the majority by declaring that he had made the most satisfactory arrangements with Charles, at the same time as he threw sweetmeats from the windows of his palace among the crowd, and ordered wine to be poured out in the street with a lavish hand.

The next day Sunday (9th of November, 1494), he came to the palace of the Priors with armed retainers, intending to summon a parliament of the people, and possess himself by a *Coup d'État* of the entire government. But the Signoria refused to admit the greater part of his companions, and receiving himself with great coldness, advising him to dismiss his paid defenders, unless he wished to provoke an insurrection. Piero, disconcerted, said he must take time to reflect, and gaining his home he ordered his kinsman, Orsini, to occupy the gate of San Gallo, while he returned with all his soldiers as before to the palace. But on arriving there he was told that this time not even the principal entrance would be opened to him; he must enter, if at all, by the little door. Such humiliation was intolerable, and Piero was furious, the more so that the crowds in the Piazza had been witnesses to the treatment inflicted upon him. Meanwhile all the shops had been shut and the standard-bearers of the guilds were arriving from all sides. The air was full of shouts for liberty; the days of the Ciompi riots seemed returning; and even the children threw stones at Piero. He drew his sword, but could not make up his mind either to use it or to return it to the scabbard; and his brother, the Cardinal, in order to secure a passage for him through the crowd, was reduced to crying "Liberty and the People!" with his own lips.

Piero did not attempt to return to his own house, but made haste to reach the gate of San Gallo, where behind Orsini's fortifications he alone felt himself secure. Here he endeavoured by entreaty, and even by scattering gold to get up a popular movement in his favour. The inhabitants of the quarter, poor and wretched, had always been attached to the Medici, having been won by the arts which Cosimo and

Lorenzo had so successfully practised. But even they had come to despise and distrust Piero who, his last hope gone, made his way with such speed as he could to Bologna. He had barely passed outside the gate when it was closed behind him, as a sort of expression of the determination of the Florentines to be rid of him once for all.

In the interval the Cardinal had gone to the Riccardi Palace, and there was busy collecting objects of value when the unwelcome cry of "Abbasso le Palle!" ("Down with the Medicean balls") met his ear.

The mob conducted by Francesco Valori was in front of the palace, and threatening to attack it. The Cardinal went down on his knees in the balcony, and recommended himself to God, but apparently deciding at the same time that his best chance of safety lay in flight, he donned the habit of a Franciscan, and escaped to join his youngest brother, Giuliano, who was still helping Orsini to guard the San Gallo gate. Before finally quitting Florence, however, the Cardinal, who had kept a cool head, saved as much as he could of the family property, and confided it to the care of the monks of San Marco.

His final exit was attended with difficulty and danger, being only accomplished at all by his condescending once again to cry "Liberty, Liberty!" and scattering gold among the crowd at San Gallo. He escaped in the same direction as Piero, and finally all three brothers reached Venice, where they met with a courtesy in striking contrast to the very rough reception from Bentivoglio of Bologna, who informed Piero that he should have let himself be cut in pieces rather than fly.

The Medici were no sooner gone than the Signoria of Florence set a price upon their heads. Five thousand florins was to be the reward of anybody who brought them back alive; while even two thousand would be paid for them dead. The fury of the people against their late rulers increased every hour. The houses of two subservient instruments of tyranny, Giovanni Guidi and Antonio Miniati were sacked, and a similar fate befell the palace of the Cardinal, and even the beautiful garden of San Marco, which Lorenzo had founded.

Bloodshed was only averted by the strenuous efforts of Savonarola's following, and by the knowledge that King Charles's ambassadors were soon to arrive and must find a reception worthy of a people who had just recovered their liberties.

But the feelings with which the Florentines looked forward to the entry of the French grew more and more unfavourable. Charles and Piero had become fast friends, and the King would promise nothing satisfactory: this much was known and caused angry fears. The best hopes of the citizens lay in Savonarola and Piero Capponi. The monk inspired everybody with a portion of his lofty faith, and the layman, resolute, daring, and able, was busy providing material means of defence.

The solemn entry of Charles was heralded during a few days by the arrival of a few Frenchmen, fifteen or sixteen at a time, who carried no arms and went about chalking the doors of the houses where the soldiers were to be lodged. They affected careless, contemptuous airs, but were unable entirely to conceal their astonishment at the splendour and luxury of this city of merchants. Great was also the impression which they received from the sight of the lofty, sombre palaces, with their grim towers eloquent of the street-fights whose tragedies and triumphs had echoed throughout Europe. The Frenchmen were quick to perceive what inexpugnable fortresses these houses could become, and soon had an object-lesson in their uses. For a rumour arose that Piero dei Medici was at the gates; the tocsins sounded, the street swarmed in an instant with furious crowds; every house, every workshop, sent forth armed men; doors were barred and towers bristled, and the ancestors of the Girondins witnessed the making of barricades. The rumour was found to be false, and peace returned as suddenly as it had been broken; but the foreign soldiers understood how little their magnificent host could do if once trapped in those narrow streets between those palace fortresses.

At last, on the 17th of November, Charles entered. He was dressed in black velvet with a mantle of gold brocade; was mounted on a superb war-horse, and sat in a martial attitude with his lance against his hip, which in those days was a sign of conquest. But all this display only brought into stronger relief his own grotesque appearance.

He had a big head, a long nose, a wide mouth; he was small of stature, with tiny legs, and feet so deformed that to conceal them he wore round-toed velvet shoes, a fashion which, out of reverential imitation, his courtiers also adopted, so that they could only hobble even when most hurried.

But if the kingly person was a disappointment to the curious crowd, the king's army was very imposing indeed. Behind Charles came a hundred archers chosen from the flower of the French youth and forming the royal guard. They were followed by two hundred knights on foot, dazzling in the splendour of their arms and dress, behind whom again advanced the Swiss Guard in parti-coloured uniform and bearing battle-axes of gleaming steel. They formed then the finest infantry in Europe, and most of them had disdainfully laid aside the breastplate as constituting too great a protection against their foes. In the centre of the host were the Gascons, small, agile, apparently swarming like ants.

The cavalry was magnificent with inlaid arms of gold and steel, mantles of gold and silver cloth, banners of velvet embroidered in gold; but the wealth they displayed was forgotten in the amazement—almost terror—excited by the cuirassiers mounted on horses of which the tails and ears had been cut, and by the gigantic archers, natives of Scotland and other northern countries, who looked to the Italians more monstrous than human.

The procession passed over the Old Bridge, where it was welcomed with flags and music, crossed the Piazza della Signoria, where triumphal cars and statues had been erected, and sweeping round the Cathedral Square, stopped finally in front of the church. To the acclamations of the crowd and the cries of "Viva Francia!" Charles had been unable to find any better response than an embarrassed smile and a few words of Italian—mostly said wrong. Inside the Duomo he was received by the Signoria, and joined in their prayers. That evening and the next the town was illuminated; two days passed in rejoicing, and then came the turn of business.

The Signoria had elected to represent the town four of its most distinguished citizens—Guidantonio Vespucci, Domenico Bonsi, Francesco Valori, and Piero Capponi. The latter was the most remarkable of the four. He belonged to an ancient Florentine family, and had been educated for commerce. But Lorenzo dei Medici, detecting his ability, had often sent him on embassies wherein the opportunities he had of studying human nature sharpened his natural insight into character. But if he was a good diplomatist he was a still better soldier, and had that fine contempt for half-measures which is the hall-mark of the truly daring. He had served Lorenzo, but had no faith in Piero, and was one of the first frankly to espouse the popular cause.

The mother and the wife of Piero dei Medici had the ear of Charles, and promised that if the tyrant were reinstated the King should be the real lord of the town. Charles was very well inclined to fall in with these views, but at the first hint of it to the delegates their faces lowered. The news of the proposition spread through the town, and from that moment the French and the Florentines could not live in peace. The situation became menacing; already there had been one tumult, another might follow at any moment, and the Signoria made haste to get rid of the King and his army. Of Piero the Florentines would not hear one word, but in other respects they were conciliatory. The King was to be allowed the title of protector of the liberties of the republic, he was to retain possession for two years of the fortresses he had taken unless the war finished sooner, and he was to receive a good sum of money.

All was nearly arranged when Charles, perhaps influenced anew by the Medicean following, asked for more money. Endless discussions ensued, and every day the population grew more exasperated. Piero Capponi himself felt his patience ebbing, and when at last the King haughtily declared that he would not give way another inch, and if further resisted would sound his trumpets, Capponi made the famous reply, "Then we will sound our bells."

The French had seen the effect of the tocsin once, and were able consequently to appreciate the full significance of this answer. So the negotiations were concluded, and the republic undertook to give the King one hundred and twenty thousand florins in three instalments. Even then Charles seemed little inclined to leave, but was prevailed on eventually to do so by the representations of Savonarola, who seemed to exercise even over this foreign prince some of his extraordinary characteristic authority.

Finally, on the 28th of November (1494) the French departed, and the Florentines began to occupy themselves with a new form of government.

The bell of the Palazzo summoned a parliament of the people, which arrived in the usual divisions, each headed by the Standard-bearers of the Companies—a spectacle which had become unfamiliar during the Medici supremacy.

The priors read out a project for naming twenty Accoppiatori who should constitute a Balià and name the Signoria and principal magistrates during one year. Permission to execute this plan was asked of the multitude, which accorded it with frantic enthusiasm, although, as the power exercised by Lorenzo's Seventy was transferred to the Twenty, and everything else left much as before, there was nothing changed but the persons and the names of the governors.

Very soon it became evident that without the will of a tyrant or an oligarchy to control them, and, above all, without money, the Twenty simply constituted a board of divided counsellors absolutely incapable of ruling. The old machinery of government was worn out: something brand new was needed, and the Venetian form offered itself as the one example of unshaken stability and power in Italy. The Grand Council of Venice transported to Florence would be an essentially popular institution, and enable the people to elect their magistrates and vote their own laws. Paolo Antonio Soderini also proposed to abolish the Councils of the Commune and the People and substitute a Grand Council. In other respects the Florentine constitution was to be left intact, no change being introduced into the Signoria, the Eight, the Ten, or the Standard-bearers of the Companies.

Vespucci was opposed to the idea of a Grand Council as unfitted to Florence, where the majority had always committed such excesses; and he was supported in his views by the undeclared partizans of the Medici as well as by the Twenty Accoppiatori, who did not wish to lose their recently-acquired power. Long discussions followed: the people grew perplexed, restless, and unhappy; a saviour was needed, and he came in the person of Savonarola. Up to now the Dominican had contented himself with preaching to the town the necessity of a moral reform, urging it to abandon pomps and vanities and dedicate itself to charity and good works. But by degrees the current of public feeling, the unspoken, unconscious yearning of the people for a leader, forced him into political life. The same instinct which made him a "prophet"—his sense, that is, of the likely and the inevitable—helped him to detect also what would be alone acceptable to the multitude, and the easiest therefore to achieve.

He consequently recommended the adoption of the Grand Council, and added also some advice as to the reform of the taxes, which were assessed in a way to oppress the poorer classes especially and to excite universal discontent, while at the same time leaving the State always short of money. He suggested further that while all the most important offices should be filled by election, lots might be drawn for the minor ones, by which system every citizen could hope to take some part in the government. He concluded with recommending public prayers and a general peace between the members of the old and new governments.

From this moment the Grand Council seemed the will of God, and so deeply had the spirit of Savonarola penetrated into the minds of the citizens, that no law was voted without one or two preliminary sermons from the friar, who explained and recommended each new measure as it arose to his hearers. Even the Signoria in council used Savonarola's words, adopted Savonarola's arguments, and seemed unable to think or speak without his authority. One reason of his influence, apart from the mystic awe with which he filled men's souls, was doubtless his intense love for Florence. He might have persuaded the republic to restore liberty to Pisa, to Siena, to Arezzo, and thus perhaps have saved Tuscany from future decadence. With his fiery enthusiasm he could have lifted the people to almost any height of momentary renunciation, but this was an idea which never occurred to him. He could interpret better than he could create, and his dream was to profit by the religious revival in Florence to make it the centre from whence should start the general movement for a reform of the Church and the world.

The new government when formed consisted of a Grand Council which was the sovereign ruler of the State, and into which entered all citizens of or above the age of twenty-nine who had either officiated in the three chief magistracies (the Signoria, the Eight, and the Ten), or whose father, grandfather, great-grandfather had done so. But as this would have made the assembly of unwieldy dimensions, a smaller council of Eighty was instituted, of which the component members were to change every six months.

The next suggestion made by Savonarola, and one which perhaps more than anything else shows a practical statesmanlike ability in him, was the reform of the taxes. He ardently advocated the abolition of forced loans and the arbitrary levies to which the government had so long had recourse, and thanks to which so many persons had been able to obtain unjust exemptions. In 1427 the Medici had established the Catasto, which, being an estimate on the property of all the citizens engaged in industry and commerce, struck at the roots of wealth and caused many workshops to be closed. Savonarola's new law introduced a tax on land, while abolishing at the same time forced loans and arbitrary assessments. Every citizen was henceforward to pay 10 per cent. on his real estate and renounce all claim to those restitutions which under the old system had enabled the government, and especially the Medici, who perfected a tool that lay ready-made to their hands, to impoverish their enemies and enrich their friends. Savonarola's influence further carried a proposal for a general amnesty, and another one for the abolition of a law known by the name of the Six Beans.

This referred to the six votes in virtue of which the Eight of Defence had the right of inflicting any punishment they chose, whether death, exile, or confiscation, upon all civil and criminal offenders. As the composition of the Eight changed perpetually it may be imagined how tremendous was the instrument of oppression which they thus possessed, and Savonarola, keenly conscious of the evil, sought to mitigate it by constituting a Court of Appeal of eighty members who might reverse excessive condemnations. The Court of Appeal was established, but the Friar's enemies—for he already had enemies—succeeded in making the Grand Council itself the depositary of the new power. Hatred of the monk had worked a very usual conversion and made the anti-democrats for the moment more democratic than himself. The significance of this fact will be appreciated later on when the course of events reveals how it was really the first step towards Savonarola's ruin. To quote a very apt Italian proverb, it was the drop of vinegar which spoils a whole barrel of honey.

The next great measure was to put an end to the parliaments of the people, those tumultuous meetings which in one hour could overturn any government or introduce any change. Now that absolute power had been conferred on the Grand Council, the parliaments obviously became superfluous. To have retained them would have been to form a state parallel to another state with the consequence that the unstable institution might at any moment cause a revolution and overthrow the republic. The necessity for abolishing the parliaments no sooner began to be recognized than once again Savonarola lifted his voice in advocacy of wisdom, only on this occasion he unfortunately allowed himself to be so far carried away by passion as to recommend the sacking of the Priors' houses and even the lawless taking of the Priors' lives, should they ever attempt to summon the multitude into the Piazza.

This, so far, is the one speck which dims the

splendour of his services and the lustre of his fame. What made him tower immeasurably above all his contemporaries and constituted his force was his disinterested love for the people he had saved. Capponi was as single-minded, perhaps, but he was passionate rather than ardent, and he had not the Friar's mystic glow. Savonarola took upon himself, and carried through, by the double inspiration of enthusiasm and genius, the task of remodelling the Florentine State in one year, and establishing a government which Guicciardini and Machiavelli have pronounced to be the best the republic ever had.

And in the midst of all these practical efforts for the people's good one idea was never absent from his mind for an instant. "I am weary, oh Florence, of the four years' preaching in which I have striven alone for thee. Much have I been afflicted at the constant thought of the punishment which I see coming, and at the fear that it may overcome thee. . . . If you, oh people, do not turn to the Lord, our joyful wishes will be saddened." This was ever the burden of his sermon, the oncoming wrath of God, and the need to avert it by prayer and penitence and purity of life. He was consumed by his own fire, and for days after one of his apocalyptic sermons he would be exhausted and unable to quit his bed. This ever-present vision of doom goes far to explain the immense effect he had upon his auditory, as well as his own strange unswerving conviction that a violent death awaited him. With Alexander VI. upon the Papal throne, with his own loved Florence, degraded like the cities of the plain by sin, it is small wonder if he felt that from such a world he could only pass to his rest through martyrdom, consumed to ashes by the forces with which he wrestled like the princess in the Arabian tale. Saturated with mysticism, and worn out with prayer and study of the Apocalypse, he soon began to have constant visions in which he reposed the blindest faith. His own predictions, some of which had been exactly realized, seem to have inspired himself generally with as much respect as they did his hearers; and yet at other times he strikes another and a truer chord. "I am not," he said, "either a prophet or the son of a prophet. I reject the terrible name. . . . In truth it is your sins and the sins of Italy which make a prophet of me. Heaven and earth prophecy against you, and you neither see nor hear."

Sometimes his visions are puerile: sometimes they rise to a grandeur of which we can feel the impression yet. Childish to grotesqueness is the description of the journey he supposed himself to have undertaken to Paradise in the character of ambassador from the Florentines to Christ. Magnificent and unsurpassed is the following, taken from a sermon which, uttered in his grave and solemn voice, must indeed have appeared like the voice of God to a people at once so imaginative and so credulous as the Florentines: "Heaven itself is fighting: the saints of Italy and the angels are on the side of the barbarians whom they called on to come, whose horses they saddled. Italy is all at strife, said the Lord: this time she shall be yours. And the Lord heads the saints and the blessed who form themselves in battle array, and who are all, all in the squadrons. Whither are they going? St. Peter marches crying, 'To Rome, to Rome!' St. Paul and St. Gregory cry, 'To Rome! and behind them come the sword, and plague, and famine.' St. John says, 'Forward, forward to Florence! and the plague is on his traces.' St. Anthony cries, 'To Lombardy'; and St. Mark, 'Let us go to the town which rises above the sea.' The patron saints of Italy visit their towns to punish them. St. Benedict and St. Dominick penetrate to their convents, and St. Francis seeks his order. All the angels of heaven, sword in hand, and all the court of heaven are marching forth to war. . . . You will see the earth, the heavens, God Himself convulsed."

To realize even inadequately the overwhelming effect on his hearers of Savonarola's visions one must take into account that the Florentines, even at the moment of their highest culture and freest thought, never ceased to believe themselves in direct contact with the inhabitants of the invisible world. Their superstitions are, under the circumstances, incredible, and were shared by the most celebrated humanists. Giovanni Pontano relates quite seriously in his "Charon" how in Naples women are inconsolable if a hen or a goose has the pip, and the most cultured gentlemen feel cast down if a horse trip or a falcon be lost out hawking. Auguries were treated quite in the spirit of antiquity. During the siege of Florence in 1529 the Signoria gravely awarded four ducats to the bearer of a wounded eagle which had flown into the town and was regarded as a good omen. Certain places and hours were regarded as lucky or unlucky. There was, for instance, one gate in Perugia which brought so much luck that through it alone would the "magnificent Baglioni" go forth on their many wars. Plagues and bad weather were held to be exorcisable by the strangest devices. Once in Piacenza in 1478 a rainfall of extraordinary duration was attributed to the fact that a well-known usurer had been buried in consecrated ground. He was dug up amid much tumult, and from that day the rain ceased, relates a chronicler.

Poggio, who in some respects was the soul of the negation, believed in ghosts, "familiars" and prodigies, strange sights, and battles between magpies and jackdaws. The very gods of antiquity reappeared upon the scene, and a terrible eruption of Mount Etna, which no prayers or processions availed to overcome, was preceded by an apparition of Vulcan and his apprentices, who meeting a merchant on his journey informed him that they intended to build something on the mountain. Shortly after Lodovico Sforza had usurped his nephew's place, a dramatic, wonderful story was current in Milan. A stranger presented himself at the dwelling of Lodovico, bearer of a letter which had been given him in the street by the ghost of the murdered Galeazzo Maria. Various persons tried to open the missive but failed—the instant Lodovico touched it, however, it unfolded. He read the contents, then was lost in thought until the bearer roused him by asking for an answer; "Reply that it is well," said Lodovico. The messenger vanished, and when war, pestilence, and famine shortly followed nobody was surprised, for that had been the meaning of the message from the dead. This story is related by Luca Landucci, the chemist, who remarks with much good sense that it is laughable, but probably indulged in equally laughable beliefs of his own.

XXVII.

FLORENCE UNDER THE INFLUENCE OF SAVONAROLA (*continued*).

NATURALLY the enthusiastic confidence which Savonarola inspired could not long be maintained universally at fever heat, and very soon Florence was divided into four camps, the Bianchi (whites), the Bigi (greys), the Piagnoni (drivellers), the Arrabbiati (the angry). The Bianchi were those who, without having any religious fervour to attach them to the Friar, were lovers of liberty, and as such voted for Savonarola's measures, while the Bigi were the secret partizans of the Medici and corresponded clandestinely with Piero, although having profited by the amnesty they professed liberal principles. The Arrabbiati were composed chiefly of rich men who had experience in government, but detested the republic and Piero dei Medici equally, and desired to found an oligarchy like that of the Albizzi. They had been the fiercest opponents of all Savonarola's proposals and continued to nourish towards him the violent hatred which justified their nickname. As to the Piagnoni they were the religious party, and their insulting appellation had been invented by the

Arrabbiati. Of all these parties the Arrabbiati were the most hampered by circumstances and the most determined. If they made one open move they knew that they would immediately have against them the Bianchi, the Bigi, and the Piagnoni, consequently they feigned to be satisfied with the government but lost no opportunity of turning Savonarola, his visions and prophecies, into ridicule, and hoped by degrees to succeed by such arts in arraying the Bigi and Bianchi against him. They also stirred up the clerical party by representing that the Friar's continual denunciations of the profligacy of the Papal Court constituted an intolerable scandal, and that intervention in the affairs of the State was unbecoming in a monk. These words found a ready echo among all who were jealous of Savonarola's eloquence and influence, or who, like Borgia, writhed beneath the lash of his unsparing invective; but while all these forces, still partly hidden, were working for his destruction, the preacher continued his passionate appeals to the people to amend their ways, and succeeded in bringing the town to an appearance of almost cloistral sanctity. Women abandoned their costly garments, sacred canticles were sung in the place of obscene lays, and in workshops when the day's task had ended recreation was sought in the Bible and the works of Savonarola. A greater miracle still was the restitution by the wealthy of ill-gotten gains which amounted to several thousand florins. Crowds of men, young and middle-aged, noble and simple, obscure and distinguished, joined the order of the Dominicans, so that the convent of St. Mark had to be enlarged.

While such was the internal condition of Florence, outside the clouds were lowering. The French though successful in Naples for a time, had soon made themselves so generally insupportable that Lodovico Sforza, who had called them into Italy, was fain to promote a league against them.

Charles eventually returned with his army to France, abandoning, although with some hesitation, the unfortunate Pisa to its fate. He would have helped it had he possessed resolution or tenacity of purpose enough to help anybody, for he had been touched by the prayers of the Pisans who, as he passed once again through their town, had renewed their supplications to be saved from Florence. They brought money and jewels to the needy king, and the most beautiful among their women clothed in mourning with bare feet and a cord, as a sign of servitude, round their necks, threw themselves on the ground before Charles, entreating him to do what he pleased with Pisa only not to surrender it again to its oppressors.

Nevertheless he did surrender it in return for Florentine gold, only his lieutenants whom he had left in the town refused to obey his orders.

They also had been moved by Pisan prayers and won by Pisan women, five hundred young girls dressed in white, who had surrounded the French asking them to be their knights: "Or if you cannot help us with your swords," they said, "then help us with your prayers," and they led the officers to a shrine of the Madonna chanting meanwhile a song so pathetic that their hearers were moved to tears.

The king was besieged with entreaties from his own people. The officers of the royal guard burst into the room where he sat at play, and one among them, Sallezard, said impetuously, " Sire, if it be money that you need, have no fear, for here is enough." They tore from their necks their silver chains and collars and offered to give up all their arrears of pay.

From Genoa, Siena, and Lucca the Pisans also received encouragement and help, the three republics joining to furnish a small force under Giacomo d'Appiano, lord of Piombino, and Giovanni Savelli, who joined the troops of Lucio Malvezzi, the Pisan ocndottiere, and inflicted a defeat upon the Florentines in the valley of the Serchio. About the same time Montepulciano revolted from the rule of Florence and placed itself under the protection, joyfully accorded, of Siena. One of the usual revolutions in the latter town had recently given a pretext to the French to occupy it, and De Signy one of Charles's officers, began to dream of establishing himself as ruler there when a fresh insurrection drove him and all his companions away.

The Lucchese, who, from their constant fear of falling into the power of the Florentines, had been very liberal with money to Charles, succeeded in persuading him to restore to them Pietrasanta and the Port of Motrone, a measure which, as interfering with their rights, greatly annoyed the Florentines who still, however, clung to the French alliance as constituting the best bulwark against the Medici.

In fact there was not a town in Tuscany which had not been stirred to new life and excited by reviving hopes at the descent upon Italy of the splendid army which achieved at first such facile and brilliant successes, only to cross the Alps once more, leaving nothing behind it but emptied treasuries and the memory of bitter deceptions.

D'Entragues, the French commander at Pisa, finally handed over the fortresses to the citizens in return for a sum of money, which the exhausted town raised by means that despair alone could teach, and then the commune, determined to resist Florence to the last, sent ambassadors to the Duke of Milan, to the Pope, and to the Republic of Venice. The Pisans succeeded in obtaining from all the states which had joined the league against Charles promises to respect their liberties, which had also been derisively guaranteed by Maximilian in the name of that Holy Roman Empire now fast becoming the shadow of a shade.

Venice responded generously to the appeal of Pisa by sending both ambassadors and troops, but as the Republic of the Lagoons was never quixotic, we must look for the explanation of her policy in the determination to prevent an alliance between the Duke of Milan and Pisa. Sforza easily penetrated these designs, and to checkmate them invited Maximilian to be crowned King of Lombardy in Milan and emperor in Rome, so that the old authority of the empire might be re-established in Italy. Maximilian had no objection to masquerade as a successor of Charlemagne provided he were paid, and he undertook to bring an imposing army, which, when it presented itself at last, was found to consist in three hundred cavalry and fifteen hundred foot. But even this small force excited uneasiness among the Florentines, who had lately met with fresh reverses in their Pisan campaign, who saw all the strength of the league against them, and found that Charles, in spite of promises, had little intention of returning to Italy to help them.

Yet they still clung to the French alliance, thanks partly to the influence of Savonarola, who preached incessantly either that Charles would again cross the Alps, or that a terrible punishment would overtake him did he fail to do so. He also prophesied that a miracle would shortly rescue the Florentines from their present perils, and when Maximilian failed in the siege of Leghorn, which was succoured in the very nick of time by a French fleet bearing provisions and soldiers, the assurances given by the Friar seemed to his fervent followers to have been abundantly justified. Maximilian, with his usual frivolity, soon tired of his Italian expedition, and went back to Germany, a move of which one result was to upset Sforza's designs on Pisa and cause him to recall his troops from Tuscany. This afforded some relief to the anxiety of the Florentines, but brought their home affairs to an acuter condition than ever. For the more Savonarola's partizans increased in number and in faith, the more determined did his enemies become to destroy him. That was the one point on which Arrabbiati and Bigi were alike agreed, and the already complicated situation was not made simpler by the efforts of the first-named to compass the establishment of an oligarchy, and the intrigues of the second class to recall the Medici. The end of April,

1497, saw an attempt made by Piero to surprise the town. Bernardo del Nero, the actual Gonfaloniere, was a friend of the exiled family, and the moment consequently seemed propitious. Piero went first to Siena, where Pandolfo Petrucci and his brother, now absolute masters of that republic, received him with every mark of friendship. There the pretender was joined by a force of eight hundred horse and three thousand foot under Bartolommeo d'Alviano, and thus accompanied he set out by night marches for Florence, but only to find on arriving at the Roman gate that every warlike preparation had been made to receive him and that Bernardo del Nero's authority was a dead letter. He remained four hours before the gate without having the courage to attack it, then sneaked away, leaving nothing behind him but a bitterer hatred than ever in the hearts of the Florentines against himself and his name.

An accident revealed somewhat later the names of those who had been in correspondence with Piero and had encouraged his attempt, and Niccolò Ridolfi, Lorenzo Tornabuoni, Giovanni Cambi, Giannozzi, Pucci, and Bernardo del Nero were condemned to death. The sentence was not executed without a tremendous struggle, in which all the forces of a determined democracy were arrayed against the open protests and secret opposition of the government's enemies. In accordance with the law which Savonarola had helped to pass, an appeal against the decision of the Eight could have been made to the General Council, but this measure, when proposed, was outvoted, thanks in great part to the resolution of

Franceso Valori, one of the most violent and fanatical among the Piagnoni. The Standard-bearers of the Companies, who had been summoned to assist the Signoria in its deliberations, threatened to massacre the four Priors whom they suspected of wishing to defraud them of vengeance, and the appeal of the Council having been rejected at last unanimously, the beheadal of the five conspirators took place the same night. Bernardo del Nero was seventy-three years of age, Lorenzo Tornabuoni was but twenty-nine, but all alike were conducted barefoot and in chains by the light of torches to the courtyard of the Bargello, which, filled with a howling crowd, resembled, said a contemporary, "a cavern of hell" They met their fate courageously, and the odour of their blood seemed to intoxicate the mob, but even among the Piagnoni many felt that such triumphs of democracy might be bought too dearly.

Savonarola, although he had once proposed and carried a general amnesty, on this occasion made no attempt to induce his own followers to temper justice with mercy. He seemed indeed to have concerned himself with the details of government but little just now, being absorbed in his correspondence with the Pope, and more and more plunged in visions and ecstatic contemplation. His moment of action was over, and he was fast losing hold of a world which he still dreamed of reforming, while outside his convent cell human passions were seething, and the men whom they swayed hungered and thirsted for the Friar's destruction. These designs found an eager partizan in Alexander VI., who had already forbidden Savonarola to preach, and in May, 1497, excommunicated him and all who should hold intercourse with him. The Dominican paid no heed to the excommunication, declaring it to be unjust, and consequently null, and on Christmas Day he publicly celebrated mass in his own church of St. Mark, communicated with all his monks and a large number of laymen, and shortly afterwards resumed preaching in the Duomo before a more numerous congregation than ever. Nevertheless, the excommunication had its effect. We can see this in the diary of Luca Landucci, who, ardent Piagnone though he was, could not reconcile it to his conscience to listen any more to Savonarola's sermons after the publication of the Papal bull. The truth was also that the Friar had strained his influence too far. He had caused a pyre to be built in the Piazza, and thereon burnt all the obscene books and indecent pictures which his acolytes could collect, together with playing cards and dice, lutes, harps, and musical instruments, false hair, perfumes, cosmetics, carnival masks, and other vanities. This ceremony, which attracted immense crowds, took place on Shrove Tuesday, a day formerly marked by orgies, but now celebrated with prayers and sacred songs and fastings among all except the unregenerate, who did their best to disturb such holy scenes. Dolfo Spini, one of Savonarola's bitterest enemies, was at the head of a band of dissolute youths who were known as Compagnacci, in reference to the unceasing and unseemly war which they waged against the Friar and all his works.

Their methods might be reprobated, but the example

of their scoffing could not but be contagious among a population who had been worked up to an impossible altitude of purity and renunciation. The reaction against such sacrifices was inevitable, and all the more so that Savonarola, absorbed, possessed, dominated through every fibre of his being by his own idea, had instituted a moral tyranny to which no free soul could long submit with tameness. He was accused of encouraging espionage in families, urging wives to leave their husbands and live as nuns, servants to report when gambling or other vicious amusements went on in the houses of their employers, and even children to testify in season and out of season before their parents.

His notion of using children for his propaganda cannot be applauded. There is something ludicrous and sad in the spectacle of these young creatures taught to penetrate uninvited into houses for the purpose of discovering whether forbidden occupations were indulged in; to pursue and denounce blasphemers; to address richly attired women in the streets, and urge them in the name of Christ, the "King of Florence," and His mother, to renounce their vain adornments if they did not wish to be punished by disease.

And as always happens in such cases, while beneath the surface a reaction had already set in against the Dominican, the society which he had so strangely transformed and travestied, being now fully organized, presented an aspect of piety so aggressive and uncompromising that all the enemies of the Piagnoni, from the Pope down to the humblest and basest

Compagnaccio, felt that Savonarola must be got rid of at any price. The chief foes of his order, the Franciscans, were exasperated beyond endurance, and their general, Mariano di Ghinazzano, never ceased representing to Alexander the necessity of striking some decisive blow. Out of all these circumstances, by a process too long to relate, arose the famous and fatal ordeal of fire. A Franciscan friar, Francesco da Puglia, had been despatched to Florence to preach against Savonarola in the church of Santa Croce, and he suddenly made the startling proposition that the Dominican and himself should voluntarily mount a burning pile for the purpose of proving whether or not a miracle from heaven would testify to the genuineness of Savonarola's doctrines. "I feel sure of perishing myself," said the Franciscan, "but Christian charity teaches me not to consider my own life, if by sacrificing it I can deliver the Church from an heretical teacher who has already led, and will lead many more, souls into eternal damnation."

Savonarola's first impulse was to refuse the ordeal, but his disciple and friend, Fra Domenico Buonvicini, declared himself ready to enter the flames, in the firm conviction that by his master's prayers a miracle of God would deliver him unhurt.

No sooner was this announcement made public than it became impossible for Fra Domenico to draw back, even had he wished to do so. The eager, curious, alert population of Florence, always credulous and sceptical at one and the same time, always agog for novelty and anxious for excitement, seized with frenzied inquisitiveness on the idea of the ordeal, some out of mere love for a spectacle so unique, some out of expectation of the promised miracle, some out of unholy longing for a catastrophe that would precipitate Savonarola to his ruin.

As for the Pope, he wrote to the Franciscans of Florence to thank them for the zeal with which they were about to sacrifice the life of a brother in defence of the Holy See's authority, and assured them that the memory of so sublime a deed should never be allowed to perish.

The object of Fra Francesco was to induce Savonarola himself to mount the pyre, but in this he failed. If the master himself were tepid, however, not so his followers. The difficulty was to cool their ardour. All the Dominican monks in Tuscany, many priests and laymen, even women and children, supplicated the Signoria to allow them to undergo the ordeal, but, fortunately, the government kept its head, and decreed that there should be only two participants—Fra Domenico Buonvicini for the Dominicans, and Fra Andrea Rondinelli for the rival order, Fra Francesco da Puglia having withdrawn when he found that Savonarola was not to be induced to expose his own life on this occasion.

A scaffold five feet high by ten broad, and eighty feet in length was erected in the middle of the Piazza della Signoria. It was covered with earth and bricks to preserve it from the fire. Along the whole length of the construction on each side combustibles four feet thick were heaped up, a space of two feet in breadth being left free for the friars to traverse. They were to enter the path of fire from the Loggia dei Lanzi, which was divided by a partition into two tribunes, one for the Dominicans and the other for the Franciscans. The ordeal was fixed for the 7th of April, 1498, and on that day, as may be imagined, the Piazza, the windows and roofs of the adjacent houses were crowded, not only with the whole population of the town, but with hundreds of people from the surrounding country who had been attracted by the news of the forthcoming miracle.

Savonarola arrived in the priest's robes which he had put on to celebrate mass, and carried the sacrament enclosed in a crystal tabernacle. Fra Domenico bore a crucifix, and behind him came all the monks of the order, chanting psalms and carrying each a red cross. A crowd of citizens followed with lighted torches. The fervour of the Piagnoni, the faith of the Dominicans, the excitement of the crowd, were raised to the highest pitch, but the Franciscans remained strangely cool. Probably they had not taken the thing quite seriously in the beginning, and had committed themselves irrevocably somewhat unawares. Their one object had been to destroy Savonarola, and this design had so far been partially foiled; and now, when the hour for the ordeal had come, perhaps the solemnity of the Dominicans, their array of red crosses and lighted torches, their apparent firm belief in the coming miracle had its effect in awing and discouraging their rivals. Certain it is that while the crowd waited in frenzied suspense, the Franciscans raised one objection after another. They said Fra Domenico might be a magician and carry some charm beneath his habiliments, and they insisted that he should lay aside the clothes in which he had come and put on others chosen by his opponents. The Friar, after much argument, submitted to this change of vestment, and declared himself ready for the flames. But as Savonarola handed him the tabernacle containing the Holy Sacrament a fresh outcry arose among the Franciscans, who maintained that it would be an act of intolerable impiety to expose the Host to be burned. But on this point Savonarola himself would not yield, declaring that Fra Domenico's one certainty of safety lay in the God whom he carried: a curious contention, which throws a side-light on the perplexities of the great strange soul, and doubting, if fervid, and noble mind of the monk who regarded himself as the chosen instrument of Heaven, who accepted his own visions as realities and believed in his own prophecies, yet had such unexpected flashes of common sense, and was more sceptical than any of his followers now that the opportunity for a real miracle presented itself. On Savonarola's refusal more wrangling followed; the day wore on; a violent downfall of rain drenched the pyre and the crowd, and finally the Signoria announced that the ordeal must be deferred and ordered the assembly to disperse.

By these means, unpremeditated or not, the Franciscans had gained their ends. The revulsion of feeling in the disappointed populace was too violent not to include friends and foes alike in its overflow. Savonarola was insulted as he passed through the Piazza on his way to the convent, and his subsequent explanation did not avail to convince the perplexed multitude that he had been innocent of any wish to avoid the ordeal. The Compagnacci, on their side, urged the people no longer to allow themselves to be duped by a hypocrite, a heretic, and a false prophet who had been weighed in the balance and found wanting.

An angry mob broke into the cathedral during the evening sermon on Easter Sunday, and the cry arose "To arms!" The Compagnacci led the way to the convent of St. Mark, which stood a siege of some hours, being defended by the laymen who were assembled in the church for divine service and by a few monks, while Savonarola and the greater number of his friars passed the time in prayers to Heaven. Alas! the saintly hierarchy, the hosts of the Most High stirred not, and no sign from an outraged divinity fell on the impious town. The doors of the convent were finally fired and then the besieged surrendered. Savonarola and two companions, the faithful Fra Domenico and Fra Salvestro Maruffi, were seized and conducted to prison amid insults and contumely and outrages too coarse to relate.

All night long the fury against the Piagnoni grew, and next morning Francesco Valori, who had taken such a leading part in the destruction of the five conspirators, was arrested, and on his way to prison killed. A like fate befell his wife as she came to a window of her home with a vain prayer for mercy on her lips; and another principal adherent of the Friar Andrea Cambini was also murdered.

The Signoria, which had entered on its functions a month previously to these events, was mostly hostile to Savonarola, and took advantage of the situation to depose the Ten of War and Eight of Justice and replace them with enemies of the Piagnoni. The Pope was bent on the death of Savonarola and at the request of the government of Florence despatched thither two ecclesiastical judges who were practically executioners.

The trial was a tragic farce varied by horrible tortures, during which the unhappy prisoner, wracked through every nerve of his delicate frame, muttered delirious phrases, and repeated dictated avowals which were embodied in a so-called confession. Even now, after four hundred years, one cannot read without passionate pity the story of the long agony of that pure and noble soul. A month passed, and then on the 23rd of May a new scaffolding and a new pile were erected on the Piazza. Again the cruel crowd assembled, breathless for a satisfaction which this time was not to be denied them. Savonarola and his two disciples descended the principal staircase of the Palazzo and after being divested of their chief clothes were conducted before the altar of the palace chapel and there arrayed in sacerdotal garments, only to be despoiled of them, as a mark of degradation, immediately afterwards. "You are separated from the militant and triumphant church," the officiating bishop said to Savonarola. "Triumphant, no! That is not in your power," replied the condemned man. Despoiled of their priestly robes and degraded, the three were taken before the ecclesiastical tribunal and had to listen to their sentence of death "for heresy." They were offered absolution and—pathetic faith!—

accepted it humbly. After a few more formalities they reached the foot of the scaffold, and there, kneeling, surrendered themselves into the hands of the executioners. Maruffi and Buonvicini were hanged first, then came the turn of Savonarola. They had not bandaged his eyes nor bound his arms, and when he was suspended in mid-air and his poor body underwent the final convulsions of death, his hand extended above the heads of the shrieking mob seemed to bless them in the very moment that they rushed forward to fire the faggots amid insulting cries of "Prophet! now for your miracle." And in the universal excitement it almost seemed to the yelling foes, as to the Piagnoni, silent with terror and grief, that a miracle was about to be worked when a sudden gust of wind blew aside the flames. What! would God now, at the last, forbid the fire to touch the martyred bodies? "Alas! they were already as black," says a spectator, "as rats."

A perfect explosion of basest hatred, a mad return to vice and folly followed on these events, and so low for the moment had the memory of Savonarola fallen that a month after his execution, at the celebration of the Feast of the Baptist, when there was a grand display of fireworks, the populace were delighted with the spectacle of dogs, a dead lion, and a pig, or in other words, the Piagnoni, Francesco Valori, and Savonarola. But this obscene farce did not represent the general opinion, for the great memory of Fra Girolamo could not long be degraded by calumny however vile. This is proved by the very divergence of opinion concerning him among contemporary and successive historians. It is a testimony to his grandeur of soul that he should have been, and to a certain extent should remain, incomprehensible. Pope Benedict XIII. said, "If by God's grace I reach Paradise I shall inquire whether Savonarola be there;" and Pius VII. expressed the same idea in the words, "In heaven I shall solve this problem."

XXVIII.

GENERAL EVENTS FROM 1498 TO 1512.

STRANGELY enough Charles VIII. died on the very day of the trial by fire, April 7, 1498. His early death, preceded as it had been by that of the infant Dauphin, seemed a justification of Savonarola's prophecies.

Louis XII. lost no time in asserting his pretensions to the Duchy of Milan, which he claimed to be entitled to in right of his direct descent from Valentina Visconti. On mounting the throne he caused himself to be described as King of France, of the Two Sicilies and Jerusalem, and Duke of Milan, thus at once disclosing views which boded but little tranquillity to Italy. As far as the Tuscan Republics are concerned, however, Louis' policy is interesting only in so far as it influenced these. He had need of alliances, and lost no time in conciliating Florence.

The war continued against Pisa, which was supplied with means of resistance by Venice. The Florentines, irritated at the long-delayed fruition of their hopes, began to suspect their commander, Paolo Vitelli, of treacherously serving the designs of the Medici. He was seized and tortured, and although no avowal could be extorted from him, and no authentic proofs of his guilt existed, he was beheaded on the 1st of October, in one of the rooms of the Palazzo Pubblico.

Siena ever since 1495 had been ruled by Pandolfo Petrucci, who pretended to govern only by favour of the Nove, and was ostentatiously simple in his mode of life, never even attempting, like the Medici, to ally himself with the nobility. He was not usually bloodthirsty, but could commit a great crime on occasions, as, for instance, when he caused his father-in-law, Niccolò Borghese, who had resisted his authority, to be cut to pieces, *coram populo*, on the city Piazza.

On the 29th of June, 1500, Pisa was again besieged by the French troops, commanded by Hugues de Beaumont, but once more the unhappy town had awakened pity and preference in French hearts; and after one attack had failed, the disaffection reigning in the camp prevented De Beaumont from carrying through a second. The French soldiers allowed reinforcements to reach Pisa, and did not conceal their hostility to their paymasters, the Florentines, and finally De Beaumont, having broken all his engagements, returned to Lombardy.

At Pistoja civil war broke out again between the Cancellieri and the Panciatichi, whose feuds were supposed to have been long over. The Panciatichi were driven away; their houses burnt, their goods pillaged. The Cancellieri pursued them outside the gates, and besieged them in the church of San Michele, but were finally overcome by a fresh contingent of the foe. Florence without troops, now that the French had left, and without money now that the King of France made continual demands for subsidies, could neither continue the war against Pisa nor suppress the sedition of Pistoja. The situation of the republic thus impoverished and enfeebled was full of danger, and what made it worse was the now manifest intention of Cæsar Borgia to possess himself if possible of Tuscany. He began by intriguing in Bologna, and revealed to Bentivoglio, the tyrant there, certain designs formed against him by the rich and powerful Marescotti. Hermes Bentivoglio assassinated Agamemnon Marescotti, the chief of the house, and there followed a butchery in which two hundred and thirty-four persons of both sexes fell. Bentivoglio ordered the gates of the town to be shut while the massacre was going on, and, with the satanic astuteness of Italian tyrants, forced the sons of the noblest families to join in the carnage, thus attaching them to himself for fear of future reprisals.

After the conquest of Naples, Louis XII., by an act of extreme bad faith, made an alliance with Borgia, by which he undertook to furnish him with three hundred horse, to be employed in expelling the Bentivoglio family from Bologna, the Baglioni from Perugia and the Vitelli from Città di Castello. This agreement increased the alarm of the Florentines, who did not know but what they might be the next victims of some secret compact, and the instability of their government appeared as an evil which increased all the other difficulties of their situation. The Grand Council on the Venetian model was to have been a radical remedy, one which would infuse new vitality into the exhausted frame of the republic. Machiavelli and Guicciardini both pronounced it the best government which Florence ever had, and no doubt theoretically it possessed transcendent merits. But the era of free communes in Italy was past, and no machinery of government could resuscitate these institutions. They had yielded all the splendid and unique results of which they were capable, and needed to be superseded by a spirit of nationality which as yet was unborn. But Florence still clung passionately, like Pisa and Lucca, to the idea of independence, and in its perplexity could think of only one device, that, namely, of a Gonfaloniere for life, who would correspond to some extent to the office of Doge in Venice. He was to be lodged in the palace, with a salary of a hundred ducats a month, to be invested with the right of assisting at the deliberations of the councils and tribunals, and share, with the president for the day of the Signoria, the right of initiating public measures. But with all these extended powers he was not placed above the risk of capital punishment, should he incur sentence on the part of the Eight of Justice.

This reform was finally passed on the 19th of August, 1502, and Piero Soderini appointed to the new office for the 1st of the following November. Only a short time previously a change had also been introduced into the legal procedure of Florence, the Captain of Justice and the Podestà being finally suppressed and replaced by five judges. The president of these five received, however, the title of Podestà, and as each judge was to be Podestà in turn for six months, the new tribunal was given the well-known appellation of the ruota (wheel).

On December 2, 1502, a treaty had been signed at Imola between Giovanni Bentivoglio and Cæsar Borgia, by which the former, in return for abandoning the cause of the Vitelli and Orsini, was confirmed in the sovereignty of Bologna, subject only to a tribute of twelve thousand ducats, to be paid annually to Borgia for the maintenance of a hundred lancers. But death came suddenly to put an end to Cæsar's project, and once again to save Florence from a pressing danger. Alexander VI. died, and his son's power fell like a house of cards. The Baglioni flew back to Perugia, the Vitelli to Città di Castello; and an army, despatched by Cæsar to attack Perugia and Florence, was defeated by Gianpaolo Baglioni, who was fighting for both towns.

In 1506, by the determined efforts of Pope Julius II., Bologna was finally incorporated with the States of the Church, Giovanni Bentivoglio being paid off, and the republican constitution of the city being guaranteed by the Pope, who nevertheless replaced the sixteen Anziani by an oligarchy of forty senators.

Genoa for some time past now had been unusually tranquil. On the conquest of Milan by Louis it had passed naturally under French domination, and a commandant of that nation had replaced the Doge. But the old bitterness between the "nobles," that is the descendants of the Fieschi, Doria, Spinola, and Grimaldi families, and the "people," under which term were included all, however rich and illustrious, who did not belong to the four great clans, had been increased by the refusal of the governing class in Genoa, and especially of Giovanni Luigi Fieschi, to take possession of Pisa when that republic offered itself in 1504. The refusal was considered to have been dictated by motives of personal calculation and by subserviency to the French, and irritated the more democratic party extremely. The French governor also envenomed the feud by not concealing a preference on all occasions for the nobles, who grew very insolent in consequence, and went about armed with poniards, on the handles of which were engraved the words, "Castiga-villano" ("Chastise the villein"). On July 18, 1506, the long-brooding storm broke, and an insurrection took place, which ultimately compelled Philippe de Ravenstein, the governor, to banish Giovanni Luigi Fieschi, to redistribute the public offices, by which the nobles were excluded from two-thirds, and to allow the creation of eight tribunes, charged to protect the people. But Louis XII. soon caused fresh exasperation by insisting that Fieschi should recover possession of all his fiefs along the eastern Riviera. No proposition could have been more unwelcome to the Genoese democracy, who desired not only to retain these fiefs which were redoubtable coigns of vantage for the enemies of the republic, but also to seize the castle and town of Monaco—a fastness which constituted all the pride and force of the Gramaldi, but had none the less been formerly the property of the commune. Louis finding the Genoese unsubmissive, proceeded to send an army against them, on which they offered themselves to Maximilian, but soon experiencing the incurable untrustworthiness of that volatile prince, resorted to more radical measures still, by declaring that they would no longer accept French rule, and naming a Doge on the old pattern. The only person whom they could get to accept the post was Paolo di Novi, a master dyer of no birth and apparently no fortune, but who had many qualities which might in happier times have made him a good ruler.

The French army meanwhile had advanced close to the valley of the Polcevera, where it soon put to flight the citizen soldiers who had been hastily enrolled. Genoa filled instantly with fugitives, and the wildest terror reigned. Nevertheless Paolo de Novi succeeded in making some preparation for resistance, and at Rivarole, where the Genoese again met the French, the latter had some difficulty in carrying off a victory. Still they were victorious, and the Genoese submitted. On April 29, 1507, Louis XII. himself made his entry into the town, and was met by women and children carrying olive branches and pleading for mercy. This attitude—a new one among the once-indomitable population—seemed to touch the French king, who announced that he would pardon the rebels. He understood the word in a kingly sense, and hanged a good number of the forgiven after a very expeditious trial.

A false friend with whom Paolo de Novi had taken refuge, sold him to the French, and he was taken back to Genoa to be executed. His head was exposed on the end of a pike on the tower of the Pretoria, and his limbs, which had been quartered, were fastened to the gates of the town. Two hundred thousand florins, exacted from the entire population, the erection of an inexpugnable fortress, and the public burning of the privileges of the commune completed the king's act of mercy. He did, indeed, restore municipal government, but as a favour, and he reinstated the nobles in one half of the public offices.

These events in Genoa constituted a fresh disaster for Pisa, and made another station of the *via dolorosa* which the heroic republic had trodden so long in want and blood and tears. From the other maritime republic, once a rival and enemy now a sister in misfortune, no further help could be expected while Lucca and Siena, friends but intimidated, could only furnish scanty and clandestine succour. The Pisans felt that their last hour of struggle was approaching. The Florentines, by the advice of Machiavelli and according to the principles laid down by him in his Treaty of the Art of War, had lately instituted trained bands intended to supersede the mercenaries, and the first use made of this militia was to lead it against Pisa. The Florentines also took into their service Bardella, a corsair of Porto Venere, who, in return for a monthly salary of six hundred florins, kept the mouth of the Arno closed with three little vessels.

Lucca, finding all further struggle useless, abandoned the cause of Pisa, entered into a treaty of alliance with Florence, and undertook to prevent all further despatch of provisions to the suffering communes.

The chief magistrates of Pisa and even the most determined among its citizens could no longer withstand the entreaties for peace of the exhausted townsfolk and the starving peasants. In the city there was no longer wine nor oil, nor vinegar nor salt, and corn could only be procured at sixty lire the quintal. Leather for making shoes was wanting, and even the soldiers went barefoot. Fourteen years and seven months the war had lasted, and now even the most undaunted accepted the necessity for capitulation. Twelve ambassadors were sent to Florence, peace was signed on the 8th, the Florentine army entered the gates of the recaptured town and distributed food to the starving people. The Pisans had prepared themselves to see their property sacked, and were stupefied at finding themselves treated with mercy and generosity. The Florentines, who had anticipated the modern spirit in so many respects, showed themselves again far in advance of their age. Not only were all offences pardoned and all property restored, but the rents and prices of produce yielded by farms on the Pisan territory during the current year were restored to their rightful owners. The ancient privileges and independent offices of the commune were guaranteed to it, and it re-entered into possession of its commercial and manufacturing franchises. Appeal in criminal cases was allowed to the same tribunals as those which judged the offences of Florentines, and, in short, no effort was spared to render the capitulation of Pisa as little humiliating as possible. Nevertheless its richest, bravest, and most distinguished citizens emigrated from the vanquished town. Some went to Palermo, others to Lucca or Sardinia, but the majority sought French soil or enrolled themselves in French armies. To this day in the South of France there exist descendants of Pisan families, whose names revive the memory of a commune's tragedy.

In Florence the surrender of Pisa after so many years was welcomed with an enthusiasm which may easily be imagined. Louis XII., now that the accomplished fact confronted him, hastened to send his congratulations. "You have become the first power in Italy," he said to the Florentine ambassadors. "How will you call yourselves henceforward: Serenissimi or Illustrissimi?" The moment was indeed a proud one, and the opportunity seemed given to Florence of playing once more a conspicuous part in European politics. But the poison of discord still worked in her veins. Piero Soderini, conspicuously honest, had yet neither the qualities which attract the popular imagination nor the force of character which can direct the popular will. He lived more soberly than Cosimo had done with no ulterior designs, but he took no interest in art or literature, and his rule seemed dull to the men who recalled the magnificent traditions of Lorenzo. Public order was also much relaxed, and public morals at the lowest ebb, and against the deadness of the general background these facts stood out in unnatural relief. Soderini was blamed for everything, and a reaction began in favour of the Medici. Piero was dead, but his widow, Alfonsina, still lived in Florence, and never ceased intriguing socially if not politically against the government. Cardinal Giovanni had succeeded in marrying his niece Clarice, Piero's daughter, to Filippo Strozzi, whose influence and wealth were enormous. The marriage at first caused the greatest scandal, and Filippo was fined and exiled for five years to Naples; but before the term ended he was allowed to return to Florence, and Soderini did not improve his own position by his piteous and abject attitude. He had but one desire which was to remain neutral in the midst of enemies whose vigilance and unscrupulousness rendered such a policy insane.

Julius II. at war with the French and exasperated against the republic for not frankly taking his side, determined to restore the Medici; and at last, on the 21st of August, 1512, the tidings spread that Ramon da Cordova, the viceroy, was already at Barberino with an advance force of two hundred, which was to be followed by five thousand of the valorous soldiers who had fought at Ravenna.

The general alarm was intense, and thousands of fugitives flocked into Florence. The Signoria took hasty measures, ordered a levy of troops, and garrisoned Prato, which was considered favourable to the Medici, but at the same time despatched commissioners to negotiate if possible with Ramon. His intentions were frankly avowed. "I mean," he said, "to carry out the views of the allies by deposing your Standard-bearer, establishing a government which cannot be suspected of French sympathies, restoring the Medici as simple citizens, and exacting eighty or one hundred thousand ducats for the 'league.'"

These terms not being immediately accepted, Ramon marched forward, and on the 29th of August took Prato, with two pieces of artillery, one of which burst, and with only a very feeble resistance to overcome on the part of the trained band of whom Machiavelli was so proud. The sack of the town lasted until the 19th of September, and several thousands were reported to have perished. The streets and churches were full of corpses—corpses of civilians, not of soldiers. In the midst of the general horror the people of Pistoja counselled by fear sent the keys of their town to Ramon.

The Florentines, consternated, began already to think of submitting in their turn, but Ramon demanded fifty thousand florins now, and while waiving other points stood out for the recall of the Medici. Hence arose fresh discussions, more confusion and another plot against the Gonfaloniere. On the morning of

MEDAL SHOWING ST. PETER'S.

the 31st of August, 1512, Antonfrancesco degli Albizzi, Paolo Vettori, Gino Capponi, and even Baccio Valori, who had married Soderini's niece, rushed armed to the palace and signified to the Gonfaloniere that he must come to some decision which would save Florence from the fate of Prato.

He tried to temporize, but Albizzi the youngest and boldest of the band seized him by the front of his dress and threatened him with death unless he resigned. Soderini, heart-sick and weary, hid himself for some hours in the house of a friend, and finally escaped to Ragusa. Several of his adherents followed his example, the long prepared revolution was accomplished, and amid cries of "Palle, Palle!" Giuliano dei Medici, mounted on the same palfrey as Antonfrancesco degli Albizzi, made his entry into Florence. He feigned to have returned as a simple citizen, with no pretensions to govern, but these declarations took in nobody, for in point of fact the Florentines were anxious for the old yoke.

XXIX.

THE SIEGE OF FLORENCE. DECADENCE AND END OF THE REPUBLICS.

THE first act of Giuliano was to summon a parliament of the people, and to institute a new Balià invested with full powers, and empowered to prolong its own existence from year to year. In this way it continued to exist until 1527, when the Medici were, as we shall learn, again expelled.

The Medici family now consisted in Giovanni and Giuliano (sons of Lorenzo), Giulio, Prior of Capua, and bastard son of the Giuliano killed by the Pazzi, Lorenzo, grandson of the Magnificent, and Ippolito, the illegitimate son of Giuliano II., with Alessandro, supposed to be the bastard either of Lorenzo II. or Cardinal Giulio. On the death of Julius II., in February, 1513, Giovanni de' Medici was raised to the Papal throne under the name of Leo X., and lost no time in enriching his family, beginning with Giulio, whom he made Archbishop of Florence, and even Cardinal, getting over the difficulty of his cousin's illegitimate birth by making the maternal uncle of Giulio and some religious swear that a marriage had taken place before Giuliano's assassination.

Leo X. interfered violently in the affairs of Siena, and drove away Borghese Petrucci, who, on the death of his father Pandolfo, had succeeded to supreme power in that town under the title of head of the Balià and commandant of the guard. Leo favoured Raffaello Petrucci, Bishop of Grosseto, a devoted adherent of his own, but a man of dissolute habits. The Pope caused him to be escorted to Siena by Vitello Vitelli and an armed force, and installed him in the place of Borghese, who meekly retired.

But Cardinal Alfonso, Pandolfo's second son, could not so easily forgive, more especially as the Pope's exaltation had been largely owing to his efforts in the conclave. The violence of his language alarmed Leo; two subordinates, one of them a doctor, were arrested, and under torture confessed to a real or false conspiracy to poison the Holy Father, and Alfonso was degraded from his sacred rank and strangled. The Doctor, Battista da Vercelli, and two companions perished amid intolerable sufferings, and the whole college of cardinals was frozen with horror and dismay.

These events were not forgotten when Leo died in December, 1521, and they contributed to the defeat of Giulio dei Medici, who, aspiring to succeed his cousin and patron, saw himself superseded by Adrian VI. He returned to Florence in a humiliated mood, and feeling perhaps that his position was not secure even there, made professions of intending to resign his position as head of the State. Personally he was the least unpopular of his family, and his assurances came just in time to disconcert a conspiracy that had been forming against him and included the famous name of Machiavelli, besides those of Gian Battista Soderini, Luigi Alamanni, Zanobi Buondelmonte, Cosimino Rucellai, Alessandro dei Pazzi, and Francesco and Jacopo da Diacceto, all members of the famous academy which met in the beautiful Oricellari Gardens.

These young and cultured patricians, although inspired with ideas of antique patriotism, were not all of the stuff of which successful conspirators are made, and they lent a willing ear to the Cardinal's promises. Already they saw the new republic constituted, and Machiavelli, Buondelmonti, and Pazzi wrote three theoretical works concerning it which they dedicated to Giulio dei Medici. He, however, either had wind of the machinations which had existed, or his liberal professions were all the time a blind. At any rate, the correspondence of Jacopo da Diacceto with French agents was discovered, and he completed the revelations which it contained by confessing under torture that he had intended to assassinate the Cardinal. Luigi Alamanni the poet had time to make his escape, but another conspirator of the same name was executed with Jacopo on the 7th of July. Zanobi Buondelmonte got safely away, as did also the sons of Paolo Antonio Soderini, but the property of the latter was sequestrated.

In 1523 Giulio at last became Pope under the name of Clement VII. The condition of abject dependence on his house into which the Florentines had fallen, and which his rule, a tolerable one on the whole, had confirmed, is shown by an incident which attended his translation to the Papal chair.

Pietro Orlandini, a respected Florentine citizen, already sixty-three years of age, and who ought to have been made Standard-bearer of Justice at the next extraction of names, had made a bet that Giulio would not be elected Pope. When the news came that proved him mistaken and he was summoned to pay his bet, he exclaimed that the Cardinal could not have been elected according to canonical rules. For this simple remark, which appeared disrespectful to the popular fetish, he was arrested by order of the Eight and beheaded two hours later.

Of the Medicean family only the two youths Alessandro and Ippolito now remained to claim the lordship of Florence. Clement VII. sent them to Florence, where the young Ippolito was regarded as chief of the State and given the title of Magnifico, while the real government was in the hands of the legate, Silvio Passerini, Cardinal of Crotona.

In April, 1527, the whole of Tuscany, but especially Florence, so often terrified throughout its history by the advance of invading hordes, saw itself threatened anew by the army of the Constable of Bourbon.

Ippolito dei Medici with the legate and two other cardinals happened to leave Florence to visit the camp at Olmo, and this incident sufficed to create the suspicion that they were fleeing from dangers of which the people had been kept in ignorance.

The opponents of the Medici had increased of late, as a portion of the Florentine population keenly felt the disgrace of submitting to a youth governed by a Roman prelate, and in a few hours an insurrection was prepared and accomplished. The Medici were proscribed and the government as it had existed under Piero Soderini re-established. Of course the three cardinals returned on hearing the news and brought with them fifteen hundred infantry, which proceeded to besiege the Palazzo inside which the insurgents had fortified themselves. Never had Florence been in such grave peril, for if the Medici in order to triumph had been forced to call in the remainder of the troops, the fair town would have been sacked.

Nor was this all, for Bourbon was at Santo Stefano, and any weakness of the Italians made his opportunity. Guicciardini, impressed with the dangers of the situation, interposed, and succeeded in alarming both parties as to the consequences of persisting in a struggle. The insurgents were eventually induced by him to lay down their arms and quit the palace, which was taken possession of by the Medici, who made promises of forgiveness which they did not observe.

On May 6, 1527, took place the famous sack of Rome by the troops of Bourbon, who thus justified all the worst and wisest of Guicciardini's previsions. The event was tremendous, but the days were past when it could send a thrill of horror throughout the Christian world. The captivity and eventual capitulation of the Pope had their counterblast in Florence, where the influence of Clement alone had propped up the now feeble fortunes of his family. The news of the events in Rome reached Florence on the 11th of May, and immediately afterwards a number of citizens, arrayed not as soldiers, but in the dignified garb of every-day life, presented themselves before the legate, and summoned him to restore its liberties to their town.

The chief spokesmen were Niccolò Capponi, and Filippo Strozzi, the first being inspired by patriotism, while the latter had grievances against his kinsman the Pope which made him quite as resolute for the moment as his colleague. The legate had no force of character, and disregarding the instances of Onofrio di Montedoglio, commandant of the garrison of six thousand men who wished to make a stand for his master, he quickly came to terms, by undertaking that Ippolito and Alessandro should quit the town, and simply stipulating that their property should be secured to them, and that they should be exempt during ten years from the payment of extraordinary taxes.

The Balià created by the Medicean party came to an end, and the constitution existing in 1512 was revived. The Grand Council was summoned to pass the decrees, but first the great hall in which it always met had to be restored to its former condition, the Medici having transformed it into a barrack.

All the young nobles in Florence assisted in the work, and when the hall had been cleaned and redecorated it was sprinkled with holy water by priests and a solemn mass celebrated within its walls. So great had been the general zeal that ten days sufficed to effect the necessary transformation, and on the 21st of May the two thousand two hundred and seventy members of the council met. Niccolò Capponi was elected Gonfaloniere of Justice for thirteen months, with the faculty of being reconfirmed in his functions at the end of that time ; new representatives were appointed to all the important offices of the State, and the members of the new government, the clergy, and devout crowds went in solemn procession to the different churches to render thanks for their newly found freedom.

Genoa had been sacked by the Imperial troops, and this disaster inspired a resolution to free her in the heart of the noblest of her sons. It is characteristic of the history of the ever unhappy republic that Andrea Doria, who loved his native city dearly, should hardly ever have lived within its walls. In the service of the French he had created a splendid fleet, and was considered the first sailor of his age. The ingratitude and ill-faith of Francis I. had embittered him, and he hated his employers only a little less than the Spaniards. He could not forgive the latter the sack of Genoa, and whenever afterwards he took any Spaniards prisoners he refused ransom for them, and forced them to row in the galleys. To a man of such a character it is easy to understand how unbearable was the contempt with which Francis treated the Genoese. Savona, having always remained faithful to the French cause, was regarded by the king with peculiar favour, and he endeavoured to increase its prosperity by ruining Genoa. One of the gravest of his measures was to transfer the salt monopoly to Savona, and the Genoese addressed a petition for help to Doria. His engagement with the French was about to expire, and he consequently offered his services to the Emperor, on the condition that Genoa should recover its liberties, and full dominion over Savona and all the Ligurian towns. The proposition met with eager acceptance, and on the 4th of July the fleet, which had been blockading Naples for the French, passed to the orders of Spain.

After the capitulation of the French army at Aversa, Doria hastened to Genoa to help in freeing it from the stranger. Teodoro Trivulzio, who was holding the town for Francis with a very feeble garrison, not being able to obtain any reinforcements, withdrew to Castelletto, and the Genoese, although decimated by the plague, found sufficient energy to drive out all the remaining French, and afterwards, under the command of Doria, to besiege Savona and Castelletto. Both capitulated without much delay, and Genoa, like Florence, recovered its independence, and, more fortunate than Florence, was destined to three centuries more of relative prosperity.

Both republics set about the oft-repeated task of remodelling their constitutions, and in both the spirit of reform proved itself aristocratic and exclusive.

Charles V., who was opposed to the idea of independent republics, offered to make Andrea Doria Prince of Genoa, and to support him in that position, but the great patriot refused the offer, and insisted on the maintenance of the republic. In order to put an end, if possible, to the eternal factions of Genoa, a curious and arbitrary device was adopted. In Genoa, as in Florence, it had long been the custom for poor and obscure individuals and families to merge themselves in great houses, and the twelve Reformers now appointed to reconstruct the republic determined to extend this principle. Twenty-eight houses were ordered to adopt among them all the remaining citizens who were entitled to a share in the government, and to do it in such a fashion that nobles and plebeians, Guelphs and Ghibellines, partizans of the Adorni and partizans of the Fregosi, should find all their old distinctions lost, and all their old rallying cries forgotten under cover of the new and grand names which they had to assume. This singular device lasted forty-eight years, and although it extinguished many hatreds, it could not make peace between the classes privileged to govern and the classes who were excluded from State affairs.

The other changes made in 1528 were the institution of a Grand Council, consisting of all citizens qualified to govern, who named the Doge. His office was appointed to last for two years only, and shorn of many prerogatives.

In Florence a large class were excluded from the rights of citizenship, and consequently from the government. Nevertheless, all the old political divisions revived, and the more aristocratic faction headed by Niccolò Capponi, caressed the time-worn theory of an oligarchy on the Venetian pattern, and inclined, if not towards the Medici themselves, at least towards the party favouring them as being opposed to a democracy which they abhorred. Capponi had also been an adherent of Savonarola, and round him gathered the now diminished Piagnoni, all those whose fervour had survived the reaction against the prophet, and who now entered into a secret and unholy alliance with the Palleschi.

Leaders of the democratic faction were Baldassarre Carducci, a fiery old man, who detested Capponi and the grandi; and Dante da Castiglione, whose strongest animosity was reserved for the Medici. His dream was to create a breach between the town and its former masters, which nothing should ever heal; but the means employed by him were not always of the most intelligent description. One day, he entered the Church of the Assumption with a troop of armed and masked followers, who threw down and destroyed the statues of Lorenzo and Giuliano dei Medici, of Leo X. and Clement VII., after which they proceeded to remove the Medici arms from the Churches of San Lorenzo, San Marco, and San Gallo. This active expression of opinion went unpunished, however, for no party in Florence was strong enough now to assert itself without foreign protection to back it.

In July, 1527, the plague raged to such an extent in Florence that everybody not too ill or too poor to fly left the doomed city. It became impossible to assemble the Signoria, or any officers of the State, in sufficient number to give validity to the public acts. At last the Priori summoned to the Grand Council all the members of the Eighty and other chief functionaries, for the purpose of suspending the ordinary forms of government until the plague should cease. Barely ninety citizens responded to the call, and they sat as far away one from the other as they could in the over-mastering anxiety to avoid contagion. The

MICHAELANGELO.

immense hall of the Grand Council echoed like the circle of the Inferno with sighs and lamentations as friends and relatives who for weeks had not met, now learnt from one another's lips the deaths of young and old. The scourge ceased about November, but its memory dwelt in the minds of the regenerate, who still seemed to hear the voice of their murdered master reproaching them for their sins. At one of the first meetings of the Grand Council in February, 1528, Niccolò Capponi made a speech which dwelt on the punishments and the clemency of God. He repeated some of Savonarola's own phrases, and ended by throwing himself on his knees and imploring the compassion of Heaven. The Council followed his example, and at his instance renewed the Friar's former dedication of Florence to Christ as king; but to revive the spirit of Savonarola among the sceptical population, now parting fast with all its old ideals, was a task as hopeless as to call Savonarola himself from the waters of the stream where his tortured body had found unhonoured rest.

During the Gonfalonierato of Capponi (who was elected for a second year to the office), a fresh effort was made to infuse a military spirit into the Florentines. Three hundred young men volunteered to form the Palace Guard, and as they consisted of enemies of the Medici, Capponi himself sought to neutralize their influence by the creation of a city militia of four thousand members, all belonging to families entitled to sit in the Grand Council. It was also decided to terminate the fortifications of Florence, and Michaelangelo furnished the plan of the works.

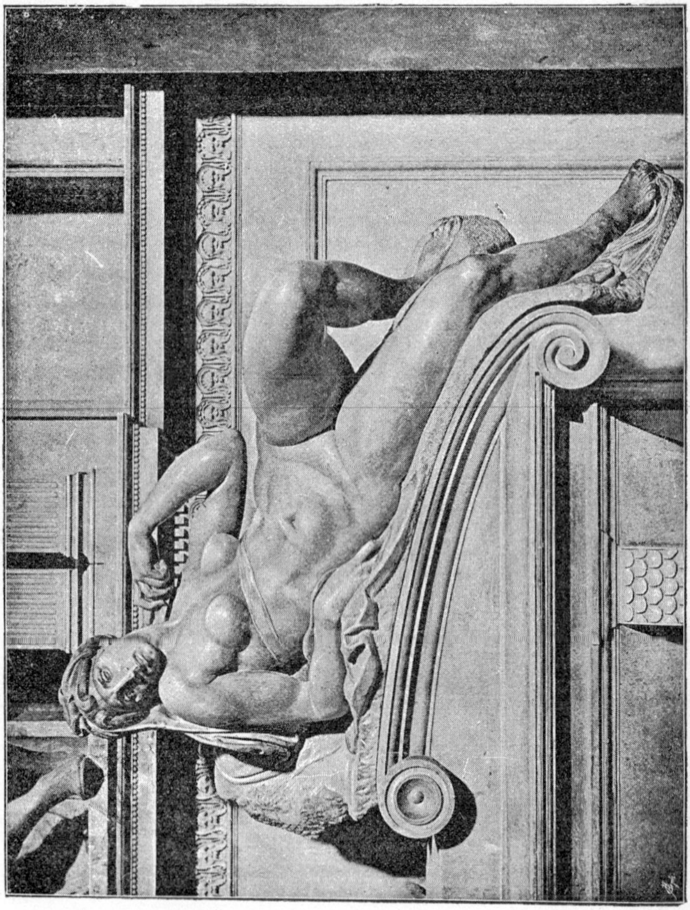

The longest headed Florentines, such as Machiavelli and Guicciardini, together with Capponi himself, were inclined now to desert the French alliance and conciliate Charles V., but Francis I. made such specious promises, while the atrocities and ill-faith of the German and Spanish commanders had filled Italy with such horror, that Florence could not be persuaded to abandon its old ally, even when warned by Andrea Doria that Clement VII. was seeking to reconcile himself with the Emperor, and would stipulate for the restoration of his family.

The fortunes of this family were now centred in Alessandro, for the Pope, feeling himself the prey of a mortal malady, and desirous to keep alive in the Sacred College influences favourable to the Medici, had bestowed a Cardinal's hat on Ippolito. Francis I. and the Pope were the arbiters of the destiny of Florence, and both betrayed her. Clement promised to crown Charles, Emperor in Italy, and Charles, on his side, pledged himself to reinstate the Medici. Francis, in order to release his sons, who were detained by the enemy as hostages, sacrificed all his allies, the faithful Venetians and the Florentines among them. The age was not one of political good faith, and Florence itself had never been conspicuous for chivalry. This consideration, however, does not excuse the French king, and the only consolatory thought is that the republic had now reached a stage in its political evolution when the spirit of independence was too effete for the forms of liberty to revive it. Various causes, chief among them the discovery of the New World and the constitution of

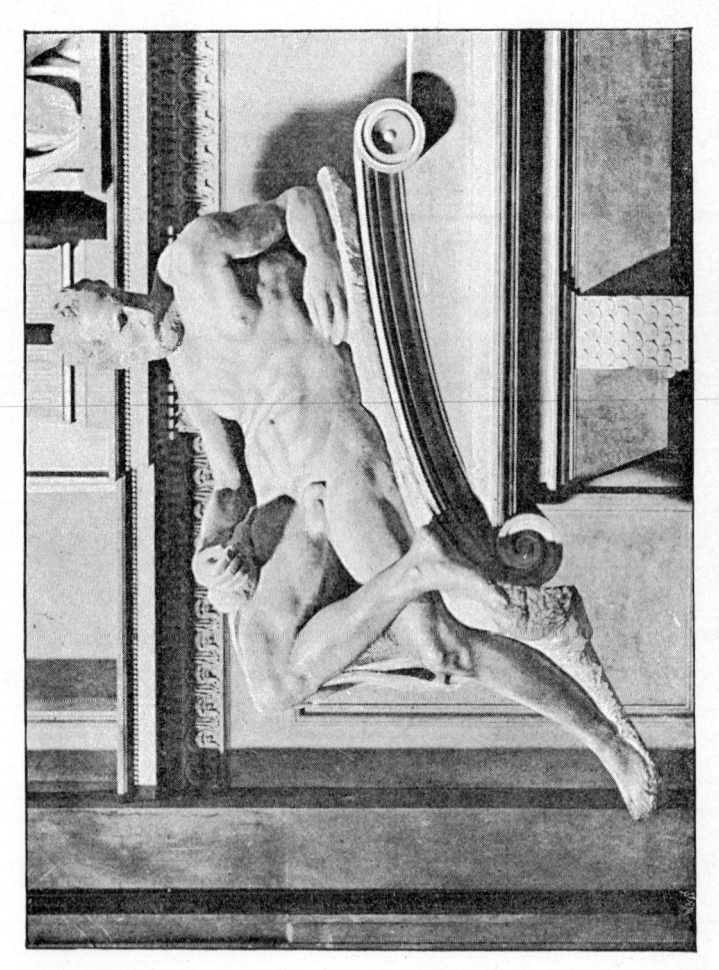

EVENING.

great monarchies, were now working for the destruction of the communes, and we may see by the republics which did survive how dead they were organically.

If Charles had wished to imitate the old Emperors he would have gone to Milan for the iron crown, and to Rome for the imperial diadem. He contented himself, however, with receiving both from the hands of Clement in the Church of San Petronio at Bologna. In all its varied history, influenced now by the Pope and now by the Emperor, Italy had never, not even in the days of Charlemagne or of Otho, lain so helpless at the feet of a foreign sovereign as now. Her own divisions, the separate struggles of communes and tyrants and vassals to be mutually independent, had achieved what armed conquest could not do. The Two Sicilies acknowledged the supremacy of Charles; the States of the Church were at his mercy; the Dukes of Milan, of Mantua, of Savoy, and Ferrara, the proud Marquis of Montferrat, were equally his slaves, and even Genoa, while still claiming to be free, was to find its only salvation in following the policy and supplying the wants of Spanish masters. Lucca and Siena had always been Imperialists; they reasserted the title now, and Venice retained a simulacrum of political existence simply by withdrawal from the scene of the world's great deeds.

There remained Florence, which was still to make a gallant struggle before sinking into torpor under the blighting rule of Medican dukes. Deserted by France and threatened by the armies of the Church, of the Empire, Spain, and Naples, the Florentines determined at last to depend on their own valour alone, and began energetically to organize the national militia, whose exploits up to now would have furnished a good excuse for not making any defence whatever. Several distinguished officers who had served in Giovanni dei Medici's celebrated black bands,[1] undertook to discipline the corps which speedily became equal to the best infantry in Europe. The city guard, which consisted of youths of family, counted three thousand members, while the territorial militia, amounting to ten thousand, was composed of peasants. Michaelangelo was named Director-general of the fortifications of the town. Troops were raised in Cortona and Arezzo, and Malatesta Baglioni of Perugia was engaged to fight under the orders of the republic with a thousand foot. Malatesta was the son of Giovan Paolo, whom Leo X. had put to death, and he desired to revenge himself on the Medici. Various other distinguished captains, such as Stefano Colonna, Marco Orsini, Giorgio Santa Croce, took service under the lily, and the title of Captain-General of the Florentine militia was given to Ercole d'Este whom the republic wished to conciliate.

Money was raised by forced loans from the richer citizens and by despatching to the Mint the plate belonging to private houses and to churches. The precious stones adorning reliquaries were pawned and an arbitrary sale effected of one-third of the ecclesiastical property, of the goods of rebels and of the estates of corporations. The towns of Borgo San

[1] Giovanni delle Bande Nere was the son of Caterina Sforza.

NIGHT.

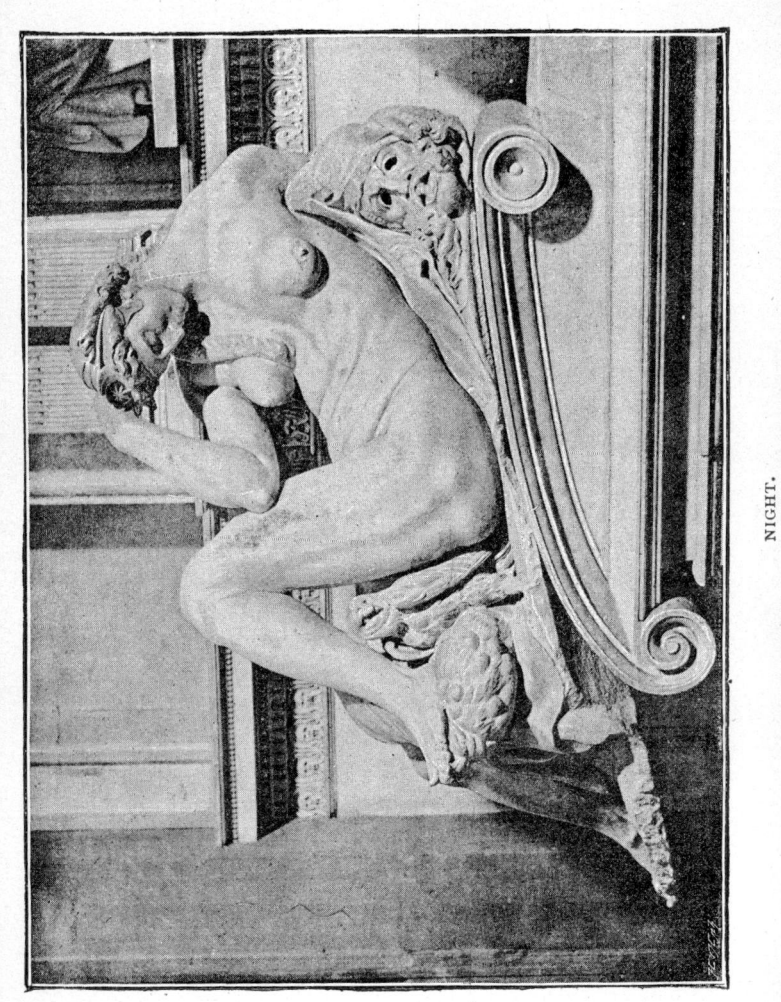

(From the Monument to Lorenzo de Medici, by Michaelangelo, at Florence.)

Sepolcro, Cortona, Arezzo, Pisa, and Pistoja, where Florence had never succeeded in making its rule acceptable to the populations, were forced to give hostages for fidelity. Then all being in readiness, and Charles V. already at Genoa with his army, Ercole d'Este received orders to repair to his post, and Florence received the first foretaste of what was to happen when he suddenly refused.

The army destined to reduce Florence was commanded by the Prince of Orange, Viceroy of Naples, and consisted of fifteen thousand men, afterwards increased to forty thousand, of German, Spanish, and Italian nationality.

As it advanced Cortona and Arezzo successively capitulated, and this example being followed by smaller places, terror began to spread in Florence and several pusillanimous citizens, among them Guicciardini the historian, precipitately left the town. Fortunately the Prince of Orange lingered in the Valley of the Arno, and the delay gave time for fresh fortifications of the walls, especially at San Miniato, and for the execution of an order given by the Eighty to raze to the ground all habitations and gardens within a mile of the town.

The owners of villas and orchards patriotically vied in destroying them, and arrived within the gates carrying faggots of olive, fig, and orange trees, which were all that remained of their estate.

At last, in October, 1529, the Prince of Orange appeared at Pian di Ripoli, and it was during the various skirmishes which took place along his route that one of the greatest of Florentine patriots, Francesco Ferrucci first became known for his valour and ability. He had served in the Black Bands, and among many other soldierly qualities possessed the great art of a commander in knowing how to inspire love and confidence in his men. He was always successful, and soon came to be thought invincible.

The Spaniards had already taken possession of San Miniato and Ferruccio resolved to dislodge them. He took the place by assault after a brave resistance, in which the enemy was assisted by the inhabitants of San Miniato themselves, but Ferrucio conquered and cut the garrison to pieces.

Some sorties from Florence were successful, but nevertheless the advance of the Imperialist troops continued steadily. Pistoja and Prato surrendered as rapidly as Cortona and Arezzo, and when the new year (1530) dawned the authority of the republic continued to be recognized only in Leghorn, Pisa, Empoli, Volterra, and Borgo San Sepolcro. Florence was now full of fugitives, and if good order prevailed, it was thanks to the discipline and endurance of the city guard, as well as to the activity of Ferruccio who found means to provision the town continually.

The engagement of Ercole d'Este having expired without his having once shown his face, Malatesta Baglione was appointed in his stead, receiving the Standard of the Republic from the Gonfaloniere, and swearing to give his life if necessary for the defence of the liberties of Florence.

All this time the government was willing enough to negotiate with the Emperor and even—strange blindness!—to receive back the Medici on condition of their respecting the liberties of the commune, and leaving its latest form of government intact. But Charles always referred them to the Pope, and the Pope was intractable.

Within the walls of Florence there had been a certain revival of religious fervour, and the monks of St. Mark had recommenced preaching that Christ would never forsake the town which had given itself to him, and that even when the Imperialists had already planted their banners on the walls, the angels of God would descend with fiery swords and disperse the enemy of the Lord of Hosts.

Although the town of Volterra had capitulated, the citadel still held out, and the Ten of War despatched Ferruccio there at the end of April (1530), to succour the garrison which was hard pressed. His departure was disastrous for Empoli, which he had fortified strongly, and where he had concentrated provisions and munitions for Florence. The Prince of Orange at once despatched troops to take the little town which resisted a formidable assault the first day, but on the second was betrayed by its leading citizens, who let in the Spaniards on condition that their property should be spared. This promise was given, but not kept, and the immense supplies collected by Ferruccio perished with the rest. That great patriot meanwhile had been successful in retaking the town of Volterra after relieving its threatened citadel. The Spaniards sent reinforcements under Maramaldo, who was at the head of some Calabrians, bandits rather than soldiers, as well as under the Marquis de Guasto and Don Diego de Sarmiento. These trained troops attacked Volterra vigorously on the 12th of June, and made two large breaches. Ferruccio, although badly wounded, had himself carried in a litter to the places where the fighting was hottest, and continued to direct the defence. On June 17th, further artillery having arrived for the besiegers, the attack was renewed. Ferruccio was now consumed with fever, but he still found strength to lead his troops, and after a desperate struggle forced the enemy to retire.

After this success he proceeded to carry out the orders of the Ten of War, who had appointed him Commissary-general in order that he might assemble all the soldiers who still remained faithful to the republic in the Florentine territory, and organize an attack on the enemy's camp. This attack was to be seconded by a vigorous sortie from Florence on which the Government insisted, in spite of the representations made by Baglione and Colonna to the effect that their militia was unfit to meet trained veterans in the open field. Ferruccio raised fresh levies in Leghorn and Pisa, and, on the 30th of July, left the latter place, and began his hazardous march among the Lucca mountains. He was surrounded on all sides by the enemy, and when he reached Gavinana at last, not only Maramaldo, Vitelli, and Bracciolini were menacing him from different quarters, but the Prince of Orange in person advanced to meet him with two thousand German and Spanish soldiers. The Prince could not have left the camp before Florence with safety had the republic not been betrayed. But Baglione had been in secret negotiation with the Imperialists for some time, and now, having been promised the sovereignty of Perugia, had engaged himself, not to effect the sorties which were to have seconded Ferruccio. Colonna was won over to the same policy of baseness, and both generals protested against the orders of the Signoria. Even when finally forced to march out they delayed as much as possible, and before they fairly left the gates the doom of Florence had been sealed at Gavinana.

The battle had been fierce; the Prince of Orange himself was killed, and victory seemed certain for the Florentines, when a fresh attack was made by the landsknechts. They surprised Ferruccio and Giovan Paolo Orsini at a moment when they were resting, and had around them but a few officers. The valiant little band defended itself a long time, and when Orsini, wounded, covered with dust and blood, and feeling himself obviously overpowered, asked Ferruccio if he would not surrender, all he got for answer was a determined "No." But Ferruccio himself was presently surrounded, and, covered with mortal wounds, fell a prisoner at last to a Spanish soldier, who, to gain a ransom, undertook to save his life. He was taken before Maramaldo, who, base-hearted, had learnt to hate him in many a bloody encounter. By his orders Ferruccio was disarmed, and then Maramaldo plunged a dagger into his heart. As the hero fell he said, "You have killed a dead man."

The news of this defeat, so dearly bought that it was still glorious, caused the wildest alarm in Florence; and although the patriotic Signoria would still have made a stand, Baglione unfortunately found all the partizans of the Medici to support him in his determination to surrender. Fear also played into the traitor's hands, for it was felt that the Perugian might obtain better terms from the Imperialists than the Government could hope for. On the 12th of August, 1530, a treaty was signed at Santa Margherita di Montici, by which the Emperor undertook to regulate the government of Florence within four months, but promised to respect its freedom.

A Balià of Twelve was appointed, who deposed the existing Signoria, the Ten of War, and Eight of Defence, and, amid cries of " Palle, Palle ! the Medici, the Medici ! " all that was best and bravest in Florence sank into a grave made glorious by the memories of Dante, of Michele di Lando, and Capponi, of all the great brains and intrepid hearts to whom the brilliant republic had been dear.

The Balià included among its members Baccio Valori, Francesco Guicciardini (the historian), Francesco Vettori, and Roberto Acciajoli. They were the real chiefs of the republic, and worked a bitter vengeance upon all their opponents. By their orders the property of patriots was ruthlessly confiscated, and the people were disarmed. The late Gonfaloniere Bernardo Carducci and four of his colleagues, old like himself, were beheaded, and about one hundred and fifty citizens were exiled for three years—a term which was afterwards prolonged to three more.

Alessandro, to whom the Emperor had promised his natural daughter in marriage, and who was consequently supported by the double authority of the Emperor and the Pope, made his entry into Florence on the 5th of July, 1531. He came back as recognized "Chief of the Republic," which title was to descend to his children or, failing these, to the male line of the Medici in perpetuity.

A year later a new constitution elaborated by the Pope conferred on Alessandro the title of Duke, or Doge, with remainder to his successors, and instituted two life councils to assist him in governing. Four councillors replaced the Signoria, but the Duke's power was absolute.

He very soon made himself so hated that many leading citizens voluntarily emigrated. Among these was Filippo Strozzi, who, together with various members of the Valori, Ridolfi and Salviati families, gathered in Rome round Ippolito dei Medici, who regarded his cousin as an alien, and was jealous of the power conferred on him. A protest was addressed to Charles V. detailing the crimes and cruelties of Alessandro, and the Emperor being at Naples on his return from Tunis, Ippolito, accompanied by Dante da Castiglione, and Berlinghiero Berlinghieri, set out thither for the purpose of further enlightening the monarch in a personal interview. Alessandro is supposed, however, to have taken his own measures, for, when Ippolito and his two companions died in atrocious suffering on their journey, it was generally believed that they had been poisoned. The Duke also made several attempts to assassinate Filippo Strozzi, but failed. He set out for Naples himself, accompanied by his satellites Baccio Valori and Francesco Guicciardini; and, as Strozzi and other malcontents were already there, Charles had an opportunity of hearing both sides. Jacopo Nardi, the historian, gave a detailed account of Alessandro's crimes. Guicciardini replied; and the Emperor in his decision took a middle course, ordering that the Florentine exiles and emigrants should be reinstated in their native town and their property, but refusing to make any change in the government of the republic. But the exiles answered that they would not return as slaves to their birthplace; that they were determined to live and die free, and that all they asked of Charles was to relieve their unhappy town from the barbarous yoke which oppressed it.

How vain was this appeal they could all recognize when, on the 28th of February, 1536, Charles married his daughter Margaret of Austria to the tyrant.

But Alessandro's own vices sharpened the weapon by which he was to fall.

Lorenzino dei Medici, his cousin, was one of those depraved, dramatic characters in which the Renaissance was fertile. Cultivated in mind, deformed in body, and base of heart, he aided the Duke in disgraceful amours, but all the time loathing him and stealthily watching for an opportunity to work his ruin. He promised to arrange a meeting between Alessandro and a lady of the Ginori family—decoyed him under the promise to his own house, which adjoined the Medicean palace, and there murdered him, with the help of a hired bandit called Scoronconcolo.

The Duke, tired out, had thrown himself on a couch while waiting for the moment of the rendezvous, when Lorenzino entered the room, with the bravo some paces behind him. "Do you sleep?" asked the young man of his cousin, and at the same moment pierced him through with a short sword. Alessandro tried to struggle, but Lorenzino, while saying "Fear not," suffocated his cries by thrusting two fingers down his throat. The Duke nearly bit them through, and might have overcome his slender assailant but for the help of Scoronconcolo, who with some difficulty succeeded at last in plunging a knife into Alessandro's throat, and turned it round and round until life was extinct. For some hours the murdered man was not missed, and Lorenzino, with his accomplice, had time to escape to Venice, where Filippo Strozzi embraced him with enthusiasm and hailed him as a second Brutus.

Guicciardini and his three principal companions, Francesco Vettori, Roberto Acciajoli, and Matteo Strozzi, immediately proposed to appoint as Alessandro's successor Cosimo, son of Giovanni delle Bande Nere, but some ardent spirits like Palla Rucellai rejected the idea with indignation. But the streets, by the orders of Guicciardini and his colleagues, had been filled with armed men, who cried, "Long live the Duke and the Medici!" and thus carried the election of Cosimo by surprise. He was confirmed in his position, and formally declared Duke of Florence by an Imperial Bull, and an army led by Piero Strozzi, which had been got hastily together by the united funds of Francis I., Filippo Strozzi, and some other exiles, met with a total defeat at Montemurlo, on the 31st of July, 1537. Vitelli, the commandant of the Spanish and German troops who now held Florence at the point of the sword, on returning victorious from this encounter, brought with him as prisoners members of all the most distinguished families of Florence. Among them was Baccio Valori, so long a creature of the Medici, but who had at last joined the party of liberty. His tardy conversion cost him his head, and Filippo Strozzi himself, one of the most brilliant figures of a brilliant age, immensely wealthy, and of cultured tastes, the very type of a grand seigneur, died miserably in prison by his own hand rather than undergo the frightful sufferings of the torture-room. His son Piero died a Marshal of France.

From this time henceforth the history of the Italian republics is the history of decay, relieved only by the obscure prosperity of Genoa, which found a compensation for the loss of its colonies by becoming the banker of the Spanish Crown.

Arezzo had recovered its republican liberties during the siege of Florence, but soon lost them again, all the inhabitants of the town, like those of Pistoja (where faction fights went on to the last) being disarmed by order of Duke Cosimo.

Lucca retained a rather useless independence by paying large sums to the Emperor; but Siena, in spite of its imperialism, speedily fell a prey to the ambition of the Florentine ruler.

In 1538 Alfonso Piccolomini, Duke of Amalfi, at the recommendation of Charles V., had been chosen head of the Sienese republic, but he fell entirely under the influence of seven brothers of the Salvi family, who literally terrorized the town. The

SALT-CELLAR. BY BENVENUTO CELLINI, IN THE UFFIZI GALLERY, FLORENCE.
(After a Phototype by Alinari.)

citizens complained of them to the Emperor, who at the same time received from Cosimo tidings of French intrigues carried on with the Salvi. Charles immediately instituted in Siena an oligarchy of forty members under the orders of an Imperial governor and backed by Imperial troops.

On the 6th of February, 1545, the people rose against the garrison and the nobles of the Nove at one and the same time, and Don Juan de Luna, the Spanish commandant, not being a man of energy, allowed himself to be overcome, but this success of the insurgents was short-lived.

Suddenly Francesco Burlamacchi Gonfaloniere of Lucca formed the bold project of driving out the Germans by a confederation of all the republics in which he fondly thought there might still be life. Pisa, Siena, Bologna, Pistoja, Arezzo were to enter into the league, and Piero Strozzi, now fighting under the banners of France, promised the help of that power, and of all the Florentine emigrants and exiles. Naturally the project failed: a Lucchese betrayed Burlamacchi to Cosimo, who caused the patriot to be arrested, taken to Milan, subjected to torture, and executed.

The Emperor sent a new Spanish garrison into Siena under the command of Don Diego Hurtado de Mendoza, whose name soon became a by-word of avarice, arrogance, and perfidy.

The cruelties of the Spaniards were so excessive that Siena at last, cured of imperialism, began to turn its eyes for help to France. The war between Charles V. and Henry II., and the unceasing desire

JUDITH. BY BOTTICELLI, IN THE UFFIZI GALLERY, FLORENCE.
(After a Photograph by Alinari.)

for vengeance of Piero Strozzi, who longed to overthrow Cosimo, encouraged these hopes.

Two Sienese emigrants, Enea Piccolomini and Amerigo Amerighi, put themselves at the head of a small force of insurgents, and in the evening of the 26th of July, 1552, presented themselves, with cries of "Liberty," before the gates of Siena. The people rose to the sound of the beloved delusive word, the Spaniards (ill equipped, thanks to Mendoza's avarice) were driven away, and Henry II. promptly seized the opportunity of sending some French soldiers to Siena, and a French governor, the Duc de Termes. A treaty of peace was concluded with Cosimo, who, however, only intended to observe it until the danger caused by the machinations of Piero Strozzi and the exiles had abated; and in a few months he was able to despatch an attacking force, under Giovanni Giacomo Medici (of Milan, a namesake but no kinsman of the Florentine family), Marquis de Marignan, one of the Emperor's best generals. Piero Strozzi came to the rescue, and fortified Siena, which proceeded to stand a siege. Marignan ravaged the whole surrounding territory, but everywhere met with a most determined resistance from the garrisons of the various castles belonging to the republic, and all his cruelties could not break the spirit of the peasants.

Piero Strozzi received constant supplies of money from Florentine merchants in Rome, Lyons, and Paris, and further aided by French reinforcements he drove the enemy in panic to Pistoja. But the fortune of war changed: on the 2nd of August, 1554, at Lucignano, Piero was beaten; and then Siena, after horrible sufferings from famine, surrendered to the Emperor, who guaranteed its liberties. In July, 1557, it was ceded by Philip II. to the Duke of Florence.

Some great names in art and science still illuminate the obscurity which from this time forth gathers fast round the republics.

Michaelangelo's stern and sorrowful spirit only quitted the scene of its many labours on the 18th of February, 1564. He was followed to the grave five years later by Benvenuto Cellini, at the age of sixty-nine. Andrea del Sarto, who died at forty-four, in 1531, belongs, like the two we have named before him, to the period of the full Renaissance, and was only two years younger than Sodoma, who revived the glories of art in Siena, and left two worthy pupils in Girolamo del Pacchia and Baldassare Peruzzi.

Passing by with a mere mention the infamous but brilliant Pietro Aretino (born 1492), the literary bandit so mercilessly lampooned by the still more brilliant Berni, we find some consolations for all Pisa's woes in the fact that the "Starry Galileo" was her son. He was born in 1564, but withdrew to Florence at the age of twenty-seven.

Genoa was not renowned for Art or Literature, but she had one transcendently famous citizen at this time in Christopher Columbus, whose discovery of the new world at the beginning of the fifteenth century ruined the commerce of the land which gave him birth.

Of Lucca in intellectual fields there is nothing to be said.

About the end of 1556 Martino Bernardini, the

SWOON OF ST. CATHERINE, CHURCH OF ST. CATHERINE, SIENA.

Gonfaloniere of the commune, following the now prevailing tendency, succeeded in getting a law passed which deprived all but a limited number of families of the rights of citizenship and the power to govern. From this time all the efforts of Lucca were directed to preventing its own incorporation with Florence, and the little republic continued in passive security until the ambition of Napoleon disturbed even the slumbering commonwealths of the Peninsula.

There is something at once pathetic and ludicrous in the efforts made by the poor little commune to preserve its independence at this time. While French armies poured over the Alps Lucca tremblingly counted out its money, and tentatively "popularized" its institutions by admitting a few more families of its governing classes. In 1798 Serrurier arrived in the town, and overturning the aristocrats called the popular party to power. But the joy of the democrats was short-lived, for the Lucchese speedily became mere slaves of the French.

In June, 1805, Lucca was given by Napoleon as a duchy to his sister Elisa and her husband, Felice Baciocchi, Prince of Piombino. By the Treaty of Paris, in 1817, Maria Luisa Bourbon, formerly Queen of Etruria, came to reign in Lucca, which was finally united to the Grand Duchy of Tuscany in 1847.

When Andrea Doria grew old his place in Genoa and in the confidence of the Emperor was taken by his nephew Giannettino, who soon succeeded in calling forth the latent discontent of the Genoese people at their present condition. This state of public mind offered to Gian Luigi Fieschi the

ARCHITECTURAL DETAILS. BY BALDASSARRE PERUZZI, IN THE UFFIZI GALLERY. (*After a Phototype by Alinari.*)

opportunity which as an enemy of the Doria he had long desired. He organized a widespread conspiracy which was entirely successful, but of which the instigator himself did not reap the fruits. Fieschi's bands had seized the fleet; Giannettino was killed, old Andrea had fled to Sestri, and the

ALFONSO D'ESTE.
(*From Die Italienischen Schaumünzen des Fünfzehnten Jahrhunderts.* (1430-1530.) *Von Julius Friedlaender. Berlin*, 1882.)

insurgents were only waiting for the word of command to march to the Palace and possess themselves of the government, when it was found that Gian Luigi, when passing from one galley to another, had fallen into the sea, and, overpowered by his heavy armour, been unable to rise. The insurgents then

FRANCIS SFORZA.
(*From Die Italienischen Schaumünzen des Fünfzehnten Jahrhunderts.*
(1430–1530.) *Von Julius Friedlaender. Berlin,* 1882.)

lost courage, and negotiated for a peace. Fair promises were made to them, but Andrea did not know how to forgive, and he employed the remaining thirteen years of his life in wreaking vengeance on his fallen foes. He died at last in November, 1560, at the age of ninety-four.

During the remainder of the sixteenth century Genoa remained under the protection of the Spaniards, and her merchants profited somewhat by their position as bankers to the Spanish Crown.

In 1566 the republic had lost the Isle of Scio and had some difficulty in suppressing an insurrection in Corsica.

Spain involved the republic in two wars, in 1624 and 1672 respectively, with the enterprising Dukes of Savoy, who even encouraged an insurrection in Genoa itself. This was headed by Giulio Cesare Vachero, who was a rich merchant belonging to the rich, popular, and even titled class whom the insolence of the oligarchy excluded from power.

An Act of Reconciliation between the factions in 1576 had established that the dominant class should be increased each year by ten new families; but care was taken to elude the law by inscribing only single men or men of very limited means in the book of nobility. It was against this intolerable state of things that Vachero rebelled, but his plot was discovered, and he, with five or six others, was arrested and executed in spite of every effort openly made to save him by the Duke of Savoy.

In 1746, during Maria Theresa's struggle, the Austrians, helped by the presence of an English fleet, had actually taken possession of the gates of Genoa, when the citizens, mindful of their ancient traditions, rose *en masse* against the troops, whose tyranny and rapacity had been worthy of the old sinister fame of their nation. On every side from the windows of every house the exasperated populace assailed the Austrians with stones, and succeeded in driving them out of the town. The insurgents then seized the town artillery and armed all the bulwarks, thus presenting such a formidable front that the Austrian commander, whose artillery had been left in the town, had no choice but to retire on Lombardy.

This popular insurrection was the last flicker of the old communal spirit, even among the Genoese. In May, 1768, Corsica, the very name of which recalled the strenuous rivalry of the republics in their youth, was ceded to France, and the decadence of Genoa was complete.

In 1800 it stood a terrible siege, when Massena held it against the Austrians; and in 1814 it rose against the French.

Lord William Bentinck pledged his word that the independence of the republic should be respected, but in spite of these assurances it was incorporated at last with the kingdom of Sardinia, by which name (since the cession of the island by the Austrians in 1720) the gallant little state of Savoy has been known.

During the whole of the seventeenth century Tuscany played hardly any part in European politics.

CASA GUIDI. (THE HOUSE ELIZABETH BARRETT BROWNING OCCUPIED IN FLORENCE.)

The Grand Duke of Florence, Ferdinand II., had a long reign, which owes some lustre to the encouragement accorded by the Court to the study of natural science. Under the auspices of the Duke's brother, Cardinal Leopoldo dei Medici, the celebrated Academy of the Cimento was founded in 1657.

By the marriage, in 1714, of Elisabetta Farnese to King Philip V. of Spain, the Duchies of Parma and Piacenza passed to the house of the Spanish Bourbons, and the treaty made by the quadruple

Obverse. *Reverse.*
MEDAL OF LEO X.
(*From Die Italienischen Schaumünzen des Fünfzehnten Jahrhunderts.* (1430–1530.) *Von Julius Friedlaender.* Berlin, 1882.)

alliance in 1720 handed over Tuscany to the same family.

The prince chosen was Don Carlos, whom the last of the Medici, Gian Gastone, a feeble, dissipated and childless man, was forced to acknowledge as his heir. This arrangement, however, did not last; Don Carlos went to Naples, and the wars of the Austrian succession next ensued, and Tuscany was eventually assigned to Francis, Duke of Lorraine, the husband of Maria Theresa, to whose second son, Peter Leopold, it passed in September, 1765,

The communes were dead; but above their ruins the star of Savoy rose in glowing splendour—to shine at last with promise for the future over the destinies of a redeemed and united Italy.

FINIS.

CHRONOLOGICAL TABLE OF EVENTS.

IN FLORENCE.

A.D.

405. Florence invaded by the Goths under Radogasius.
545. Another invasion by Totila.
570. Occupation by the Longobards.
786. Charlemagne comes to Florence, which is now governed by a Count.
1068. Pietro di Pavia, Bishop of Florence, having been accused by San Giovanni Gualberto of simoniacal practices, the truth of the charge was submitted to a trial by fire at Badia a Settimo, on the 13th of February, and resulted in the discomfiture of the Bishop.
1078. This is the date usually assigned for the construction of the second circle of the walls of Florence.
1115. Consular Government, in the hands of the Grandi, is now fully established; and Florence, in the struggle between Pope and Emperor, declares for the former.
1125. The Florentines marched out against Fiesole, took and destroyed it.
1162-3. Archbishop Reinhold, of Cologne, sent by Barbarossa into Tuscany, filled all the castles round Florence with German Counts and garrisons, by which means San Miniato became the centre of the foreign government, whose representatives were the Podestas.
1167. In the autumn of this year Barbarossa quitted Italy, and did not return thither for some years. Pisa and Florence then concluded an alliance against Genoa, Lucca, Pistoja, and the Counts Guidi, and a constant state of war ensued for six years.

A.D.
1197. The Emperor Henry V. having died, his brother Philip, whom he had created Duke of Tuscany, returned to Germany, and Florence formed a league against the Imperialists, which included the Pope, Lucca, Siena, Volterra, and Pistoja.

1200. By this time Consuls had disappeared, and were replaced by a Podestà.

1215. Florence is torn by the faction fights of the Buondelmonti and Amidei.

1248. Frederick, Prince of Antioch, a natural son of the Emperor Frederick II., entered Florence to assist the Ghibellines, and the Guelphs were driven out of the city on the 2nd of February, 1249.

1250. The people of Florence, oppressed by Ghibelline rule, effected a revolution, deprived the Podestà of a portion of power, and appointed a Captain of the People, with twelve councillors to assist him. A little later the leading Ghibellines were ejected.

1260. Florence marched against Siena, which had afforded an asylum to Ghibelline refugees. On the 4th of September, the battle of Mont' Aperti took place, and the Florentines were defeated. The leading Guelphs went into voluntary exile, and the Ghibellines reasserted themselves.

1266. Battle of Benevento, in which Charles of Anjou was defeated. Manfred restored the supremacy of the Guelphs.

1282. Three Priors of the Guilds replaced the fourteen Buonuomini as chief magistrates of Florence.

1289. On the 11th of June the battle of Campaldino took place, in which the allied Guelphs, headed by Florence, defeated the allied Ghibellines, headed by Arezzo.

1293. Giano della Bella drew up the Ordinances of Justice against the Ghibellines.

1300. The Papal Legate Cardinal d'Acquasparta is sent by the Pope to Florence to restore peace, if possible, between the Bianchi and Neri, headed respectively by the Cerchi and Donati.

1304. Florence, assisted by Lucca, besieged Pistoja, which was

A.D.
in the power of the Bianchi, and reduced it finally by famine on the 10th of April, 1306. Fall and death of Corso Donati, who had become obnoxious to the predominant Neri faction.

1311. The arrival of the Emperor Henry the VII. in Italy revived the hopes of the Ghibellines.

1313. Death of Henry VII.

1342. On the 8th of September, Walter de Brienne, Duke of Athens, usurped supreme power in Florence, but was driven away some ten months later.

1343-4-5. Overthrow of the power of the Grandi, and popular reforms in the government.

1375. Creation of a new Magistry, the Eight of War. Florence alarmed at Cardinal Albornoz', encroachments on Bologna and Perugia, went to war with Pope Gregory XI. Is placed under an interdict.

1378. The Ciompi riots.

1382. Beginning of the Oligarchy known as the Ottimati.

1434. Cosimo de' Medici becomes the supreme authority in Florence.

1464. Cosimo died on the 1st of August.

1469. Piero de' Medici, dying on the 2nd of December, Lorenzo the Magnificent becomes head of the house.

1471. Appointment of the Accoppiatori, practically Lorenzo's creatures.

1478. The Pazzi conspiracy broke out on the 26th of April, and Giuliano de' Medici was murdered.

1492. Death of Lorenzo the Magnificent on the 8th of April.

1494. The Florentines, encouraged by the arrival in Tuscany of the French Prince, expelled the Medici on the 9th of November, and on the 17th Charles de Valois entered Florence. He remained eleven days, and on his departure the Florentines remodelled their government, and eventually appointed a Grand Council.

1498. On the 7th of April the failure of the ordeal by fire gave a fatal blow to the influence of Savonarola. On the 23rd of May the Friar was executed.

1502. On the 19th of August, Piero Soderini was appointed Standard Bearer for life.

A.D.

1512. In the autumn of this year the Medici are re-established in Florence.

1522. Jacopo da Diacceto and Luigi Alamanni were executed on the 7th of July for conspiracy against the Medici.

1527. Tuscany was invaded by the Constable of Bourbon. Expulsion from Florence of Ippolito and Alessandro de' Medici in April. Revival of the Constitution of 1512.

1530. Final struggle of Florence against the Imperialists and the Medici. Defeat and death at Gavinana of Ferruccio on the 8th of August.

1531. Return of Alessandro de' Medici on the 5th of July. A year later he was created a Duke by the Pope.

1537. Alessandro was assassinated by Lorenzino de' Medici in Florence, and Cosimo, son of Giovanni delle Bande Nere, succeeded him.

1552. Siena, with the assistance of Piero Strozzi and the encouragement of the French, rose against the German garrison, and stood a siege, but had eventually to surrender.

1557. Siena was ceded by Philip II. to the Duke of Florence.

1765. The Grand Duchy of Tuscany, of which Florence was the capital, passed by treaty to Peter Leopold, second son of the Duke of Lorraine.

IN GENOA.

958. Berengarius and Adalbert, joint kings of Italy, guaranteed the property and the rights of the commune of Genoa against interference on the part of Crown functionaries.

1190 (or thereabouts). Consuls appear in Genoa.

1130. Consuls of Justice are created for civil suits; the consuls of the commune retaining final jurisdiction in all criminal matters.

1132. Lothair, anxious to be crowned Emperor in Rome, came to Pisa, and established peace between that commune and Genoa by dividing Corsica (of which both claimed possession by right of conquest) between them; and raising Genoa to the rank of an Archiepiscopal See.

A.D.
1147. The Genoese stormed and took Almeria from the Moors on the 26th of October.
1148-9. Taking of Tortosa from the Moors.
1160 and following years. Genoa, on Barbarossa's first appearance, showed a hostile and determined front, but eventually took the oath of fealty to the Emperor and paid one thousand two hundred marks in return for pledges of undisturbed possession of all conquests and full liberty of internal government.
1200. A Podestà now governed in place of the Consul.
1246. War between Genoa and Frederick II., during which Genoese archers helped the troops of Parma to take Vittoria.
1250. On Frederick's death, Savona, Albenga and other insurgent towns along the Riviera, returned beneath the rule of Genoa.
1284. On the 6th of August, in a battle off the island of Meloria, the Genoese inflicted a crushing defeat on the Pisans.
1339. Election of the first Doge in the person of Simone Boccanera.
1353. Brief interregnum of government by Giovanni Visconti, Archbishop of Milan.
1362. Simone Boccanera, who had been proclaimed Doge for the second time, was poisoned.
1379. Genoa took Chioggia from Venice, but the Genoese ships are afterwards shut inside Chioggia by a brilliant surprise on the part of the Venetians.
1380. Genoese inside Chioggia surrendered to famine.
1396. Antoniotto Adorno, Doge of Genoa, unable to govern, resigned his functions to the French, who made him governor of the town.
1401. After fresh anarchy, Boucicault arrived in Genoa, despatched thither by the French king.
1407. Sarzana passed into possession of Genoa.
1409. French occupation brought to an end by a popular rising, and twelve councillors appointed to govern Genoa, under the Marquis of Montferrat as Captain.
1420. War between Alfonso of Aragon and Genoa for Corsica, which the former had seized, but had eventually to surrender.

A.D.
1435. Genoese galleys inflicted a great defeat on Alfonso off the island of Ponza, on the 5th of August. On the 27th of December, Genoa shook off the yoke of Milan, imposed on it fourteen years previously by the Doge, Tommaso Campofregoso.

1453. The Republic lost its finest colony, Pera, which was taken by the Turks.

1458. Unable to continue the struggle against Alfonso, the Doge Pietro Campofregoso transferred the lordship of Genoa to France.

1461. French protectorship ceased.

1464. The factions in Genoa solicited and obtained the protection of Francesco Sforza.

1475. Genoa lost Caffa, which surrendered to the Moslems.

1477. Galeazzo Maria Sforza having been assassinated, Prospero Adorno became Governor of Genoa, and a year later the Genoese beat the troops of Milan in battle and recovered some liberty, but no peace.

1498. On the death of Charles of Valois, and the conquest of the Milanese territory by Louis XII., Genoa passed under French protection and a French commandant replaced the Doge.

1507. On the 29th of April, Louis XII. entered Genoa after his troops had inflicted a defeat on the soldiers of the Republic.

1527-8. Genoa was sacked by the Imperial troops, but saved by Andrea Doria, who made favourable terms with Charles V. of Germany.

1547. Fieschi conspiracy.

1560. Death of the Doge Andrea Doria, in November, at the age of ninety-four.

1746. The Genoese rose *en masse* against the Austrians, who had taken possession of the gates of the city, and succeeded in driving them away.

1800. Genoa was besieged by the Austrians and defeated by Massena.

1814. Genoa rose against the French. Afterwards incorporated with the kingdom of Sardinia.

IN PISA.

A.D.
980. Pisa, already important, carried Otho II.'s troops to Magna Greecia.

1081. Henry the Fourth of Germany granted a diploma to Pisa guaranteeing her in the exercise of her ancient customs.

1087. Daibert, Bishop of Pisa, established peace between the factions in the town and founded a government to which all subscribed.

1094. The Consular government is now fairly established in Pisa, and the town begins to describe itself as a commune.

1112. The Pisans proceeded against the Balearic Isles, and thence dislodged the Saracens.

1135. Pisa, which had sent a fleet to assist Pope Innocent II. against Roger of Sicily, took and ruthlessly destroyed Amalfi.

1162. Pisa declared for Barbarossa, and from this time forth remained steadily Ghibelline. Security in her conquests and freedom were guaranteed to her by the Emperor.

1174. Frederick summoned delegates from Pisa, Lucca and Genoa to Pavia, and imposing peace on these warring republics, ordered that one-half of Sardinia should belong to Genoa while Pisa kept the other.

1197-8. Pisa declines to enter the league against the empire initiated by Florence.

1200. A Podestà had fairly replaced consuls.

1245-6. Pisa assisted Frederick II. with galleys and arms.

1284. In the battle of Meloria, Ugolino della Gherardesca betrayed Pisa, and succeeded afterwards in establishing himself as leader of a Guelph faction at the head of the commonwealth.

1287. Overthrow and imprisonment of Ugolino, who was allowed to die of starvation.

1311. Pisa, alarmed at the ruin of the Ghibelline cause on the death of Henry VII., called in Uguccione della Faggiuola from Genoa, where he was acting as Imperial Vicar. He governed Pisa with energy, revived the war against the Guelphs, forcibly occupied Lucca, and beat the Florentines under the Duke of Gravina at Montecatini. But his tyranny rendering him insupportable, he was eventually driven away.

1325. The King of Aragon occupied Sardinia.

1326-7. Castruccio Castracane, supported by Louis of Bavaria, besieged and entered Pisa, which had to accept him as Imperial Vicar.

1351-2-3. Long negotiations resulted finally in the entry into Italy of the Emperor Charles IV., who, finding the Guelph Gambacorti family at the head of the government, caused three of the number to be decapitated; and invested the Elders of Pisa with Lucca as a perpetual fief, thus confirming the previous assignment of Lucca to its rival made by the Visconti of Milan.

1375. Pisa joined the league got up by Florence against Pope Gregory XI.

1392-3-4. Pietro Gambacorti who had governed Pisa for twenty-seven years, was assassinated by order of Gian Galeazzo Visconti, who coveted the town. Jacopo d'Appiano, Visconti's tool, had himself proclaimed captain, but practically surrendered the republic to the tyrant of Milan. Pisa eventually sold, on d'Appiano's death, to Visconti for two hundred thousand florins.

1406. Gabriele Maria Visconti having in his turn sold Pisa to Florence, the town was besieged, and after a desperate struggle surrendered on the 9th of October.

1494. Entry of Charles of Valois on the 8th of November. He is hailed as a deliverer.

1509. The French having abandoned Pisa, to its fate the town at last surrendered to Florence, and the Florentines entered it on the 8th of June. This was the end of the republic of Pisa.

IN LUCCA.

1081. Henry the Fourth of Germany guaranteed the security of Lucca within her walls, and released her from the obligation to erect an imperial palace.

IN LUCCA.

A.D.
1160. Guelph of Este sold his rights over the town of Lucca and its territory to the consuls of the commune. Lucca declared for Barbarossa, but only with a view of preserving its communal independence by conciliating the emperor, who guaranteed the possessions and liberties of the republic.

1197–8. Lucca joined the league against the empire initiated by Florence.

1202. Rising of turbulent nobles against the authority of the Podestà, eventually defeated by that functionary, Inghirame Porcaresi.

1264. The Lucchese, whose sympathy with the Guelphs had been cooled by the battle of Mont' Aperti, recognized Manfred as their lord. The five consuls about this time were abolished, and replaced by ten Anziani or Elders, whose office was to last only two months.

1266. On the arrival of Charles of Anjou, Lucca returned to Guelph allegiance.

1322. Castruccio Castracane, now tyrant of Lucca, directed his arms against Florence, but with no conspicuous success until

1325. When, on the 23rd of September, at Altopascia, the Lucchese troops under Castruccio completely defeated the Florentines.

1329. Death of Castruccio Castracane on the 3rd of September, after which Lucca, by paying Louis, recovered its liberties, but was sold by Marco Visconti, a condottiere, to the Genoese Gherardino Spinola, who claimed to govern in the name of the Emperor.

1369. Charles IV. being again in Italy, went to Lucca and thence despatched troops against Pisa, which was restive under his attempts at interference. His soldiers were defeated, but nevertheless he declared Lucca released from Pisan rule and invested the town with the Val di Nievole. Republican government then restored in Lucca, with two councils and a Signoria of Ten.

1375. Lucca joined the League got up by Florence against the Pope Gregory XI.

A.D.

1392-3-4. The mercenaries of Visconti overrun the Lucchese territory. The Guinigi family rise to power, and Paolo Guinigi eventually rules alone.

1402. Death of Gian Galeazzo saves Lucca from probable extinction.

1432. Paolo Guinigi died in the fortress of Pavia, where he had been imprisoned by Visconti, to whom he had been handed over by Lucchese conspirators.

1527-8-9. Lucca became Imperialist once more when Italy lay at the feet of Charles V.

1545. Francesco Burlamacchi Gonfaloniere, of Lucca, conceived the project of uniting Pisa, Siena, Bologna, Pistoja, and Arezzo, in an attempt to free Tuscany from the Germans. He was betrayed, and executed by order of Duke Cosimo.

1805. Lucca, which had remained a republic, was given by Napoleon as a Duchy to his sister Elisa.

1817. Maria Luisa Bourbon made Duchess of Lucca.

1847. Lucca was finally incorporated into the Grand Duchy of Tuscany.

INDEX.

A

Abbot of the people, 114; Acciajoli Roberto, 417-420; Accoppiatori, the, 301
Adalbert and Berengarius, 4-10
Adelheid, her marriage with Lothair, 9; subsequent adventures, 10
Agricultural proprietors, their misery, 75-76
Alamanni Luigi, 396
Alberti, the, *see* Florence
Alberti Leo Battista, 273, 337
Albertinelli, Mariotto, 278
Albizzi, the, *see* Florence
Alfani, Gianni, 257
Alfonso of Aragon, *see* Genoa
Almeria, 38, *et seq.*
Altopascia, battle of, 144, 145
Amalfi destroyed by Pisa, 35
Amidei and Buondelmonti in Florence, their feuds, 74-75
Ammonizioni, *see* Florence
Anaclet II., Pope, rival to Innocent II., 33; allies himself with Roger II. of Sicily, 34
Andrea Pisano, 267, 268; Angelico, Fra, 275
Angiolieri, Cecco, 259, 260
Antioch, Frederick, Prince of, entered Florence, 76; cause and consequences of his coming, 77
Anziani, *see* Elders
Aragon, Alfonso of, *see* Genoa
Architecture, Italian, 267
Aretino, Pietro, 426

Arezzo, 151, 197, 421
Arnolfo del Cambio, 267; Arnulf, 9
Arrabbiati, the, 363
Arrighetti Azzo, *see* Mirabeau
Arti Maggiori and Minori, 50, 54, 104, 236, 237, 245
Arte di Calimala, *see* Guild of Wool
Assisi, Guglielmo di, *see* Duke of Athens
Athens, Duke of, 146, 152, 154, 155, *et seq.*, 159, 185

B

Banking in Florence, 240, 241; institution of the Public Debt, 241; value of the florin, 242; fluctuations of the lira, *ib.*; value of money, 243
Bank of St. George in Genoa, 251, 252
Bankers of the Holy See, 243, 244
Barbarossa, his designs, 41; despatches Reinhold to Tuscany, 57; concessions to Lucca and Pisa, 58; action towards Genoa, 58, 59; crowned in Rome, 60; disasters, *ib.*; defeat at Legnano, 62; death, 68
Bardi, *see* Peruzza, also 160, 161
Bartolommeo, Fra, 278
Bella, Giano della, 121, 123, *et seq.*; his ordinances, 123, *et seq.*; his measures against the Guelph party, 127; fall and

448   INDEX.

banishment, 129, 130; his aim, 130
Benedetto da Majano, 271
Benevento, battle of, *see* Manfred
Bentivoglio, Hermes, his astuteness, 383
Berengarius of Friuli, 9; of Ivrea, 10
Berengarius and Adalbert, 4
Berlinghiero Berlinghieri, 418
Bernabò, Visconti, *see* Visconti
Bianchi and Neri, *see* Neri
Bianchi, the, 363
Bigi, the, 363
Bishops, their authority, 2; insignificant in Tuscany, 3
Boccaccio, Giovanni, 264; his works, 265-7
Boccanegra, Guglielmo, 113
Bologna, 168-9, 174-5, 177, 202-3, 209-10, 213, 221-2; intrigues of Borgia in, 383, 385; consequences of his death, 385; final settlement of, *ib.*
Bontura, *see* Dati
Borgia, Cæsar, *see* Florence and Bologna
Botticelli, Sandro, 275
Brienne, Walter of, *see* Duke of Athens
Brunelleschi, 269, 271
Boucicault, Marshal, in Pisa, 214, 215; in Genoa, 231-235
Bracciolini Poggio, 335, 340
Bruni, Lionardo, 339
Buondelmonti and Amidei, 74-75
Buondelmonti, Zanobi, 396
Buonuomini, 6, 92, 95, 101, 103, 143

C

Caffaro, 260
Cambio, Arnolfo del, 267
Campagne of Genoa, 18-19
Campaldino, battle of, 118, 119
Cancellieri of Pistoja, 131
Capponi, Gino, 214-217, 240
Capponi Picro, 348, 351, 352
Captain of the people in Florence, 78; when first named, *ib.*; his council, 95; in Genoa, 113
Carducci, Baldassare, 403

Carroccio, the, of Florence, 81, 82, 84
Castiglionchio, Lapo da, 182, 183
Castruccio, Castracane, 141, 143; victorious at Altopascia, 144, 145, 147; dies, 148; his aims, *ib.*
Cattani Lombardi, their Teutonic origin, 49
Cavalcanti, Guido, 132-134, 257
Cellini, Benvenuto, 426
Cerchi, Niccolò dei, 135
Cerchi, Vieri dei, *see* Campaldino; also 131-133
Charles the Bald, 8
Charles the Fat, 9
Charles of Anjou, 89, 90, 95, 98, 108, 116
Charles of Calabria, 146
Charles of Valois, 134-136
Charles of Bohemia, 165, 166; cruelty towards the Gambacorti, 167; subsequent action, 168 *et seq.*
Christian of Mayence, Archbishop, 58; imperial vicar, 61; his action in Tuscany, 61, 62
Cimabue, 273
Cimento, academy of the, 435
Cino da Pistoja, 103, 257; Ciompi, the, *see* Florence
Ciullo d'Alcamo, 256
Civitale, Matteo, 271
Commerce of Florence, 236 *et seq.*; usurious interest, 241, 247; good quality of coinage, 242; commercial failures, 243; commerce with the East, 245; first galleys, 245; commerce ruled politics, 244, 246
Commerce of Genoa, 248; with the East, 248-251
Communes, Italian, their origin, 1; different in different towns, 2, 3
Compagni, Dino, 132, 257, 260
Compagnacci, the, 371
Companies, fighting, 78, 79
Consuls, 6; their first appearance, *ib.*; when mentioned first in Florence, 54; how elected, *ib.*

INDEX. 449

Consuls of the Guilds, 92
Corsica and Sardinia, rivalries of Pisa and Genoa for possession of, 11, 14. 31, 32; Corsica divided by Pope Innocent II., 35; obtained by Genoa, 224; subdued under Boucicault, 234; ceded in 1768 to France, 433
Corso, Donati, see Donati
Councils, governing, in Florence, 70, 92, 95, 96. 105, 148; changes in, 193; the Two Hundred, 301; the Grand Council, 353–355; the Eighty, 355
Council, Grand, in Genoa, 402
Council governing in Lucca, 106, 108
Council of the Guelph Party, 97
Crisolora, 335

D

Daibert, Archbishop of Pisa, 16, 17
Dante, 102, 118, 119, 130, 132, 133, 136, 255, 256; his "Vita Nuova," 261; his "Divina Commedia," 261–3, 278
Dante da Castiglione, 403, 418
Dati, Bontura, 141, 142
Decamerone, the, 265–267
Desiderio da Settignano, 271
Diacceto, Jacopo da, 396
Donatello, 269
Donati, Corso, see Campaldino, also, 129, 131–133, et seq.; his death, 139
Donati Simone, 135, 136
Doria, Andrea, 400, 401
Duccio of Siena, 273, 274
Durazzo, Charles of, 198, 199

E

Elders (*Anziani*) of Florence, 78, 95; of Lucca, 108; of Genoa, 114, 231, 235; of Bologna, 385
Empoli, parliament at, see Uberti

F

Faction, spirit of, 71; fights, 64
Faggiuola family, disabilities of, 151

Farinata degli Uberti, see Uberti
Ferdinand of Naples, see Florence
Feast of St. John in Florence, 120
Ficino, Marsilio, 336–7
Fiesole, Mino da, 271
Filelfo, 335
Flagellants, 151, 253–255
Florence, early aggressions of, 37, 38; origin of city, 43, 44; name, 44; legendary history, *ib.*; walls, 45; invasions, *ib.*; its first feuds religious, 47; its expansion, 63; how effected, *ib.*; how regarded, 64; hatred excited by the Commune, 65; initiates a league against the empire, 68; for what purpose, 69; first Podestà at Florence, 70; history of Florence in the thirteenth century, 70, *et seq.*; Buondelmonte Buondelmonti, 74, 75; commerce of Florence, 75; entry of Prince of Antioch, 76, 77; rising against the Uberti, 78; fighting companies, 78; year of victory, 80; war with Siena, 81; defeat at Monteperti, 84, 85; dismay of the Guelphs, 86; Florence saved by Farinata, 87; Ghibellines in jeopardy, 91; calls in two knights of St. Mary, *ib.*; changes in constitution, 92; street fight, 94; departure of Ghibellines, 95; the Twelve, *ib.*; Guelph magistracy, 97; victory over Sienese, 98; the Pope endeavours to reconcile the factions, *ib.*; Florence excommunicated, 99; a fresh illusory peace, 100, 101; institution of Priors, 103–5; Guelph league, 117; battle of Campaldino, 118; increase of luxury, 119, 120; in the fourteenth century, 121; Giano della Bella's "Ordinances," 123, 124; Standard Bearer of Justice created, 125; Leagues of the people, 125; tranquillity in Florence, 126; Giano's unpopularity, 127,

128, 129, and exile, 130; Blacks and Whites, 131; Cerchi and Donati, *ib.*; Cardinal Matteo d'Acquasparta, 133; arrival of Charles of Valois, 134; feuds of Cerchi and Donati, 134, 135, 136; the Bianchi expelled, 136; great fire, 137; death of Corso, 139; defeat at Altopascia, 144; necessity for mercenaries, 145; Duke Charles of Calabria, 146, 147; attack on Pistoja, 147; constitution again remodelled, 148; life led by the Priors, 148, 149; great flood, 150, 151; Flagellants, 151; failures of banks, *ib.*; the Duke of Athens, 152, 153, *et seq.*; consequences of his fall, 159; twelve Priors appointed, 159; street fights, 160, 161; four changes of government, 162; exclusion of the Grandi, 163; the plague, 164; alliance with Charles of Bohemia, 165; he is forbidden to enter Florence, 166; ill-feeling between the Minor Guilds and the Guelph magistracy, 168; the Ammonizioni, 168, 173; defeat of Florentines at Cascina, 173; the Ricci and Albizzi, *ib.*; the Ten of Liberty, *ib.*; war with the Pope, 174; the Eight of War, 175, 177, 179, 180, 181; league against the Pope, 175, *et seq.*; religious revival, 179; St. Catherine of Siena, *ib.*; interdict disregarded by the Eight, 179; end of the league, 180; peace, 181; city feuds, 181; reign of terror, 182, 183; Salvestro de' Medici, 183; armed gatherings of the Minor Guilds, 185; the Ciompi, 185; their demands, 187, 188; Michele di Lando, 188, *et seq.*; the Eight of Revolution, 191; end of the rising, 193; the Eight of War quit office, 193; prevailing confusion, 194; Strozzi and Scali attack the palace of the Podestà, 195; death of Scali, *ib.*; banishment of Salvestro de' Medici and Michele di Lando, 196; wealth of Florence, 196; Florence arrayed against the Visconti, 200-4; what the war cost, 205; financial devices, 205; governing oligarchy of the Ottimati, 205-6; supposed conspiracies, 206-7; severities towards the Alberti, 207; measures against Gian Galeazzo, 207; increasing danger to the Commune, 210, 211; death of Gian Galeazzo, 211; Florence acquires Pisa, 214-8; Ladislaus of Naples, 218; his demands, 219; his ill-success, *ib.*; peace, 221; conditions, *ib.*; death of Ladislaus, 222; statistics of, 246, 247; decay of Guilds in, 279; difference between Florence and Venice, 280-81; checks the designs of Filippo Maria Visconti, 282; decay of the government of Ottimati, 282; character of Rinaldo degli Albizzi, *ib.*; exile of the Medici, *ib.*; their recall, 284; methods of Cosimo, *ib.*; Leghorn bought from Alfonso of Aragon, 285; money the root of Cosimo's power, 286, 287; his munificence, *ib.*; his death, 291; enigmatic character, 292; conspiracy against Piero, 293-95; his clemency, 295; his death, 297; Lorenzo and Giuliano proclaimed chiefs, 297; Lorenzo takes the lead, 298; Sources of his fascination, 298-99; conspiracy of the Pazzi, 299; how caused, 301; the Accoppiatori, 301; Minor Guilds reduced to five, 302; Franceschino dei Pazzi, 302-3; Jacopo dei Pazzi, 304; details of the conspiracy, 305-7; murder of Giuliano de' Medici, 308; failure of the conspiracy, 309; terrible

INDEX. 451

reprisals, 310; fate of Jacopo, 311; Florence excommunicated, 312-3; war with Ferdinand of Naples, 313; Florence under Lorenzo, 328; Savonarola's first sermons, 329; effect of his predictions, 330; his fearlessness and independence, 331; Lorenzo's three sins, 331; his deathbed, 332; his death, 333; first humanists in Florence, 334; their quarrels, 335; Poggio and Filelfo, *ib.*; Giorgio Scolaro and Teodoro Gaza, 335; Giorgio Gemisto Pletone, *ib.*; the Platonic Academy, 335-6; Marsilio Ficino, 336-7; the Oricellari Gardens, 336; Cristoforo Landino, 336; Pico della Mirandola, 337; poets and historians, 338-40; loss of influence under Piero II., 341; Lodovico Sforza calls in the French, 342; Savonarola favours Charles VIII., *ib.*; French fleet at Genoa, 344; sack of Rapallo, *ib.*; consequences of Piero's weakness, 344-5; attempted *coup d'état*, 345-6; Piero escapes to Bologna, 347; his brothers expelled, *ib.*; Savonarola and Piero Capponi, 348; entry of the French, 348-9; splendid army, 350; early dissensions, 351; Capponi's famous reply, 352; departure of Charles, *ib.*; a new Balià, 353; impotence of the Twenty, 353; the Grand Council and Savonarola, 354-5; Savonarola's statesmanship, 356; law of the Six Beans, *ib.*; abolition of the Parliaments, 357; Savonarola's immoderation, 357; his visions, 358-60; superstitions of the Renaissance, 360-1; four parties dividing Florence, 363; violence of the Arrabbiati, 364; religious revivalism, *ib.*; Savonarola's prophecies, 368; attempt of Piero to surprise Florence, 369; reprisals, 369-70; change in Savonarola, 370; he is excommunicated, 371; faults of his system, 372; proposed ordeal of fire, 373; preparation, for the ordeal, 374-75; its failures 376; siege of St. Mark, 377; trial and death of Savonarola, 378-79; judgments on his character, 380; Louis XII. seeks the alliance of Florence, 381; war against Pisa continues, 381; torture and beheadal of Paolo Vitelli, 382; critical condition of Florence, 383; designs of Cæsar Borgia, *ib.*; appointment of a Gonfaloniere for life, 384; the Ruota, *ib.*; consequences of the death of Cæsar Borgia, 385; final surrender of Pisa, 389; weakness of Piero Soderini, 390; sack of Prato, 391; return of the Medici, 391-93; a new Balià, 394; the conspirators of the Oricellari Gardens, 396; abject dependence of Florence on the Medici, 397; advance of the Constable of Bourbon, *ib.*; expulsion of the Medici, 399-400; aristocrats and democrats, 402-3; the plague, 403; a vain religious revival, 405; Gonfalonierato of Niccolò Capponi, 405; Florence fortified by Michelangelo, 405; betrayal by pope and king, 407; organization of the City Militia, 410; efforts to raise money, 410; advance of the Prince of Orange, 412; Francesco Ferruccio's defence, 413, *et seq.*; betrayal by Baglione and Colonna, 416; death of Ferruccio at Gavinano, 416; treaty of Santa Margherita di Montici, 417; the new Balià, 417; entry of Alessandro de' Medici, *ib.*; he is made Duke, 417; married to Margaret of Austria, 419; assassinated, 419-20, succeeded by Duke Cosimo I.; 420; Peter Leopold of Lor-

452   INDEX.

raine, Grand Duke of Tuscany, 435
Folgore, da San Gemignano, 259
Francesco della Piera, 275
Francesco da Carrara, 199, 200, 201-4
Francesco Ferruccio, 412-3, *et seq.*; his death, 416
Frederick II., 77, 80, 110, 111, 256
Frescobaldi, Dino, 257

G

Galileo, 426
Gambacorti of Pisa, *see* Pisa
Genoa, its uprise, 11, 12; resemblance to Pisa, 17; governed by bishops, 18; consuls of justice, 28; of the commune, 29, 30; council of conciliators, 30; parliament of the people, 30, 31; absorption of feudalism, 31; expedition against Almeria, 39, 40; general history, 108, *et seq.*; battle of Meloria, 114, 115; submission to Visconti, 165; monotony of annals, 223-24; struggle with Alfonso of Aragon for Sardinia, 224; Simone Boccanera, Abbot, 225; then Doge, 226-27; war with Venice, 227; siege and surrender of Chioggia, 228; faction fights, 228-30; Adornò and Montaldo, *ib.*; French occupation, 230; more anarchy, 231; advent of Boucicault, 231; his administration, 231-34; his fall, 235; republic handed over to Filippo Maria, 285; victory over Alfonso at Ponza, 285; Genoese recover their freedom, 286; civil war, 315; loss of Pera, *ib.*; lordship of Genoa given to Charles VII., 316; discontent and sedition, 317; French defeat at San Piero d'Arena, 317; anarchy, 318; intervention of Milan, 318; loss of Caffa, 318-19; Prospero Adorni proclaimed Doge, 320; deposed, 321; further anarchy, *ib.*; intervention of Lodovico Sforza, 322; fresh events, 385; French preference for the nobles, 386; popular discontent, *ib.*; Paolo di Novi, doge, 387; French victory, *ib.*; entry of Louis XII., *ib.*; execution of Paolo, *ib.*; severities of Louis XII., 387-88; sack of town by Imperialists, 400; Andrea Doria, his character, *ib.*; frees Genoa, 401; arbitrary device, 401-2, 421; Christopher Columbus, 426; Fieschi conspiracy, 428-32; wars with Savoy, 432; insurrection and execution of Vachero, 432; resistance to Austria, 433; siege of Genoa, *ib.*; incorporation with Sardinia, *ib.*

Gherardesca, *see* Ugolino
Ghibellines and Guelphs, 77, 78, 79, 80, 86, 88-91, 93, *et seq.*; 99-101, 116, 117, 121
Ghiberti, 269-71; Ghirlandajo Domenico, 275
Gianni Lapo, 256
Gian Galeazzo Visconti, *see* Visconti
Giano della Bella, *see* Bella
Giotto, 273, 278
Giovanni Pisano, 267
Gozzolo, Benozzi, 275
Grandi, the, of Florence, 49, 53; "Ordinances" against them, 123, *et seq.*; 130; exclusion from power, 163
Gualberto San Giovanni, 47
Guelphs and Ghibellines, *see* Ghibellines
Guicciardini, 34, 398, 417, 418, 419, 420
Guido of Novello, 86-88, 93-94, 118
Guido of Spoleto, 9
Guido of Siena, 273

Guido Cavalcanti, 257
Guido Guinicelli, 256
Guilds of trade, 7, 55, 56, 92, 93, 103, 104–5, 212, 236, *et seq.*, 245; money changers' guild, 245; major and minor, 278, 302
Guilds of wool, 55, 103, 104; Arte di Calimala and Arte della Lana, 237; the Umiliati, 238–39; supremacy of Florentine wool-trade, 239
Guittone d'Arrezzo, 256

H

Hawkwood, Sir John, 169, 173, 175, 177, 178, 202–4
Hermengard of Ivrea, 9
Hugo of Provence, 9
Humanists, the, *see* Florence

I

Innocent II., Pope; rival to Anaclet II., 33; ally of Lothair of Germany, 34; appeals for help to Genoa and Pisa, 35

J

Justice, ordinances of, *see* Bella

L

Ladislaus of Naples, *see* Florence
Lambert and Guido, joint kings, 9
Latini, Brunetto, 258, 259
League of the Guelphs, 117; of the people, 125
Lippi, Fra Filippo, 275
Lothair of Germany, 34, 35
Louis of Provence, called into Italy, 9
Lucca, privileges accorded to, by Henry IV., 5; sided with Matilda, 22; sold to its consuls by Duke Guelph, A.D. 1160, *ib.*; diploma of freedom obtained from Barbarossa, A.D. 1162, *ib.*; consular government, 23; commercial rivalry with Pisa, *ib.*; ferocity of war between Lucca and Pisa, 38; strength of the army of Lucca, *ib.*; general history, 106, *et seq.*, 141, 142, *et seq.*; expels Castruccio's sons, 150; town sold to Gherardino Spinola, 150; commune assigned to Pisa, 152; buys its release from Charles of Bohemia, 172; harassed by Gian Galeazzo, 208; Lazzaro Guinigi, 208; assassinated and succeeded by Paolo, 209; Paolo made captain and defender of the people, 281; deposed, 282; final events in, 421, 423, 428; union with the Grand Duchy of Tuscany, 428

M

Machiavelli, 340, 396
Majano, Benedetto da, 271
Majores, 5, 6
Manetti, Giannozzo, 288, 289
Manfred, his difficulties, 80; his death, 90, 91; his love of poetry, 256
Marquises, their courts, 3, 4
Marsili Luigi, 334
Marsuppini, Carlo, 339, 340
Martinella, the, or war-bell of Florence, 81, 84
Masaccio, 275
Matilda, Countess, 52
May-time in Florence, 120
Medici, Salvestro de', 183, 186; Cosimo de', 282 *et seq.*; Piero, 293–97; Lorenzo and Giuliano, 297; Lorenzo's policy of equilibrium, 324–26; his sumptuousness, 326; his dishonesty, 326–28; his poetry, 338; Piero II., his character, 341; Leo X., 394; Clement VII., 394–96; Alessandro and Ippolito, 397; captivity of Clement VII., Ippolito made a cardinal, 407; Giovanni delle Brande Nero, 410; Alessandro dei Medici, 417–20; intrigues of Ippolito, 418; Lorenzino dei Medici, his character, 419; murders Ales-

sandro, 419, 420; Duke Cosimo, his election, 420; encouragement of science by Duke Ferdinand II. and Cardinal Leopoldo, 435; Gian Gastone, the last Medici, 435
Memmi, Simone, 274-5
Mercenary troops, 145, 211-13
Michelangelo, 275, 278, 405, 410
Michele di Lando, *see* Ciompi
Michelozzo, 271, 282
Mino da Fiesole, 271
Mirabeau, 97
Mirandola, Pico della, 333, 337-38
Mont' Aperti, battle of, 83-5
"Morgante Maggiore," 338-39

N

Neri and Bianchi, 130-34, *et seq.*
Niccolò Niccoli, 334
Niccola Pisano, 267

O

Orcagna, 269, 273, 278
Ordine dei Nove, dei Dodici, dei Reformatori in Siena, 73, 170
Ordinances of justice, *see* Bella; revival of ordinances, 163
Otho the Great, 8; invades Italy, 10; what followed, *ib.*
Ottimati, the, *see* Florence

P

Pacchia, Girolamo del, 426
Pawnbrokers' shops, 247
Pazzi conspiracy, the, *see* Florence
Pazzi, Alessandro, 396
Pecora, 127, 130
Peruzzi and Bardi, their failure, 151, 243
Peruzzi, Baldassare, 426
Peter Igneus, 48
Petrarch, 136, 264
Petrucci, Antonio, *see* Siena
Piagnoni, the, 363
Pisa, privileges accorded to, by Henry IV., 6; its early importance, 13; struggles with the Moslem, 14, 15; spirit of faction, 15, 16; its early luxury, 19, 20; expedition against the Balearic Isles, 23-25; chivalry of the Florentines, 26, 27; terms imposed on by Florence, 80; remains Ghibelline, 98, 112; battle of Meloria, 114; disastrous for Pisa, 115; calls in Uguccione della Faggiuola, 140; welcomes Emperor Charles of Bohemia, 166; who beheads the Gambacorti, 167; Pietro Gambacorti and Gian Galeazzo, 201; betrayal of Pietro by Jacopo d'Appiano, 205; triumph of Gian Galeazzo, 205; he is momentarily withstood by Jacopo d'Appiano, 208, 209; death of Jacopo, 209; Pisa sold to Visconti, 209; receives Gabriele Maria coldly, 214; sold once more to Florence, 215; resistance of the Pisans, 215; ferocity of the Florentines, 216; the city is betrayed and provisioned, 216; unbroken spirit of Pisans, 216, 217; decay of the town, 218; entry of Charles VIII., 345; abandonment of Pisa by the French, 365-67; Fresh siege by Hugues de Beaumont, 382; French compassion, *ib.*; frightful sufferings of population, 388-89; peace, 389; Florentine generosity, *ib.*
Pistoja, 130, 131, 138, 143, 144; sacked by Florentines, 147; recovered by Castruccio, *ib.*; accepts jurisdiction of Florence, 151; gives itself to Charles of Bohemia, 166; revival of civil war in, 382
Pistoja, Cino da, *see* Cino
Pitti, Bonaccorso, 207
Pitti, Luca, 291, 293
Poliziano, his poetry, 333, 338
Priors, of Florence, 103, *et seq.*, 148, 149; number increased, 159; proportion of parties among, *ib.*
Pulci, Luigi, 338-39
Podestà, the, 67; disputes with

INDEX.

the Florentine consuls, 67, 68; cause of bloodshed in Genoa and Lucca, 70; alternation of the office in Florence with that of Consuls, *ib.*; the later podestas not imperial functionaries, 71; instituted against the Grandi, *ib.*; in Lucca, 106; in Genoa, 109

Poetry, Italian, 255, *et seq.*

Q

Quercia, Jacopo della, 269

R

Reinhold, Archbishop, 57, 58
Ricci, the, *see* Florence
Robbia, Luca della, 269
Roger II. of Sicily, 34, 35; takes Innocent II. prisoner, 36
Rosselli, Cosimo, 278
Rossellino, Antonio, 271
Rudolph of Upper Burgundy, 9

S

Sacra Rappresentazione, 255
Salvani, Provenzano, 98
Salviati, Francesco, *see* Pazzi conspiracy; 304, 308–10
Sardinia and Corsica, 11, 14, 31, 32
Sardinia finally possessed by Alfonso of Aragon, 224
Sarto, Andrea del, 426
Savonarola, *see* Florence
Sculpture, Italian, 267–73
Settignano, Desiderio da, 271
Sforza, Lodovico, 313, 322; story concerning him, 361, 362, 365, 367
Siena, factions in, 73; the Maggiori, *ib.*; Consuls and Podestà, *ib.*; banking, 73, 74; Ghibellinism, 98; defeated by Florence, *ib.*; Tolomei and Salimbeni in, 146; Commune surrenders to Charles of Bohemia, 166; changes of government, 167–70; victory over Charles, 170; other changes, 201; submission to Gian Galeazzo, 209; regains independence, 213; governed by Antonio Petrucci, 281; rule and character of Pandolfo Petrucci, 382; interference of Leo X. in, 395; supposed conspiracy against the pope, 395; reprisals, *ib.*; terrorism of the Salvi brothers, 421–3; oligarchy of Forty, 423; popular rising, *ib.*; cruelties of the Spaniards, *ib.*; fresh rising, 425; siege of, *ib.*; cession to the Duke of Florence, 426

Signorelli Luca, 275, 278
Sodoma, 426
Signoria of Florence, 159
Silk manufacture, 240
Sordello, 255
Spinola, Gherardino, 150
St. Mary, Knights of, 91; allusion to, in Dante, 92; driven from Florence, 94
Standard-bearer of Justice, 125, 148, 155, 160, 162, 183, 188, 192
Strozzi, Filippo, 418, 420, 421
Strozzi, Matteo, 420
Strozzi, Palla, 334
Strozzi, Piero, 420, 421, 423, 425
Sumptuary laws in Florence, 147; rescinded, *ib.*

T

Towers, Companies of the, 51, 54, 55
Traders, early Italian, 8

U

Uberti, the, of Florence, 53, 64, 65, 80, 81; Farinata, 83, 87, 88; mentioned by Dante, 88 a youth of the name, 97
Ubertini family, disabilities of, 151
Uccello, Paolo, 275
Ugolino della Gherardesca, 99, 115, 116

Uguccione della Faggiuola, 140; defeats the Guelphs, *ib.*
Uzzano, Niccolò da, 207

V

Valori, Baccio, 417, 418, 421
Vettori, Francesco, 417, 420
Villani, Filippo, 260
Villani, Giovanni, 260
Villani, Matteo, 260
Vinci, Lionardo da, 278
Visconti, the, 99, 152, 164, 165, 169, 172, 173, 175, 177, 200, *et seq.*, 207-11; death of Gian Galeazzo, 211; Filippo Maria, 281
Visconti, Marco, 150
Visdomini, Cerrettieri de', *see* Duke of Athens

The Story of the Nations.

MESSRS. G. P. PUTNAM'S SONS take pleasure in announcing that they have in course of publication, in co-operation with Mr. T. Fisher Unwin, of London, a series of historical studies, intended to present in a graphic manner the stories of the different nations that have attained prominence in history.

In the story form the current of each national life is distinctly indicated, and its picturesque and noteworthy periods and episodes are presented for the reader in their philosophical relation to each other as well as to universal history.

It is the plan of the writers of the different volumes to enter into the real life of the peoples, and to bring them before the reader as they actually lived, labored, and struggled—as they studied and wrote, and as they amused themselves. In carrying out this plan, the myths, with which the history of all lands begins, will not be overlooked, though these will be carefully distinguished from the actual history, so far as the labors of the accepted historical authorities have resulted in definite conclusions.

The subjects of the different volumes have been planned to cover connecting and, as far as possible, consecutive epochs or periods, so that the set when completed will present in a comprehensive narrative the chief events in the great STORY OF THE NATIONS; but it is, of course, not always practicable to issue the several volumes in their chronological order.

The "Stories" are printed in good readable type, and in handsome 12mo form. They are adequately illustrated and furnished with maps and indexes. Price, per vol., cloth, $1.50. Half morocco, gilt top, $1.75.

The following are now ready:

GREECE. Prof. Jas. A. Harrison.
ROME. Arthur Gilman.
THE JEWS. Prof. James K. Hosmer.
CHALDEA. Z. A. Ragozin.
GERMANY. S. Baring-Gould.
NORWAY. Hjalmar H. Boyesen.
SPAIN. Rev. E. E. and Susan Hale.
HUNGARY. Prof. A. Vámbéry.
CARTHAGE. Prof. Alfred J. Church.
THE SARACENS. Arthur Gilman.
THE MOORS IN SPAIN. Stanley Lane-Poole.
THE NORMANS. Sarah Orne Jewett.
PERSIA. S. G. W. Benjamin.
ANCIENT EGYPT. Prof. Geo. Rawlinson.
ALEXANDER'S EMPIRE. Prof. J. P. Mahaffy.
ASSYRIA. Z. A. Ragozin.
THE GOTHS. Henry Bradley.
IRELAND. Hon. Emily Lawless.
TURKEY. Stanley Lane-Poole.
MEDIA, BABYLON, AND PERSIA. Z. A. Ragozin.
MEDIÆVAL FRANCE. Prof. Gustave Masson.
HOLLAND. Prof. J. Thorold Rogers.
MEXICO. Susan Hale.
PHŒNICIA. Geo. Rawlinson.
THE HANSA TOWNS. Helen Zimmern.
EARLY BRITAIN. Prof. Alfred J. Church.
THE BARBARY CORSAIRS Stanley Lane-Poole.
RUSSIA. W. R. Morfill.
THE JEWS UNDER ROME. W. D. Morrison.
SCOTLAND. John Mackintosh.
SWITZERLAND. R. Stead and Mrs. A. Hug.
PORTUGAL. H. Morse-Stephens.
THE BYZANTINE EMPIRE. C. W. C. Oman.
SICILY. E. A. Freeman.
THE TUSCAN REPUBLICS. Bella Duffy.
POLAND. W. R. Morfill.
PARTHIA. Geo. Rawlinson.
JAPAN. David Murray.
THE CHRISTIAN RECOVERY OF SPAIN. H. E. Watts.
AUSTRALASIA. Greville Tregarthen.
SOUTHERN AFRICA. Geo. M. Theal.
VENICE. Alethea Wiel.
THE CRUSADES. T. S. Archer and C. L. Kingsford.
VEDIC INDIA. Z. A. Ragozin.
BOHEMIA. C. E. Maurice.
CANADA. J. G. Bourinot.
THE BALKAN STATES. William Miller.
BRITISH RULE IN INDIA. R. W. Frazer.
MODERN FRANCE. André Le Bon.
THE BUILDING OF THE BRITISH EMPIRE. Alfred T. Story.
THE FRANKS. By Lewis Sergeant.

Heroes of the Nations.

EDITED BY

EVELYN ABBOTT, M.A.,

FELLOW OF BALLIOL COLLEGE, OXFORD.

A SERIES of biographical studies of the lives and work of a number of representative historical characters about whom have gathered the great traditions of the Nations to which they belonged, and who have been accepted, in many instances, as types of the several National ideals. With the life of each typical character will be presented a picture of the National conditions surrounding him during his career.

The narratives are the work of writers who are recognized authorities on their several subjects, and, while thoroughly trustworthy as history, will present picturesque and dramatic "stories" of the Men and of the events connected with them.

To the Life of each "Hero" will be given one duodecimo volume, handsomely printed in large type, provided with maps and adequately illustrated according to the special requirements of the several subjects. The volumes will be sold separately as follows:

Large 12°, cloth extra $1 50
Half morocco, uncut edges, gilt top . . . 1 75

The following are now ready:

Nelson, and the Naval Supremacy of England. By W. CLARK RUSSELL, author of "The Wreck of the Grosvenor," etc.

Gustavus Adolphus and the Struggle of Protestantism for Existence. By C. R. L. FLETCHER, M.A., late Fellow of All Souls College.

Pericles and the Golden Age of Athens. By EVELYN ABBOTT, M.A.

Theodoric the Goth, the Barbarian Champion of Civilisation. By THOMAS HODGKIN, author of "Italy and Her Invaders," etc.

Sir Philip Sidney, and the Chivalry of England. By H. R. FOX-BOURNE, author of "The Life of John Locke," etc.

Julius Cæsar, and the Organisation of the Roman Empire. By W. WARD FOWLER, M.A., Fellow of Lincoln College, Oxford.

John Wyclif, Last of the Schoolmen, and First of the English Reformers. By LEWIS SERGEANT, author of "New Greece," etc.

Napoleon, Warrior and Ruler, and the Military Supremacy of Revolutionary France. By W. O'CONNOR MORRIS.

Henry of Navarre, and the Huguenots of France. By P. F. WILLERT, M.A., Fellow of Exeter College, Oxford.

Cicero, and the Fall of the Roman Republic. By J. L. STRACHAN-DAVIDSON, M.A. Fellow of Balliol College, Oxford.

Abraham Lincoln and the Downfall of American Slavery. By NOAH BROOKS.

Prince Henry (of Portugal) the Navigator, and the Age of Discovery. By C. R. BEAZLEY, Fellow of Merton College, Oxford.

Julian the Philosopher, and the Last Struggle of Paganism against Christianity. By ALICE GARDNER.

Louis XIV., and the Zenith of the French Monarchy. By ARTHUR HASSALL, M.A., Senior Student of Christ Church College, Oxford.

Charles XII., and the Collapse of the Swedish Empire, 1682-1719. By R. NISBET, BAIN.

Lorenzo de' Medici, and Florence in the 15th Century. By EDWARD ARMSTRONG, M.A., Fellow of Queen's College, Oxford.

Jeanne d'Arc. Her Life and Death. By MRS. OLIPHANT.

Christopher Columbus. His Life and Voyages. By WASHINGTON IRVING.

Robert the Bruce, and the Struggle for Scottish Independence. By SIR HERBERT MAXWELL, M.P.

Hannibal, Soldier, Statesman, Patriot; and the Crisis of the Struggle between Carthage and Rome. By W. O'CONNOR MORRIS, Sometime Scholar of Oriel College, Oxford.

Ulysses S. Grant, and the Period of National Preservation and Reconstruction, 1822-1885. By LIEUT.-COL. WILLIAM CONANT CHURCH.

Robert E. Lee, and the Southern Confedracy, 1807-1870. By Prof. HENRY ALEXANDER WHITE, of the Washington and Lee University.

The Cid Campeador, and the Waning of the Crescent in the West. By H. BUTLER CLARKE, Fellow of St. John's College, Oxford.

Saladin, and the Fall of the Kingdom of Jerusalem. By STANLEY LANE-POOLE, author of "The Moors in Spain," etc.

To be followed by:

Moltke, and the Military Supremacy of Germany. By SPENCER WILKINSON, London University.

Bismarck. The New German Empire, How it Arose and What it Displaced. By W. J. HEADLAM, M.A., Fellow of King's College.

Judas Maccabæus, the Conflict between Hellenism and Hebraism. By ISRAEL ABRAHAMS, author of "The Jews of the Middle Ages."

G. P. PUTNAM'S SONS, NEW YORK AND LONDON.